DELIVER

DELIVER

Why Some Leaders Get Results & Most Don't

RUSS HILL
JARED JONES
TANNER CORBRIDGE

Deliver: Why Some Leaders Get Results & Most Don't

Copyright © 2025 Lone Rock Leadership

All rights reserved. No part of this publication may be reproduced, distributed, or transmitted in any form or by any means, including photocopying, recording, or other electronic or mechanical methods, without the prior written permission of the publisher, except in the case of brief quotations embodied in critical reviews and certain other noncommercial uses permitted by copyright law.

Hardcover ISBN: 978-1-7363374-1-7
eBook ISBN: 978-1-7363374-2-4

First Edition

Interior design: Adina Cucicov

This book is dedicated to Erin, Reagan, Noelle, Wesley, Lily, Christy, Brooklynn, Hallie, Ashley, Kate, Janelle, Michael, Marlane, Tyler, Makenna, Camden, and Colby.

Our spouses. Our kids. Our everything.

TABLE OF CONTENTS

Foreword ix
Introduction xix

PART ONE. Leader Modes 1

    Chapter 1.   Founder Mode 3
    Chapter 2.   The Consensus Revolution 17
    Chapter 3.   The False Choice 35

PART TWO. Welcome to Chaos 49

    Chapter 4.   Gate C24 51

PART THREE. Installing LeaderOS: Create Clarity 67

    Chapter 5.   The Clarity Crisis 69
    Chapter 6.   The Clarity Extremes 83
    Chapter 7.   Define the Destination 99
    Chapter 8.   The Clarity Playbook 113

PART FOUR. Installing LeaderOS: Build Alignment 125

    Chapter 9.   The Alignment Gap 127
    Chapter 10. Make the Case 147
    Chapter 11. Gauge & Discuss 159

DELIVER

Chapter 12. Get Involved 179
Chapter 13. The Alignment Playbook 195

PART FIVE. Installing LeaderOS: Generate Movement 209

Chapter 14. Movement, Not Motion 211
Chapter 15. High-Leverage Activities 225
Chapter 16. Rewrite the Script 241
Chapter 17. The Movement Playbook 259

PART SIX. The Search for The Third Leader 271

Chapter 18. Menlo Park vs. Highland Park 273
Chapter 19. The Answer's In Dayton 287

PART SEVEN. The Manifesto 307

Chapter 20. The Third Leader Manifesto 309

PART EIGHT. Appendix: Assessment & What's Next 325

Chapter 21. Leader Mode Assessment 327
Chapter 22. What's Next? 335

Endnotes 343
Index 375

FOREWORD

Tom Smith
Co-Founder of Partners In Leadership
Co-Author of *The Oz Principle*

It's been over three decades since we first published the New York Times bestseller, The Oz Principle, and began witnessing the extraordinary results leaders and organizations achieve when they commit to building a Culture of Accountability. Since then, millions have engaged with our framework to achieve the outcomes that matter most.

Not long after graduate school, I realized success didn't come from being the smartest in the room—it came from surrounding yourself with the smartest people and creating an environment where they could unleash their potential. That's exactly what we did when we brought on Tanner Corbridge, Jared Jones, and Russ Hill. Over the years, I've had the privilege of watching them take the principles we introduced to thousands of organizations and apply them at the highest levels, advising executives at some of the world's most prestigious companies.

DELIVER

This book is the powerful result of that experience. It builds on the principles we first introduced, but it does more: it provides a timely, relevant, and actionable guide with one clear objective—delivering results!

In my work with leaders across the globe, I observed that the best created space for others to step into. Wisely, we created space for Jared, Russ, and Tanner, and they filled it exceptionally well! They are my friends, and they have my deepest respect! As you absorb their insights and experience their work, I am confident that your teams and organization will rise to new levels of performance—and Deliver, over and over again!

Greg Ulmer
President, Lockheed Martin Aeronautics

LOCKHEED MARTIN

Our mission in support of our customer is core to our foundation as a company. When you design, build, and sustain aircraft that protect freedom and liberty around the world, you have to deliver! I came to know the authors of this book about 15 years ago—long before I assumed leadership of Lockheed Martin Aeronautics and the 35,000 professionals and artisans who build and maintain F-16s, F-22s, F-35s, C-130s, C-5s, U-2s, and the next generation of aircraft at Skunk Works. They helped me to focus on three core leadership tenets of Clarity, Alignment, and Movement that an organization must have in order to be successful. Those became our rallying cry in our effort to meet our commitments. There are so many leadership skills that are important, but none of them matter if your teams don't deliver results. The authors of this book have helped us do just that and become friends and trusted colleagues along the way."

Chris Fox
Executive Vice President, U.S. Commercial
Teva Pharmaceuticals

When your team develops critical medications, you can't waste time talking about abstract leadership ideas or putting your managers through training that doesn't move the needle. For almost a decade, I've invited the authors of this book into my executive team meetings on a quarterly basis and put them in front of our mid-level managers because what they teach affects performance.

I believe deeply in transparent leadership that treats people as adults, empowering them to make decisions while creating a culture that demands performance for our shareholders, patients, and team members. I've read this book. I can't recommend it more enthusiastically because the concepts in it aren't new to me. They're proven. If you're a manager who wants to scale your career and impact, you should not just read this book but study it.

Dr. Tony Bridwell
Former Chief People Officer, Brinker International & Ryan, LLC
Chief Talent Officer for The Encompass Group

As Chief People Officer for two global organizations, Brinker International, parent company of Chili's Grill & Bar, and Ryan, LLC, a leading tax consulting and services firm, I've experienced firsthand the transformative power of creating Clarity, Alignment, and Movement. In this book,

DELIVER

the authors masterfully guide you through creating Team Key Results. Once you discover this approach, you'll wonder how you ever led teams without it. Simple, yet often underutilized, this approach is essential for leaders aiming to drive alignment and movement.

Whether leading thousands across diverse regions or a small local team, consistency is critical, yet variability in results can quickly undermine success. The way to ensure a consistent, sustainable product or service begins with clear results. This book brilliantly unpacks the art of creating that clarity, offering practical, field-tested tools to equip any leader's toolbox for success. Penned by three cherished long-time friends, its pages reflect their deep expertise and commitment to helping others realize their greatest potential, personally, professionally, and organizationally. As the author of eight books myself, I wholeheartedly endorse their work; it's a game-changer you will want to dive into.

Eva Borden
Chief Product Officer, Cigna

In the world of healthcare, you don't have time for abstract theories; you need to deliver for people who need help now. What makes Deliver so impactful is that it cuts through the noise. It outlines the essential skills needed to lead a team where clarity and alignment are absolutely critical. This book makes you think differently, and its application is so clear you can immediately put the principles into practice to drive simple, effective action.

It's a must-read for any leader in a high-stakes environment. I know the authors, and I've seen the impact of the concepts you're about to read on real-life teams dealing with real-world problems as we've implemented them for the last several years across our leadership teams. I strongly recommend you not only read this book but implement what it advocates if you want to Deliver.

Jon Rambeau
President, Integrated Mission Systems
L3Harris Technologies

I've applied the principles taught in this book at different points throughout my career to help teams achieve new levels of performance. What continues to be remarkable is their unfailing consistency. You reach a point where you shouldn't be surprised anymore because they keep working, time after time.

Yet, when I was faced with the challenge of forging a single, unified team out of 20,000 people from 100 different sites around the globe, each with its own legacy culture, there was a moment when I wondered if the task was simply too large. But I stayed disciplined and applied these simple, foundational concepts to break down those silos and unify the team. Once again, they proved their value. We have more work to do, but because of this framework, I know we are on the right path. I highly recommend reading this book and applying its contents.

DELIVER

Tony Ventry
VP, Chief Human Resources Officer
Veritiv

We operate more than 120 distribution centers in multiple countries. Our leaders are running a significant portion of the supply chain for products in all kinds of categories. When we first invited the authors of this book into our executive team meetings, we immediately saw the power of the core concepts you're about to discover in this book.

We immediately decided we needed to expand the exposure of the LeaderOS framework to all of our people leaders. That was several years ago. We've now had time to see the impact of what's in this book on performance. It's why I'm endorsing the concepts so strongly. The Leader Operating System is the foundation of leaders who Deliver!

Rodney Leonard
Head of North America Deliver for Kenvue (former Johnson & Johnson executive)

When the pandemic hit and stores were running out of Children's Tylenol I knew our team had to Deliver! The odds were stacked against us. The global supply chain was offline and our employees could have leaned on tons of legitimate excuses for why some kids simply wouldn't get the medication they needed. Leaders don't allow something like that to happen. And the leaders inside our company responded and pulled off miracles.

People have asked me how our team rallied in that moment. How we pulled it off. They ask how we have the highest employee engagement scores and are rated one of the best vendors by Walmart, Walgreens, Target, Amazon, and many others. I tell them it's due in large part to what you'll read in this book! The core concepts, models, and tools laid out in these pages teach leaders how to deliver. We've put our leaders through the training in this book. Multiple times! LeaderOS changed everything for us!

Carole Bennett, PhD
VP of Sutter University
Sutter Healthcare

Deliver completely reframes the conversation by shifting the leadership development focus from 'soft skills' to tangible 'impact.' It's a simple, relatable approach that just works. When I shared the Leader Operating System framework taught in this book with a room full of HR leaders across our hospital system of nearly 20,000 employees, their reaction was universal and immediate: a resounding 'Yes! We need this!' We've taken the concepts in this book to thousands of our leaders because it impacts organization outcomes!

A. Dixon
SVP, HR and Training and Development
Kumon North America, Inc.

With years of experience in leadership and training, I've seen countless leadership models come and go. What sets this book apart is its inspiration and practicality for leaders. Deliver encourages leaders to think

DELIVER

differently, act decisively, and create lasting change—all in ways that are simple and relevant for a multi-generational workforce.

When paired with the Lead In 30 training, the impact of these efforts can be transformational. My advice: read the book, and then seriously consider working with Lone Rock to ignite powerful changes in how you and your teams deliver results.

Brian Walder
Former President, Current Chairman
Nu-Way Transportation

In the trucking business, the word 'deliver' is literal and figurative. It's all about delivering. For our leaders, applying the tools taught by Lone Rock around Clarity, Alignment, and Movement aren't just buzzwords from a business book; they're what keep our wheels turning. We've brought these ideas to life in our company, and they have totally changed our conversations and teamwork for the better. It's helped everyone, from our office staff to our drivers and warehouse workers, get focused and driving in the same direction.

We have partnered with Lone Rock for years now, and their Lead In 30 training course has become a cornerstone of our leadership development because it is built for the real world. These concepts are an invaluable tool for any leader who is focused on execution and delivering results.

Manager Training Requires a License

The content, concepts, methodology, and terms in this book cannot legally be used in manager training programs without securing a per-employee license from Lone Rock Leadership. Intellectual property rights are protected under the law. Because what you're about to read actually works, the lawyers tell us we have to protect it.

AI Usage Prohibited

This book and its contents are prohibited from being used to train, develop, or improve any Artificial Intelligence (AI) systems, machine learning models, or similar technologies. Back away slowly, bots!

INTRODUCTION

"THIS IS AN EFFING waste of time," Ben declared, his voice cutting through the silence like a blade. "I have zero confidence this is going to be worth a damn. I'm only here because I was told I had to show up."

The meeting room on the fourteenth floor of the company's Philadelphia offices suddenly went completely still. No movement. No noise. Ten executives who collectively controlled billions in revenue sat frozen, watching their head of sales—a man closer to retirement than anyone else in the room—methodically destroy the other departments in the company.

"The problem isn't with my sales team," Ben continued, pointing at his colleagues. "It's your departments that are the issue. Sorry, but the truth hurts."

When Ben finished his brutal assessment and sat down, arms crossed and head down, we realized we were witnessing something profound: a leader so frustrated by his organization's inability to execute that he was willing to risk the repercussions of spewing unfiltered honesty rather than sit through another pointless meeting.

It wasn't the opening we anticipated to start that meeting, but it wasn't entirely surprising either. This was the world's tenth-largest company as measured by revenue, and it was suffering from the same disease we had seen spreading everywhere.

The Fog In Your Org Chart

Through a sequence of unexpected events, we gained access to the highest levels of many of the world's largest organizations over the last twenty years. The consulting firm we worked for and the leadership development company the three of us later founded have provided us a front-row seat to discussions, debates, and decisions that impact the lives of employees and customers worldwide.

The problem perplexing executives universally is the inability of mid-level managers to deliver. The cause isn't a lack of desire, intelligence, or ability. It's the fog that blankets the center of the org chart. Your mid-level managers are confused.

Who can blame them? Consider how they've been trained and developed. For many, that training has been nonexistent. They've had to make it up as they go along. What makes a good leader? They're combining lessons from their worst bosses, their best bosses, books they might have read, and various articles.

Those fortunate enough to undergo formal leadership training have been handed binders of complex frameworks or put through courses on how to build trust or discover their why when what they really need help with is the one thing missing from it all.

We wrote this book for three reasons. First, because what we've witnessed deserves to be shared. You shouldn't be granted the access we've had and keep what you see, hear, and learn to yourself. Second, to set the record straight. We noticed one thing missing from every leadership book on the bestseller lists over the last couple of decades, in every module of leadership training shared with us, and in all the onboarding we've reviewed for new managers at the organizations we consult. The missing word is the one we ultimately chose as our title: The job of a leader, above everything else, is to deliver.

The third reason we wrote this book is not to share what we created but rather what we discovered. It's elegantly simple yet profound. It's the Leadership Operating System used by the most successful leaders, and it delivers sustained results. This is unlike other business books. We're not showing you what worked for one executive in one industry. We're not sharing something conceived by professors at some business school. This isn't an academic theory or a blog post that went viral and led to a book deal. This is the wisdom and insight gained from more than 4,000 flights and 9,000 meetings.

The Access We Were Given

We've signed Non-Disclosure Agreements (NDAs) with every organization whose senior executives we consult and every company that uses our 30-day leadership training cohorts. Some have granted us permission to use their real names; others we've intentionally used fake first names or broad terms to identify them (for instance, a 'manufacturing company' or a 'retailer'). We've added a few details to bring real-life moments alive for you. Every person, company, and situation described here is real.

Get ready to walk inside the command center at Microsoft, where they track every meeting invite and email sent by all of you. You're about to read the email exchanges that ignited a firestorm at Amazon. You'll be in the room with the senior leaders of Target when they did the exact opposite of what Wall Street expected. We'll take you to Memphis and the warehouse where an executive decided to build the future of AI. You'll

DELIVER

go behind the scenes of the debates at Starlink, witness the day that 20% of the workforce in a tech company quit, and travel to an unexpected place to meet an executive we believe deserves to be studied by every business school in the world.

Our journey begins in Silicon Valley on a night that sparked a firestorm of debate.

We worked hard to make this book entertaining and engaging for you. We can't promise we hit that mark, but what we can guarantee is that if you implement what we discovered, it will profoundly impact your ability to do what matters most: Deliver.

DELIVER

Introduction
– Quick Start –

We wrote this book for busy executives and managers and insisted that our publisher organize it so you can grasp the main points without having to read every page. We rarely read every chapter of books, and we assumed many of you are the same. Here's your cheat sheet:

Do NOT Skip These Chapters:

- To get the main career-changing ideas of the book (trust us, that's not hyperbole), you'll absolutely want to read the following chapters:
- *Chapters 1-5, 7, 9, 14-15, 18-20*

The Tactical Chapters:

- We hope you'll read every chapter, but these chapters focus on implementing the Leader Operating System and slow down to provide plenty of tactical information:
- *Chapters 6, 7, 8, 10-13, 16, 21-22*

Key Points:

- At the end of every chapter, we provide a page called the Quick Start.
- Think of it as a PowerPoint summary of that chapter's main points.
- You won't benefit much if you only read these one-page overviews.
- But they are great quick references when you revisit the book after initially reading it and wonder where certain ideas, stories, or frameworks are contained.

DELIVER

 Action Items:

- Each chapter ends with something to consider, something to seek feedback on, and something to start doing.
- Think of these as tips from an executive coach helping guide you through implementing what you're reading.

> **The Reality:**
>
> We believe you'll discover this book is something every manager in your organization can benefit from reading. It will change your results. Dig in and see if you agree. If so, contact us for bulk discounts and information about getting your HR leaders certified in running the 30-day leadership training cohort based on this book. Go to https://www.lonerock.io

PART ONE

LEADER MODES

CHAPTER 1

FOUNDER MODE

HE EXPECTED CONTROVERSY. But he started a war.

The gathering was the kind that Silicon Valley legends are made of—a private meeting of some of the most successful people in the world, each of whom had built companies from nothing into billion-dollar enterprises. These weren't the public conferences where executives deliver polished keynotes. This was the inner circle, the sanctuary where tech's most successful leaders shared their most honest thoughts.

No recordings. No press. No one who wasn't invited.

The man preparing to address this exclusive group had built the kind of company that most Ivy League grads and dropouts only dream about. He wasn't here as a wannabe—he was one of Silicon Valley's newest stars.

But confidence wasn't what showed in his eyes as he prepared to speak. Instead, there was something that looked almost like betrayal—the expression of someone who had followed the so-called experts' advice

DELIVER

after his app exploded in popularity. They told him what he had to do to scale his company as a professional CEO. Their advice, he now believed, nearly destroyed everything he'd built.

Tonight, he was here to deliver a manifesto motivated by anger. Anger that they were wrong. That all the leadership experts, consultants, coaches, gurus, and board members didn't know what they were talking about. Tonight, he came to settle the score. To understand his rage—you have to rewind.

> > >

The rain hammered against the windows of the tiny apartment as Brian stared at his laptop screen, scrolling through yet another rejection email. The Rhode Island School of Design graduate was broke, surviving on cereal and whatever free food he could scavenge at tech meetups.

This wasn't how it was supposed to go.

Brian moved to San Francisco with the same dream that drew thousands of others: to build something that mattered, get rich, and prove that a creative kid from upstate New York could make it in the big leagues. But reality had been merciless. His previous startup attempts had crashed and burned. His savings were gone. His credit cards were maxed out.

"Maybe it's time to consider a real job," his mother suggested during their last phone call, her voice carrying that familiar mix of love and exasperation only moms can master.

But Brian couldn't shake the feeling that he was close to something, even if he couldn't quite define it. A design conference was coming to town, hotels were booked solid, and he and his roommate, Joe Gebbia, had hatched a plan that sounded far-fetched even by Silicon Valley standards:

rent out air mattresses in their living room to conference attendees who needed a place to stay.

They spent their last few hundred dollars creating a simple website called "AirBed & Breakfast." The concept felt both obvious and insane—let strangers sleep on your floor for money. Who would trust this? Who would even try it?

The early response was devastating.

Potential users dismissed the idea as unsafe and weird. "Who would stay in some random person's apartment?" one particularly harsh response read. "This will never work." It sounded creepy.

But then, a few bookings trickled in. Then a few more. Over time, people began listing space in their apartments or houses, and users started leaving positive reviews. Word spread through design conference networks, then broader travel communities. What had seemed impossible—strangers trusting strangers with their safety and shelter—was actually happening.

The momentum led to investor interest. What had started as a desperate scheme to pay rent had generated $112 million in funding and was expanding globally. This was Airbnb, and it made Brian Chesky part of the new class of Silicon Valley's most celebrated founders.

In December 2020, Airbnb went public, and within hours was valued at over $100 billion. Brian's net worth skyrocketed to more than $11 billion. Renting out air mattresses (hence the name Airbnb) had evolved into renting out rooms and houses, transforming the way the world traveled.

But with rapid growth came new challenges—and voices urging him to "professionalize" his management style. The message was consistent and

DELIVER

seductive: Hire great people and get out of the way. Delegate more. Trust your team. Scale yourself by reducing your involvement in day-to-day operations. Stop being the founder and start being the CEO.

Brian listened.

He stepped back significantly from product decisions, hiring experienced executives from Google, Amazon, and other tech giants. He created layers of management between himself and the work he'd once obsessed over.

From the outside, it looked like textbook leadership evolution. Airbnb continued growing, expanding into new markets and launching ambitious initiatives.

But something was wrong.

One day, Brian looked up and barely recognized the product they were building. The platform that had once felt personal, crafted, and intentional now seemed corporate and disconnected from the original vision. Features were being launched that he disagreed with. The company culture he'd carefully cultivated was being "optimized" by HR professionals who'd never slept on an air mattress in a stranger's living room.

The breaking point came during a product review meeting. Brian sat in a conference room, listening to a presentation about a new feature set that would fundamentally change how users discovered listings. The metrics looked good on paper, but the experience felt soulless to him. When he voiced concerns, he was told that the decision had already been made by the product team—a team that reported to executives who reported to other executives, creating a distance between leadership and execution that felt insurmountable.

DELIVER

After that meeting, Brian made a decision that would ignite one of the most contentious debate in modern management theory. It would soon spread far beyond Airbnb and Silicon Valley. Brian decided he would fire entire layers of management. He was done following the advice to delegate and elevate.

That was the backstory, the journey preceding the night in Mountain View. Brian took a deep breath and walked into the meeting he had almost decided to skip. No, he needed to be there. He needed to set the record straight.

Paul Graham, the tech kingmaker, sat in the front row. Ron Conway, the now silver-haired grandfather who years ago had written some of the first checks for Google and Facebook, found a spot near the back.

Brian was raw and completely unfiltered. He said listening to conventional wisdom about scaling leadership was the biggest mistake he'd made in his career. What was supposed to be a quick meetup stretched for hours as Brian dismantled the management orthodoxy followed by nearly every major corporation in modern times. He looked around the room at founders who'd built billion-dollar companies and said, "We've been told that great leaders hire great people and get out of the way. That's bullshit. Steve Jobs didn't get out of the way—he got deeper into the details. Bezos doesn't delegate the customer experience—he obsesses over it. We've been trained to think that caring about your product makes you a micromanager when really it makes you a founder."

Heads around the room began nodding. Someone shouted, "Yes!" from the back. These weren't just any entrepreneurs—these were people who'd felt the same frustration, who'd been told to step back from the companies they'd bled to build. For the first time, someone was giving them permission to care again.

Founder Mode > 7

DELIVER

"We've been told to worry more about employee feelings than the soul of our products. More about org charts than features. More about being liked than being right. I tried it, and it almost killed everything that made Airbnb special."

Brian paid homage to how Bezos and Musk run their companies. He talked about firing 25% of his leadership team when he realized executive layers make companies soulless. Brian was unforgiving and visceral in his manifesto. Delegating wasn't the way to scale. Taking charge, being involved in all the details, and not letting go of the reins was how the greatest modern leaders grew the world's most valuable companies.

When Brian said the words "founder mode," the room erupted. Paul Graham started taking notes furiously. Someone yelled, "Founder Mode!" and suddenly half the room was chanting it back: "Founder Mode! Founder Mode!" It wasn't just a concept—it was a battle cry for everyone who'd been told they cared too much about their own companies.

Brian felt a huge sense of relief. What had been boiling inside him had finally been said out loud.

He had no idea he'd just lit a fuse that would explode across Silicon Valley and then spread much further.

The Pushback Begins

It wasn't long after the meeting ended when Kim Scott first saw the tweets celebrating Founder Mode as some kind of brilliant breakthrough.

The enthusiasm made her feel sick. When the New York Times reached out for her perspective, Kim didn't mince words: "This is about obsession with 'one-man rule' in the tech sector. It's unsustainable and damaging for both companies and governments."

Kim had seen this pattern before, and she knew exactly how it ended—with broken people and broken companies, all in service of leaders who mistook fear for respect.

"The idea that one person, no matter how brilliant, can have all the answers is not just wrong—it's dangerous," Kim argued. "We've seen this pattern repeat itself over and over. A charismatic founder or executive has early success, becomes convinced that their personal involvement is the secret sauce, and then creates an organization that can't function without them."

After sixteen years climbing the ranks at Google and Apple, Kim had witnessed the human wreckage left behind by leaders who confused intensity with inspiration. At Google, she'd watched the company struggle with what employees called "brilliant jerks"—technically gifted individuals whose abrasive personalities and authoritarian management styles created toxic environments for everyone around them.

Rising stars whose innovative ideas were stolen by autocratic managers who then berated them for "lack of initiative." These weren't isolated incidents. And this wasn't just about tech companies either. This happened in companies across all industries. This was a debate about command-and-control leadership styles. About executives and managers who can't let go. Who think they know best and must be involved in everything. Leaders who prioritize control over collaboration, treating psychological safety as weakness rather than the foundation of innovation.

Kim had worked directly with Steve Jobs during her time at Apple. She'd seen his genius up close—the obsessive attention to detail, the impossible standards, the revolutionary products that emerged from his relentless pursuit of perfection. But she'd also witnessed the other side: the public humiliations, the impossible standards, the culture of fear that permeated certain parts of the organization. Talented employees reduced to anxiety attacks, brilliant minds second-guessing every instinct, entire teams walking on eggshells around a leader whose approval felt more like survival than success.

"The most successful leaders I've worked with create conditions where the best ideas can emerge from their teams," Kim said. "That requires humility, not heroics."

The Network Effect Skeptic

Reid Hoffman received the same types of texts Kim did after Brian's manifesto moment and knew he had to weigh in. Brian was a good guy with remarkable accomplishments, but he had gone too far that night.

None of the data supported his misguided pep rally speech that suddenly licensed every tech bro to flex and unleash their egos. Reid had spent decades studying what truly made organizations successful, and everything Brian advocated for was a recipe for disaster.

"The research on high-performing teams consistently shows that distributed decision-making drives better outcomes than command-and-control approaches," Reid fired back. "Founder Mode might work for unicorn companies with unicorn founders, but it's not a scalable model for most organizations."

Reid's frustration was personal. Growing up as the son of academics—his father a lawyer, his mother an archaeologist—he'd been raised to value evidence over ego, rigorous thinking over charismatic proclamations.

Everything he'd learned in two decades of building companies told him that Brian's Founder Mode was organizational poison disguised as leadership wisdom.

At PayPal, working alongside future titans like Peter Thiel, Elon Musk, and Max Levchin, Reid witnessed what happened when brilliant individuals became convinced they were the key to everything. Companies that should have scaled hit walls. Talented people left. Innovation stagnated because everything had to flow through one person's limited bandwidth.

Building LinkedIn had proven the opposite approach worked. The platform's value grew exponentially as more people joined and connected—not because Reid made all the decisions, but because millions of users contributed their knowledge and insights to enhance the whole system.

"I've seen this pattern play out over and over," Reid explained, his voice carrying years of watching promising companies self-destruct. "An executive has success, becomes convinced that their personal involvement is the key to everything, and then hits a scaling wall when their capacity becomes the bottleneck for the entire organization."

At Greylock Partners, Reid evaluated thousands of companies and worked closely with hundreds of CEOs. The pattern was devastatingly consistent: organizations that built strong distributed leadership capabilities outperformed those that relied on founder brilliance—not sometimes, but every time.

Reid's critique was grounded in both personal experience and rigorous research. The data was overwhelming: Organizations led by what researchers called "directive control leaders" were 34% more likely to experience significant performance drops during leadership transitions, 28% more likely to struggle with innovation metrics over five-year periods, and 45% more likely to face talent retention problems among high-potential employees.

"When we concentrate decision-making in a single individual, we're essentially creating a single point of failure," Reid argued. "That might work when everything is going well, but what happens when circumstances change faster than any one person can process? What happens when that leader makes a mistake? What happens when they're unavailable?"

The Debate Begins

While Kim Scott and Reid Hoffman were sounding alarms about the dangers of command-and-control leadership, Brian Chesky's manifesto was spreading across Silicon Valley like wildfire.

The moment Paul Graham published his essay recounting Brian's speech, the Founder Mode phenomenon transformed from a private gathering into a global conversation. He took Brian's speech and doubled down. "C-level execs, as a class, include some of the most skillful liars in the world," he wrote. "There's also another, subtler force keeping Founder Mode from being the default: the assumption that [professional] manager mode is the grown-up way to run a company. Manager Mode sounds so calm and reasonable, with its MBAs and org charts and systems of delegated authority. I predict Founder Mode will become the new default."

The speech that began as casual remarks to a small group of entrepreneurs and Graham's essay were now being dissected in classrooms at Stanford and Harvard. The manifesto spread through Slack channels at Google and Tesla, shared by employees who felt vindicated by someone finally challenging the conventional wisdom about professional management.

Elon Musk retweeted Brian's ideas. The besties on the soaring All In podcast dedicated an entire episode to debating its merits.

But the debate also revealed deeper fractures not just in Silicon Valley but across industries about leadership philosophy. What is the best leadership approach? What is the ultimate way to deliver results? How should a manager or executive drive performance? Leaders get paid to deliver results. But how they do it is ultimately their choice. They get to decide: Founder Mode or something different?

This Isn't About Tech Companies

We've seen the champions of Founder Mode up close during our twenty years of consulting executive teams. In the chapters ahead, you'll have a front-row seat to some of those moments and the debates they ignited in their organizations. One of those moments was in Dallas. A retired general entered the private sector with the task to stand up a new business line in the Fortune 50 company that hired him. In less than five years, he did something most remarkable. He and his team created more than a billion dollars in new revenue. Bob was celebrated. But he was also loathed.

In a feedback session we facilitated among the senior executive team, Bob received candid feedback. His peers praised his accomplishments but were honest about how difficult he was to work with. They detailed how their teams hesitated to collaborate with his team. They professionally and respectfully informed Bob of the tension his approach had introduced to the organization. People at all levels felt it.

When it came time for Bob to respond to the feedback, instead of choosing humility and considering that he and his team may have leaned too far into a stand-and-salute approach, he resembled a clone of Brian that

DELIVER

night in Mountain View. Bob looked and sounded like a defense attorney who heard all the prosecution's compelling witnesses and then declared them all misguided softies. He was brief, unapologetic, and unmovable.

The meeting ended. We grabbed our suitcases from the corner of the room. On our way out of the building, one of Bob's colleagues, a respected executive who oversaw a significant part of the business, pulled us aside. She had tears in her eyes but spoke calmly. "I'm done," she said softly. "I told myself if it ever got like this here, I wouldn't stay. That moment has come," she said.

Founder Mode can get you fired at some companies. At others, it appears to be the only path to promotion. Does it have merit? Without question. Does it also negatively impact organizations and individuals? The evidence is irrefutable.

The District Manager Who Couldn't Breathe

Melissa was a district operations manager for a national retailer. Her VP had a reputation for brilliance. He knew every detail of merchandising, store layouts, and weekly promotions. But what made him admired at the top left Melissa suffocating in the middle.

Every new display had to be photographed and texted to him for approval. Store managers couldn't even change an endcap without waiting for his feedback. Melissa remembers a call where she presented a simple weekend staffing adjustment. The VP interrupted and spent twenty minutes dictating exactly how many hours each store should allocate, down to which cashier would be on which shift. "It's faster if I just do it," he said.

At first, Melissa admired his passion and experience. But over time, her team stopped suggesting improvements. Why experiment when every decision was going to be rewritten? She felt her experience and opinions didn't matter to her VP. It seemed he was just looking for managers at her level to follow orders and not offer ideas. She felt ignored and overlooked constantly.

The Battle Cry and the Blind Spot

Back in Silicon Valley, Brian found himself energized by the controversy he created. Speaking requests poured in from conferences around the world. Business journalists called for quotes. A symbol of Brian's unexpected new celebrity status arrived in a package at Airbnb headquarters: a black baseball cap with huge white letters spelling out "FOUNDER MODE." Brian opened the box, smiled, and laughed as he showed colleagues what some new fan had sent him. Then he took the cap, walked into the executive conference room, and placed it on a shelf where all would see it during future meetings.

The debate Brian Chesky ignited is critical because it zeroes in on the central purpose of this book. To **Deliver** requires two things he instinctively understood: the absolute **Clarity** of a destination and the relentless **Movement** needed to reach it. His manifesto celebrated the passion and energy of a leader who could will these into existence.

But what he missed, and what so many leaders miss, is the essential third ingredient of the Leader Operating System that delivers at scale: organizations cannot sustain **Movement** *at scale* without deep team **Alignment**. The Founder Mode formula is powerful, but it's incomplete. It leaves out the very element required for compounding success. Perhaps Brian couldn't see the alternative because he, like most leaders today, had never experienced an organization that showed him the complete formula for sustained delivery of desired results.

While the battle lines were clearly drawn over Founder Mode, the public debate became a sideshow. As the media chased the unicorns and the

DELIVER

controversy, a quiet movement was already scaling organizations and advancing the careers of leaders who had discovered a new way to deliver. The real solution wasn't about choosing sides; it was about realizing that both sides were fighting on the wrong battlefield.

DELIVER

Chapter 1: Founder Mode

– Quick Start –

Key Points:

- Brian Chesky's manifesto rejected "hire great people and get out of the way."
- Founder Mode = hands-on, systematic, leader-driven control.
- Creates impressive short-term results but damages relationships long-term.
- Like performance steroids, building gains that can't be sustained without escalating costs.

Red Flags You're in Founder Mode:

- Team waits for your decisions on everything.
- High turnover among talented employees.
- You're the bottleneck for most initiatives.
- People comply but don't contribute ideas.

Action Steps:

- **Consider:** Reflect on leaders you've worked for who clearly were in Founder Mode. How did their leadership approach affect you and others?
- **Seek Feedback:** Ask a peer or a trusted direct report, "On a scale of 1 to 10, how much do you think I focus on execution (1) versus collaboration (10)?"
- **Start Doing:** Listening for evidence of when you may be in Founder Mode. If you rarely operate in that mode identify when others do and note the impact it has on others.

DELIVER

> **The Reality:**
> Founder Mode isn't sustainable because it doesn't scale beyond the leader's capacity.

CHAPTER 2

THE CONSENSUS REVOLUTION

THE EMAIL ARRIVED on a Tuesday in February 2013, and Tony knew it would change everything he'd built.

Sitting in his sparse Airstream trailer in downtown Las Vegas—200 square feet of deliberate minimalism that looked more like a monk's cell than a billionaire's quarters—Tony Hsieh read the resignation letter from one of his most talented employees.

The message was brutally simple: "I'm leaving because this place has become a bureaucratic nightmare. We spend more time in meetings about meetings than actually serving customers. I came here to make a difference, not to navigate endless approval chains and politics."

Tony stared at the screen for twenty minutes. This wasn't just any employee complaining—this was someone who embodied everything Zappos stood for. Someone who had drunk the Kool-Aid, lived the culture, and was walking away because the very thing Tony thought he'd eliminated—soul-crushing corporate bureaucracy—had somehow returned.

That single email would launch one of the most ambitious and ultimately devastating management experiments in corporate history.

Destroying the Org Chart

Tony built Zappos on a simple but revolutionary premise: hire good people and trust them completely. The famous online shoe company's culture was legendary, build on ten core values including "Create fun and a little weirdness" and "Build open and honest relationships with communication." Employees had $2,000 spending limits to solve customer problems without asking permission. Customer service representatives could send flowers to grieving customers, upgrade shipping for free, or even stay on the phone for ten hours with lonely callers who just needed someone to talk to.

The stories became corporate legend: representatives sending pizza to hungry customers at 2 AM, helping someone find the nearest late-night bar in Las Vegas, or shipping a single pair of shoes overnight to a wedding guest who'd forgotten to pack formal footwear.

It wasn't just customer service theater—it was a philosophy. Tony believed that if you created a culture where people felt trusted and empowered, they would do extraordinary things. The results spoke for themselves: Zappos grew from nothing to over $1 billion in annual sales, consistently ranked among the best places to work, and eventually attracted Amazon's attention with a massive acquisition offer.

But as Zappos scaled past 1,500 employees, the bureaucracy that Tony thought he'd banished reemerged. Layers of management appeared.

Politics crept in. Approval processes multiplied. The very culture he'd fought to create was being suffocated by the traditional corporate structures that growth seemed to demand.

That resignation email was Tony's wake-up call. If bureaucracy was the disease, the cure was obvious: eliminate hierarchy entirely.

In 2013, Tony announced that Zappos would transition to "holacracy"—a management system that would replace traditional bosses and org charts with self-organizing teams called "circles." Employees would take on multiple "roles" instead of job titles. Decision-making would be distributed throughout the organization. No more managers. No more traditional hierarchy. Just pure, democratic self-organization.

The transition began with evangelical fervor. Tony hired consultants, mandated company-wide training, and restructured the entire organization into hundreds of overlapping circles. Employees were told they were pioneering the future of work—creating a company that could scale without losing its soul.

The early signs were promising. Employee engagement scores hit all-time highs. People felt energized by the radical experiment. The business press celebrated Zappos as a glimpse into the future of organizational design. Tony appeared on magazine covers and keynoted conferences around the world, explaining how holacracy would revolutionize corporate America.

The Tomato Plant Revolution

While Tony was dismantling hierarchy in Las Vegas, something even more radical was happening in the tomato fields of Central California. Chris Rufer built Morning Star Company on a principle that sounded impossible: no bosses, no job titles, no management hierarchy of any kind.

DELIVER

At Morning Star, every employee was a "self-managed person." Instead of reporting to supervisors, workers negotiated directly with colleagues about responsibilities, performance, and compensation. There were no traditional performance reviews—instead, each person received feedback from everyone they worked with throughout the year. Salary decisions emerged from peer negotiations, not management dictates.

During harvest season, when the company processed millions of tons of tomatoes in a few intense months, there wasn't a single traditional manager directing operations. Decisions emerged from the bottom up, through peer negotiation and collective problem-solving. Truck drivers coordinated directly with processing plant operators. Quality control specialists worked with field teams without layers of bureaucracy.

The results validated the most optimistic predictions about human nature. Morning Star became one of the world's largest tomato processors, handling roughly 25% of the tomatoes processed in the United States. The company operated multiple facilities, employed hundreds of full-time workers, and managed thousands of seasonal employees during peak harvest—all without traditional management.

Chris Rufer wasn't just running a business—he was proving a philosophy. "Everyone is the CEO of their own job," he explained. "When you give people freedom and responsibility, they rise to meet it. Traditional management isn't just unnecessary—it's counterproductive. It assumes people can't be trusted, when the opposite is true."

The Morning Star model attracted attention from business schools, consultants, and executives worldwide. Here was proof that large-scale operations could function—even thrive—without traditional hierarchy. If it worked in the demanding environment of agricultural processing, it could work anywhere.

The Academic Validation

The Harvard Business School case study on Morning Star became required reading in management courses on other campuses. Professor Gary Hamel proclaimed it a glimpse into the future of organizational design. "Morning Star has proven that you can run a large, complex business without a traditional management hierarchy," Hamel wrote. "The results speak for themselves."

Academic papers began documenting the benefits of consensus-driven management. This wasn't just about Zappos or tomatoes; it was about a new, flatter approach to how we work. A landmark study from MIT found that organizations with high employee autonomy in knowledge work environments were significantly more likely to report lower turnover and better performance compared to traditional hierarchical structures. Stanford research showed that teams with highly distributed leadership generated more innovative solutions in short-term creative projects.

Researchers at INSEAD documented how consensus-based decision-making led to higher employee engagement across industries. Their multi-year longitudinal study found that organizations shifting toward distributed authority saw improvements in both employee satisfaction and financial performance.

The Gallup organization's research seemed to validate the trend. Their annual State of the American Workplace report found that only 32% of American workers were engaged at their jobs—but organizations that embraced employee empowerment and distributed decision-making consistently scored 20-30 percentage points higher on engagement metrics.

The conclusion felt inevitable: the command-and-control era was ending, and the consensus revolution was just beginning. The academic evidence seemed overwhelming: consensus worked.

DELIVER

The Anti-Consensus Alternative

Tony Hsieh and the tomato executives from Central California were never invited to visit Netflix—and if they had shown up, Reed Hastings, Netflix's CEO and co-founder, might have dismissed them like a bad indie script from a desperate studio. The idea of building a company around consensus or self-organization would have landed like a cliché pitch in a room full of editors obsessed with precision, speed, and performance. Netflix wasn't built on harmony; it was built on heat.

While Tony was reinventing management through empowerment and distributed authority, Reed Hastings and Patty McCord were quietly dismantling the prevailing myths of "friendly" leadership. Together, they created one of the most influential and unapologetically performance-driven cultures in corporate history. They didn't just reject hierarchy—they rejected anything that stood in the way of speed, accountability, and excellence.

"We're not a family. We're a team," Hastings declared repeatedly. "A dream team, not a kindergarten."

To Hastings, the family metaphor wasn't just inaccurate—it was toxic. "The classic metaphor for companies was the family," he said. "That's kind of baloney, because you'll lay someone off in a way you wouldn't your sister." He preferred the sports team model, where the goal was to win championships, not accommodate underperformance. "If you want to win a championship, you've got to have incredible talent at every position," he explained. At Netflix, the infamous keeper test was blunt: "Adequate performance gets a generous severance package." Hastings didn't want consensus—he wanted clarity, intensity, and results. "You've got to earn your job every year at Netflix."

Patty McCord, Netflix's Chief Talent Officer during its formative years, was equally allergic to consensus thinking. "When people say they want a family at work, what they usually mean is, 'I want to be safe from criticism,'" she wrote. But safety, she argued, doesn't produce innovation. "If your workplace is built on being nice, then nobody tells the truth. And if nobody tells the truth, nobody gets better." McCord believed consensus wasn't kindness—it was compromise. It dulled edges, slowed decisions, and protected mediocrity. Her strategy was subtraction, not addition: strip out every rule, policy, or approval that slowed people down.

"We didn't create the Netflix culture by adding things. We did it by removing the crutches that make people feel comfortable but unaccountable."

The Gathering Storm

The first cracks in the consensus revolution appeared gradually, then all at once.

At Zappos, the holacracy transition that was supposed to take months stretched into years. What had initially felt liberating began to feel oppressive in a different way. Employees spent countless hours in "governance meetings" just to clarify who was responsible for what. Simple decisions that once took minutes now required multiple circle consultations and complex role negotiations.

The very bureaucracy Tony had tried to eliminate was being replaced by something even more cumbersome—endless discussion without clear accountability. Employees complained that they spent more time talking about work than actually working. Projects stalled as teams struggled to reach consensus on basic decisions.

Customer service scores began to slip as representatives became unclear about their authority to make decisions. The famous $2,000 spending limit became meaningless when employees had to consult multiple circles before taking action. Response times increased.

DELIVER

By 2015, Tony realized the transition was stalling. The company was caught between two worlds—neither the nimble startup it had been nor the distributed organization it was trying to become. In a moment of desperation, he issued an ultimatum: fully commit to holacracy or take a generous severance package and leave.

One in five workers, around 260 people, walked out the door. Twenty percent of the workforce quit—all at once!

Tony was stunned. He had started this entire experiment because ONE person had quit, frustrated by bureaucracy. Now, in what felt like a single devastating day, he had hundreds of people rejecting his solution. The irony was crushing: maybe an unhealthy culture isn't just from leaders who overstretch and rule like founder-mode champions. He had just discovered that leaning too much into consensus and being too hands-off, swirling in discussion without action, yields a similar result.

Zappos's disappointment with the failed experiment affected Tony profoundly, both professionally and personally. For the first time in eight years, the company fell off Fortune's Best Companies to Work For list, with scores declining on 48 of 58 survey questions. The magic that had made Zappos special was disappearing, replaced by confusion and endless processes.

At Morning Star, the democratic approach continued, but unfortunately, it hasn't led to significant market share growth, employee headcount expansion, or major revenue increases—or any acquisition offers in a food production industry full of huge players hungry for consolidation targets.

Even Medium, one of holacracy's most high-profile adopters, quietly abandoned the system after three years. "Holacracy exerted a small but persistent tax on both our effectiveness and our sense of connection to each other," wrote the company's head of operations. "It was getting in the way of work."

Other companies that had embraced "Consensus Mode" management began quietly pulling back. Buffer, the social media management platform, scaled back its radical transparency policies after finding they slowed decision-making. GitHub abandoned its consensus-driven approach to product development when projects began stalling indefinitely.

The consensus revolution that had seemed so promising was revealing its fundamental flaw: in the real world, consensus often meant paralysis, and distributed decision-making frequently meant no decisions at all.

The Question Nobody Wanted to Ask

The research that had once seemed so compelling began to look different under closer scrutiny. The MIT study that showed the benefits of employee autonomy had been conducted primarily with knowledge workers in a few industries. The Stanford research on distributed leadership focused on short-term creative projects, not ongoing operational decisions.

Most tellingly, the longitudinal studies that claimed to show sustained benefits from consensus management had follow-up periods of only two to three years—not long enough to capture the full effects of organizational changes that took time to manifest.

When researchers began looking at longer time horizons, the picture became more complex. Organizations that had initially thrived under consensus-driven approaches often hit scaling walls. Decision-making slowed as more voices were added to every conversation. Innovation decreased as teams became focused on achieving unanimous agreement rather than pushing boundaries.

DELIVER

The very engagement scores that had initially justified the consensus approach began to reveal their limitations. High engagement didn't necessarily correlate with high performance. Teams could feel great about their inclusive decision-making process while failing to deliver results.

But perhaps the most damaging critique came from an unexpected source: the employees themselves. Exit interviews from consensus-driven organizations revealed a pattern that contradicted the research findings. High performers were leaving not because they felt disempowered, but because they were frustrated by the inability to move quickly on good ideas.

"I spent six months trying to get approval for a simple website change," wrote one former Buffer employee. "By the time we reached consensus, three competitors had already implemented similar features."

Just Make a Decision!

We saw something similar at one of the world's largest drug companies. A new director of scientists at the company's vast campus in Thousand Oaks, California, contacted our firm for assistance in helping her create a high-performing team. She had met us at a senior-level retreat a few weeks earlier.

"I'd appreciate your perspective as our team comes together," she told us during a Microsoft Teams call. We arranged to spend 30 minutes interviewing each of her new direct reports and then report back on the themes we observed.

There was complete alignment on her team regarding how much they liked their new boss. "She's a wonderful person. You can't help but appreciate her experience and how open she is to our ideas," said one team member. As aligned as they were in their praise, they all offered the same constructive feedback.

When we asked, "Where are her opportunities for growth, or what coaching would you give her after the first 90 days?" they all responded uniformly. "It's time for her to make a decision. She knows our perspectives and has heard our ideas. It's time for her to share her vision and set our priorities," one person said.

The honeymoon was ending. Their appreciation for her as a person was being overshadowed by their frustration with the endless discussion and lack of clarity on priorities and what mattered most.

Real Artists Ship

In 2010, technology blogger Ryan Tate sent a lengthy email to Steve Jobs criticizing Apple's iPad policies and arguing that the company was becoming too controlling and corporate. The email was passionate, well-reasoned, and reflected the thoughtful dialogue that Consensus Mode leaders valued.

Jobs' response was brief and brutal: "Real artists ship."

Three words that cut through all the discussion, debate, collaborative exploration, and nuanced consideration of different perspectives. Three words that captured what consensus leaders consistently missed: at some point, the talking has to stop, and the doing has to begin. Real artists ship.

The story spread quickly through Silicon Valley because it crystallized something many executives felt but couldn't articulate. While competitors held endless meetings to ensure everyone felt heard, Apple was

DELIVER

launching products that changed the world. While other companies built consensus around every decision, Apple made decisions that created entirely new markets.

Jobs understood something that Tony and Chris seemed to miss: the marketplace doesn't care about your process. Customers don't reward you for thoughtful discussions. Competitors don't wait while you build consensus.

The consensus revolution was eating its own children.

The False Promise

But this isn't about an experiment in Las Vegas or a commendable approach in California. The reality is that tens of thousands of managers across industries share Tony's dream. Perhaps they've worked for overreaching Founder Mode types and romanticize democratic rule in the departments or business units they run. These managers pride themselves on being inclusive and ensuring every voice is heard, even if they're repeating the same points. They are well-meaning managers who initially have high engagement scores and strive to be well-liked.

We've seen it in mid-level managers.

Perhaps what drove these consensus leaders wasn't a philosophical commitment to collaboration, but something more uncomfortable: insecurity about being disliked. They had watched founder-mode leaders get criticized as tyrants and autocrats, and they chose the opposite extreme.

But in avoiding the discomfort of making unpopular decisions, they created a different kind of dysfunction. Endless meetings replaced decisive action. Consensus-building became an excuse for avoiding accountability. The desire to be liked by everyone prevented them from being respected by anyone.

These leaders often seem more interested in preserving harmony than driving results. They would rather be inclusive than effective. They would rather avoid making enemies than make difficult decisions that actually move organizations forward.

Lean this way too long, and one of two things happens in teams and companies led by consensus-mode leaders: they either start to lose talent and driven people like Tony did, or they eventually realize that the team, organization, and even their own careers are stagnant. They lack progress. They are failing to deliver. And that's not sustainable.

Tony Hsieh's revolution was a well-intentioned search for the human element missing from top-down leadership. His genius was in creating a culture of psychological safety and a deep sense of team **Alignment**—the very ingredient Brian Chesky's approach lacked. But in solving for collaboration, he created the opposite problem. The endless swirl of discussion sacrificed the decisive **Clarity** of a destination and, ultimately, the forward **Movement** required to **Deliver** results. His experiment proved a critical lesson: perfect **Alignment** around going nowhere is still going nowhere.

The leadership landscape is littered with the wreckage of these two extremes. On one side, the burned-out teams of Founder Mode. On the other, the stalled projects of Consensus Mode. Leaders feel trapped, swinging from one flawed approach to the other, searching for a balance that doesn't exist. But what if the answer isn't to balance these two broken models, but to replace them? What if leaders need to stop choosing a *style* and start installing a **Leader Operating System**?

DELIVER

Chapter 2: The Consensus Revolution
– Quick Start –

Key Points:

- Tony Hsieh's holacracy experiment eliminated hierarchy completely.
- Consensus Mode = distributed authority, democratic decision-making.
- 20% of Zappos' workforce quit when forced to choose full commitment.
- Creates engagement without execution, enthusiasm without outcomes.

Red Flags You're in Consensus Mode:

- Endless meetings that don't produce decisions.
- Projects stall waiting for unanimous agreement.
- High engagement scores but missed performance targets.
- "Let's discuss this more" becomes the default response.

Action Steps:

- **Consider:** How much do you lean into discussion versus decision-making? Do your meetings typically go long? Do you like to fully consider all options before being decisive?
- **Seek Feedback:** Ask several direct reports, "In our team meetings, how often do you find yourself thinking the discussion is going on too long and we just need to make a decision? Does that happen frequently, sometimes, or hardly ever?"
- **Start Doing:** Begin to get more comfortable with making decisions when you have heard enough to make an informed

DELIVER

decision. End meetings on time. When the meeting starts to swirl, move onto the next agenda item.

> **The Reality:**
>
> Consensus often means paralysis—talking about work instead of doing work.

CHAPTER 3

THE FALSE CHOICE

THE LATE AFTERNOON sun slanted through tall windows, casting geometric patterns across polished hardwood floors in a sprawling Beverly Hills estate. In the center of this shrine to creativity sat an elderly man in a burgundy velvet armchair, his silver hair perfectly styled despite his ninety-plus years, hands gesturing animatedly as he spoke to an interviewer with the theatrical flair of a born storyteller.

"You know," he said, leaning forward conspiratorially, "people always ask me about the secret to creating heroes. They think it's about the powers, the costumes, the spectacular battles. But that's not it at all."

He paused, his gaze drifting to a framed piece of original artwork on the nearby wall, a sketch of a young man in a distinctive red and blue costume, web-lines extending from his wrists as he swung between towering skyscrapers.

"The real magic happens when you give people something they've never seen before, someone who refuses to accept that life has to be about

DELIVER

impossible choices." His voice grew more passionate. "Life's always throwing tough choices at you, like you've got to pick between saving your sweetheart or a bus full of strangers."

The man suddenly stood, moving with surprising energy toward the framed artwork. He placed his hand gently on the glass, looking at the sketch with the pride of a father admiring his child.

"But this kid?" He turned back, his eyes now blazing with creative fire. "This kid says, 'Nuts to that!' He's human, sure, he messes up, he doubts himself, but he never buys into those traps where you're supposed to sacrifice one good thing for another."

The interviewer's voice was barely audible: "Mr. Lee, can you tell us about—"

"Call me Stan. Stan Lee," he said firmly, straightening to his full height. "Creator of Spider-Man, the X-Men, the Fantastic Four, and more heroes than I can count. And let me tell you something about this particular wall-crawler here..."

He pointed dramatically at the artwork, his voice taking on the cadence of someone who had told this story a thousand times but still believed in it completely.

"When I dreamed up Spider-Man, I wanted a hero who wasn't a god or a billionaire, just a kid, Peter Parker, with bills to pay, homework to finish, and a heart bigger than his bank account. With great power comes great responsibility, yeah, but that means finding a way to do both, to save everybody, because that's what a real hero does. He's got the guts and the brains to reject false choices and keep swinging no matter how heavy the odds."

Stan Lee's philosophy played out in his most famous creation. When Spider-Man faced villains' traps, like saving forty-seven children trapped in a bus or saving the woman he loves, he rejected the premise entirely. "I choose both," he declared. It's exactly this thinking that transforms businesses when leaders refuse to accept false trade-offs.

Modern leaders face false choices every day in boardrooms, strategy sessions, and executive coaching conversations across the globe. Not with children and cable cars, but with equally impossible choices presented as the only options available: Founder Mode or Consensus Mode? Brian Chesky's hands-on control or Tony Hsieh's radical democracy? Speed or collaboration? Results or relationships? Innovation or efficiency?

This isn't just about business efficiency or team dynamics. This is about the future of how humans organize themselves around shared work. While leaders are trapped in century-old debates about control versus collaboration, entire organizations are being disrupted by entities that have transcended these limitations entirely.

The stakes couldn't be higher. In a world where competitive advantage comes from speed, innovation, and human engagement simultaneously, leaders who remain trapped in false choices aren't just suboptimal; their value is diminishing.

The Pattern We Discovered

After decades working with executives at Fortune 500 companies across every major industry, from pharmaceuticals to manufacturing to technology to healthcare, we discovered something that changes everything about how we think about leadership effectiveness. The vast majority of companies that request our firm's involvement lean heavily into either the command-and-control culture we label Founder Mode or the

DELIVER

collaborative swirl we call Consensus Mode. But not every company, and certainly not every executive and manager, is choosing one of those two options these days.

We first noticed a third alternative occasionally. These organizations, or more often just a business unit or department here or there, were transcending what we saw everywhere else. Not only were these teams delivering strong financial performance, increasing speed to market, and hitting near-impossible quality and safety metrics, but they were also leading their industries in employee satisfaction and retention of their best people.

These leaders, and in some cases entire organizations, are rejecting both Founder Mode and Consensus Mode. They don't toggle between control and collaboration depending on the situation. They don't try to balance competing approaches or find some middle ground between extremes. They transcend both approaches entirely.

We call these leaders Third Leaders, and they operate with a fundamentally different understanding of what leadership actually is. While Founder Mode Managers and Consensus Mode Managers argue about methodology, Third Leaders focus on engineering results. While others debate philosophy, Third Leaders build systems that deliver both engagement and performance, both innovation and execution, both speed and sustainability.

But before we reveal what Third Leaders do differently, we need to understand exactly why the two dominant approaches, despite their passionate advocates and impressive short-term results, ultimately fail when put to the test of sustained performance.

Leader Modes: The Two Paths to Limitation

Through research and consulting experience, we've identified that roughly 90% of leaders default to one of two distinct approaches when facing pressure, complexity, or high-stakes situations:

Founder Mode Managers: The hands-on, systematic, leader-driven approach that Brian Chesky advocates, and that Steve Jobs, Elon Musk, Jeff Bezos, and countless "visionary" CEOs have used to build dominant companies. These leaders prioritize clarity, speed, and direct control over outcomes. These companies prohibit the use of consultants, coaches, and any outsiders. They build tall walls around their campuses to keep outsiders out. And they invest almost nothing in developing or training managers. Degrees or IQs identify real talent.

Consensus Mode Managers: The collaborative, democratic, consensus-driven approach that Tony Hsieh championed at Zappos, that Chris Rufer built at Morning Star, and that Amy Edmondson validated in her Harvard research. These leaders prioritize psychological safety, distributed decision-making, and inclusive processes. They lean hard into developing their managers, often through a massively complex training approach that teaches leaders how to trust people, become better coaches, have hard conversations, discover their why, be inclusive, build psychological safety, develop emotional intelligence, and influence others. You get the point.

Both modes can generate impressive results. Both have passionate advocates who can point to research, case studies, and personal experience that validates their approach. Both address real problems that the other mode struggles to solve.

But both modes also contain the seeds of their own destruction.

DELIVER

The Fitness Book Club Problem

Imagine a group of friends who meet every week to talk about fitness. They read books on strength training, discuss the latest podcast on nutrition, and share Instagram posts about recovery routines. They even have a group text stream filled with encouragement, affirmations, and meal prep photos. There's genuine support and real camaraderie. They trust each other. They care.

But here's the problem: nobody's actually working out.

They don't meet at the gym but instead at a local bar while throwing back their favorite brews. The Fitness Book Club is having powerful conversations about doing the hard thing, but they're just not doing it.

This is exactly what happens with Consensus Mode approaches that prioritize process over performance. The Consensus Mode Manager builds a safe space, a high-trust team, and an idea factory. People feel seen, respected, and valued. But when the pressure hits, when the business pivots, or when performance is required, this high-trust culture doesn't convert to high performance. It's collaboration without consequences.

The Steroid Leader Problem

For Founder Mode advocates, directive approaches represent leadership at its most effective: decisive, focused, and results-oriented. They argue that in a world of increasing complexity and accelerating change, organizations need leaders who can cut through the noise, make tough decisions, and drive execution with unwavering focus.

But there's a problem with this approach that becomes apparent when we examine it more closely. Founder Mode, for all its apparent effectiveness, often resembles performance enhancement through artificial means.

Consider the bodybuilder on anabolic steroids. The results are impressive and immediate: muscle mass increases dramatically, strength gains exceed natural limits, recovery time between workouts decreases significantly, and physical appearance transforms in ways that seem impossible through natural training. For a while, everything appears to be successful. The mirror reflects a physique that commands respect. Other gym members seek advice, wanting to understand the secret behind such a remarkable transformation.

But underneath the impressive exterior, a different story unfolds. The steroid user becomes trapped in a cycle where stopping the enhancement means losing the gains, but continuing means accepting escalating health risks. What seemed like sustainable success was actually borrowed performance that came with a hidden cost.

This mirrors what happens with Founder Mode approaches that rely too heavily on directive control and leader-driven decision-making.

Founder Mode Managers "win" by creating immediate, visible results through hyperfocus on measurable metrics, demanding urgency and accountability across all activities, clear directives that eliminate ambiguity and debate, and centralized decision-making that speeds implementation. They often rise quickly in organizations that reward short-term performance. Quarterly numbers improve. Efficiency metrics show green. Projects complete ahead of schedule. The Founder Mode Manager gets promoted, recognized, and held up as an example of effective leadership.

But beneath the impressive results, organizational dysfunction quietly develops. Employee engagement gradually erodes as people feel micromanaged and undervalued. Innovation stagnates because experimentation and risk-taking are discouraged. Institutional knowledge walks out the door as talented individuals seek more autonomy elsewhere. Decision-making capability atrophies throughout the organization as people become dependent on leader direction. Adaptability decreases because the system is optimized for efficiency rather than learning.

DELIVER

Eventually, the gains stall. The metrics that once showed consistent improvement plateau or decline. The leader who once seemed unstoppable begins struggling to maintain momentum. And when that Founder Mode Manager departs, through promotion, termination, or career change, the system collapses.

The Research Validation

These observations align with groundbreaking research from MIT's Human Dynamics Laboratory, which conducted the largest study of team performance ever attempted. Dr. Alex Pentland and his team tracked 2,674 team members across 21 organizations over six years, measuring everything from individual capabilities to communication patterns to project outcomes.

The results shattered conventional assumptions about what makes teams successful:

- The factor that most predicted team success wasn't talent, experience, or even the quality of ideas. It was whether teams had developed what researchers called "balanced energy patterns," communication rhythms where everyone contributed roughly equally to discussions and decisions.
- Teams with the most balanced participation outperformed teams with superstars by more than 30%. Even when individual team members were less skilled, teams that learned to coordinate effectively delivered better results than those reliant on individual brilliance.
- Most remarkably, the highest-performing teams weren't those with the clearest individual roles; they were those where everyone understood the same definition of success. When researchers asked members of high-performing teams to independently write down their team's top three priorities, 89% of responses were identical. When they asked the same question of average-performing teams, only 23% of responses matched.

This research validates what Third Leaders intuitively understand: sustainable excellence comes from engineering alignment around shared objectives, not from choosing between control and collaboration. The most effective teams had transcended the false choice entirely.

Introducing LeaderOS: The Third Way

What Third Leaders have discovered, and what this book will show you how to implement, is that sustainable success requires installing a **Leader Operating System**. Think of it not as choosing a style like Founder Mode or Consensus Mode, but as engineering a system that integrates the best of both while eliminating their fatal flaws. We call this system **LeaderOS**, which will enable you to enter Scale Mode. This framework will be our focus for the rest of this book.

Just as your smartphone's operating system allows dozens of different apps to work together seamlessly, LeaderOS provides the foundational framework that enables you to deliver exceptional results while building institutional capabilities that compound over time. It consists of three integrated components that must be installed in sequence:

DELIVER

First, we install **Clarity**. This tool allows a legacy retailer like **Target** to engineer a stunning turnaround by focusing 350,000 employees on just three numbers. It's the antidote to the confusion that plagues organizations, like the **hospital system** where a well-intentioned 80-item "balanced scorecard" created paralysis instead of progress. **Clarity** is the first step: engineering a shared definition of success so precise that it ends the swirl of competing priorities.

Next, we build **Alignment**. This explains why a championship **NBA team** can collapse at the finish line of a remarkable season and moments from a championship trophy. It happened not because of a lack of talent, but from a lack of **Alignment**. It's the force that allowed a **company at rock bottom** to turn its year around, starting with an honest conversation in a basement meeting room led by a manager who understood what's required to create alignment. You'll see how **two hospitals in the same system** achieved dramatically different results because one leadership team understood how to create genuine ownership while the other simply created awareness.

Finally, we generate **Movement**. This is how **SpaceX** is dominating the commercial space race with a ruthless focus on High-Leverage Activities. It's what allowed the world's most powerful **AI supercomputer** to be built in a stunning 122 days inside an abandoned Memphis warehouse. It was the missing piece in the explosive **executive meeting in a Philadelphia highrise** where beliefs between departments halted all progress, proving that **Movement** is about clearing internal roadblocks, not just external execution.

These three components work together as a system. **Clarity** without **Alignment** creates awareness but not ownership. **Alignment** without **Movement** creates enthusiasm but not results. **Movement** without **Clarity** creates activity but not progress. When all three function together, you can finally stop hoping for success and start engineering it.

What You're About to Learn

The remainder of this book is not theory; it's a practical, step-by-step implementation guide forged from the real-world challenges of the organizations you've just read about. You'll learn the specific frameworks that tens of thousands of leaders around the world have used to transform their results.

- In the **Clarity** section, you'll learn how to distill your team's entire annual plan into three memorable numbers, your **Team Key Results (TKRs)**.
- In the **Alignment** section, you'll get the three-step process that is simple yet powerful in creating alignment on teams and between teams.
- In the **Movement** section, you'll discover how to identify the **High-Leverage Activities** that truly drive your TKRs, allowing you to reduce noise and increase efficiency on your team.

Most importantly, you'll discover that becoming a Third Leader isn't about changing your personality. It's about installing an operating system that makes you and your team profoundly more effective. The cable car doesn't have to fall. The girlfriend doesn't have to die. You can save both. The question is: Are you ready to reject the false choice and learn how?

DELIVER

Chapter 3: The False Choice
– Quick Start –

Key Points:

- Most leaders are trapped choosing either Founder Mode (control) or Consensus Mode (collaboration).
- 90% of leaders default to one mode, missing the Third Leader option entirely.
- LeaderOS transcends both approaches: Clarity + Alignment + Movement.

The Pattern:

- Consensus Mode: High trust, low results (Fitness Book Club Problem).
- Founder Mode: High results, low sustainability (Steroid Leader Problem).
- Third Leaders: High results + high sustainability through LeaderOS.

Action Steps:

- **Consider:** When facing a difficult situation, which leadership mode—Founder Mode (control) or Consensus Mode (collaboration)—do you naturally gravitate toward?
- **Seek Feedback:** Ask a mentor or peer, "When you observe me lead, do you see me prioritize getting results quickly, or do I focus more on team relationships? Which way do you see me lean more?"
- **Start Doing:** Begin to install LeaderOS in the way you lead others. Develop the skills of creating Clarity, building Alignment, and generating Movement. We'll show you how in the coming chapters.

DELIVER

> **Third Leader Realization:**
>
> Sustained results don't come from switching back and forth between these two flawed modes but by transcending them.

PART TWO

WELCOME TO CHAOS

CHAPTER 4

GATE C24

IT'S 6:47 PM ON A TUESDAY at Dallas-Fort Worth International Airport, and passengers are living through what feels like a social experiment designed to test the limits of human patience.

Flight 1247 to Chicago, originally scheduled to depart at 6:15 PM, has been delayed for the third time. The gate agent, who looks like she'd rather be anywhere else, has just announced over a crackling intercom that the new departure time is "approximately 8:30 PM, weather permitting."

Approximately. Weather permitting. In other words, "We have no idea, but please stay put and keep buying overpriced airport sandwiches."

This is Gate C24, where 200 strangers are about to demonstrate what happens when there's no clear plan, no effective leadership, and everyone starts making decisions based on their own interests.

Within minutes of the announcement, chaos begins.

DELIVER

A businessman in a wrinkled suit storms to the counter, demanding to speak to a supervisor about his "extremely important" meeting tomorrow morning. Behind him, a line forms as other passengers realize they should voice their complaints before everyone else does. The gate agent looks overwhelmed as she juggles five different rebooking requests while her computer system moves at the speed of dial-up internet.

Meanwhile, families with small children spread out across the gate area like they're setting up base camp. Diaper bags, car seats, and snack containers create an obstacle course that forces everyone else to navigate around them. The parents look apologetic but desperate; they need space, and they're going to take it whether others like it or not.

Business travelers make increasingly loud phone calls, each trying to outdo the others in demonstrating how critical their travel plans are. "I'm going to miss the Johnson presentation," one announces to the entire gate area, as if the universe might take pity and personally expedite his flight. Another paces back and forth while explaining to his colleague that the "Henderson deal is going to fall apart" if he's not in Chicago by 9 AM.

A group of college students, apparently unconcerned about the delay, decides this is the perfect time to charge all their devices. They commandeer every available power outlet, sprawling on the floor with their laptops, phones, and what appears to be a Nintendo Switch. Other passengers who need to charge their phones eye the students with growing hostility.

And then there are the vigilantes, passengers who appoint themselves as unofficial information brokers. They march between the gate counter and the departure board, providing unsolicited updates to anyone within earshot. "I heard from someone at the other gate that it's not weather, it's mechanical," one announces confidently. "Actually, my cousin works for the airline, and he says it's air traffic control," counters another. Soon, multiple contradictory rumors are circulating simultaneously, each delivered with complete certainty.

The gate agent, who began the evening trying to help everyone, has now adopted the survival strategy of avoiding eye contact and speaking in barely audible monotones. The businessman is still arguing about nonexistent upgrades. The families have created a small village of belongings. The business callers have formed a competitive loudness hierarchy. The students have established a technological fiefdom. And the information vigilantes are engaged in an increasingly heated debate about what's really causing the delay.

Nobody is happy. Nothing is getting solved. And everyone is focused on optimizing their own situation rather than improving things for the group.

The scenario is familiar to anyone who has worked in an organization with more than five people; they've been to Gate C24.

But before we explore what this chaos means for teams, let's see how different types of leaders would handle the Gate C24 situation. How a leader responds to chaos reveals everything about their approach to leadership and the results they'll ultimately achieve.

How Different Leader Modes Would Respond

The Founder Mode Leader: Spectacular Overreach

Picture someone in Founder Mode walking up to Gate C24. Let's call this manager Barb. Barb surveys the gate area with the intensity of a Navy SEAL assessing a hostage situation. This chaos is unacceptable and will end immediately. The only reason it ever started was total incompetence from idiotic softies who got promoted erroneously.

DELIVER

Barb strides directly to the gate counter, pushing passengers aside, and speaks directly to the gate agent. "You're fired!" she announces. The gate agent looks relieved and immediately sprints away as if a pit bull just broke off its leash.

Barb commandeers the PA system. "Attention minions, uh, I mean passengers. We're instituting optimal gate operations immediately. I've seen this scenario so many times I can solve this in my sleep. What I need is total silence," she says.

She designates specific seating areas by passenger type and starts issuing commands like a drill sergeant. "Business travelers, section A. Families, section B. Students, you're confined to the back wall. Move now."

When she spots the college students with their gaming console, she confiscates it and throws it in a trash can. "This is not a recreation center," she announces. "This is a transportation hub operating under emergency protocols." One student protests, and she cuts him off: "The conversation is over. You don't even have a degree yet, kid."

The vigilantes are still pacing and yelling updates. Barb walks over to them and yells while holding her open hand in the air. "Stop," she commands. She asks all five for their boarding passes. Once she collects them, she rips them up and tosses them into a recycling bin. "Your tactics are not acceptable here," she says. None challenge her. They immediately bolt for the airline assistance area to be rebooked.

Within minutes, the chaos of Gate C24 is resolved. Everyone is sitting silently in their assigned areas. Even the babies in the family section are quiet. Barb makes a few phone calls and quickly discovers the real issue is a flight crew coming in late. She contacts the airline's operations center and learns a standby crew is in the lounge. She has them reassigned to this flight. And within 15 minutes, the plane is ready to board.

DELIVER

As she announces Group One can now get on the plane, Barb wonders why no one is moving forward. She gets on the PA again and says Group Two can board now, too. A few people walk forward. As Barb surveys the gate area, she realizes what she hadn't noticed while making those phone calls. Almost all the passengers have left. Gate C24 is a ghost town.

A few minutes later, the plane is ready to take off, but it's almost completely empty. Her solution was not worth her process. Her approach left her isolated again.

The Founder Mode Leader creates impressive short-term operational efficiencies but burns down everything needed for sustained success.

The Consensus Mode Leader: Embracing the Beautiful Chaos

Picture a Consensus Mode manager walking into Gate C24. We'll call her Beth. Beth's face lights up with genuine excitement. This isn't a problem to be solved; this is humanity expressing itself authentically, and she absolutely loves it.

"This is amazing!" she announces to anyone within earshot as she starts skipping like a fourth-grade girl towards the gate agent. "Look at how everyone is organically self-organizing around their needs. This is exactly what distributed authority looks like in action!"

She immediately starts facilitating what she calls an "emergence session." She approaches the arguing businessman and says, "Hey, I love your passion about getting to Chicago. What if we created a space where everyone could share their travel stories and maybe find some collaborative solutions?"

Within minutes, she's convinced the gate agent to let her use the PA system. "Attention Gate C24 family! I love you all so much," she

DELIVER

announces with the energy of a camp counselor on Red Bull. "We're going to turn this delay into an opportunity for authentic human connection. Everyone grab a seat in our newly formed sharing circle!"

She starts passing around napkins from the coffee shop, asking everyone to write down their "emotional journey" with the delay. "No judgment, just radical honesty about your feelings," she says.

Two hours later, Gate C24 has become a therapy session. The businessman is crying. One of the moms of the small kids hands him a wet wipe. The executive has loosened his tie and shares some repressed childhood memory about his dad and his deep fear of disappointing people. The college girls are sobbing, listening to him, barely able to see through their tears as they scroll on Instagram. Everyone feels emotionally validated, included, and seen. There's just one problem: nobody has checked the actual flight status and realized it's been canceled. When one of the vigilantes finally discovers reality, he starts screaming that they're going nowhere. At that moment, Beth gets on the intercom and announces, "We must accept what we cannot control."

The Consensus Mode manager creates incredible engagement and psychological safety, but somehow the plane never actually leaves the gate.

Both approaches address real problems that teams face every day. Both have passionate advocates who can point to research and success stories. And both contain the seeds of their own destruction.

But here's what leaders need to understand: teams look like Gate C24.

This Is Every Team

Maybe it's not delayed flights and airport chaos. But every team starts as a collection of smart, capable people with different priorities, competing needs, and no clear system for coordination. Every new project, new team, merger, acquisition, or initiative begins with the organizational equivalent of Gate C24, where individuals act based on their own perspectives while lacking a shared framework that would enable effective collaboration.

This chaos isn't a sign of selfishness or incompetence; it's the starting point. It's the raw material leaders must work with.

The businessman arguing at the counter isn't a bad person; he's optimizing for his own urgent needs due to the absence of a clear process for handling the situation. The families spreading out aren't inconsiderate; they're addressing immediate problems because no one has designed a better solution. The students monopolizing the power outlets aren't selfish; they're responding rationally to their circumstances given the lack of an organized approach to shared resources.

This is the initial form of the clay that leaders get to mold. This is what naturally occurs when someone inherits a team or starts a new project. Each person does what smart individuals do when they lack clarity about how to coordinate with others: they focus on their own priorities and hope for the best.

The role of a leader is to shape this raw material into something that delivers results. Because, as we've learned from studying thousands of teams, chaos isn't the problem; chaos is where results begin.

DELIVER

The Modern Workplace

This dynamic plays out in organizations daily, and we've witnessed it firsthand in our decades of consulting with executive teams. The business world's version of Gate C24 can be even more destructive than airport delays, as airport chaos is at least temporary. Here's how real leaders are addressing team chaos:

The High-Rise Meeting
We received a call from a Fortune 10 healthcare executive: "Our leadership teams are in chaos. They're not getting along, and it's holding us back. Fix it."

At 6:00 PM in a deserted Philadelphia high-rise, ten executives arrived for a mandatory after-hours meeting. Jackets off, ties loosened, and zero faith in the process. When we called on the most senior leaders to set the tone, the first two offered forgettable platitudes.

Then came Ben, head of sales. He stood up and didn't waste time on pleasantries. He blasted the operations team and the pharmacy team telling them the performance issues in the company were absolutely and completely their fault.

This wasn't just a group of managers who didn't see eye-to-eye. It was a team at one of the highest levels of the org chart that despised each other. The chaos we saw in our initial meeting with them was jeopardizing billions of dollars in revenue at one of the world's largest companies. We'll dive more into the experience deep in this book. It was immediately obvious that they lacked clarity around a shared definition of success.

DELIVER

The Off-Site Awakening

Jason had just stepped into his role as Executive Vice President of a Fortune 50 manufacturing company, leading 20,000 people. His first executive team off-site was designed to set the tone for the future.

The meeting followed the company's formal tradition: U-shaped tables, nameplates, microphones with on/off switches. One by one, each executive delivered structured presentations while Jason's phone buzzed continuously with texts from other executives in the room.

"I can't believe she's using those numbers. She's completely off base."

"Her priorities are totally wrong. How does she not see that?"

Throughout two days of presentations, Jason received a steady stream of negative commentary about colleagues from people sitting just feet away.

At the end, he spoke up, holding his phone.

"I've been getting texts," he began. "Messages from some of you about your colleagues during this meeting." He read them aloud without naming sources.

The room sat frozen. Jason looked around and said, "This has to change. We cannot function like this anymore." In that moment, Jason began the simple but difficult work of building alignment throughout his 20,000-person team. Alignment had to start at the very top.

Telling Stories

When Russ took on a turnaround project in Phoenix, he inherited several underperforming media properties. In his first 90 days, he met with everyone to understand what was happening.

DELIVER

What he got wasn't clarity; it was chaos.

"Ken in production is your biggest problem. You've got to fire him." Others echoed this, including his boss.

When Russ finally met Ken, he found someone passionate, committed, and creative. Everywhere he turned, there was another directive: "Cancel that sports show." "Fire that talk show host." "This department is hopeless."

The team had no shared metrics, no pride, no sense of winning. Everyone was operating in silos, clinging to their own beliefs about what needed fixing. After weeks of these meetings, Russ realized the team wasn't just underperforming; it was paralyzed by unchallenged perceptions. Russ knew the clock was ticking, and his corporate media bosses expected movement. That meant identifying and changing the perceptions that had paralyzed performance.

The Shocking Truth About High-Performing Teams

When researchers at MIT set out to discover what separated high-performing teams from average ones, they expected to find the usual suspects: better talent, more resources, clearer goals. Instead, they discovered something that will fundamentally change how anyone thinks about why teams succeed or fail.

Dr. Alex Pentland tracked 2,674 team members across 21 organizations over six years, measuring everything from individual IQ scores to communication patterns. The results were stunning.

When researchers asked high-performing team members to independently write down their team's top three priorities, 89% of responses were identical. For average teams, only 23% matched.

DELIVER

High performance had little to do with individual capabilities; it was all about alignment. Teams with greater energy in communication patterns and tangible alignment outperformed teams with individual superstars by more than 30%.

The difference wasn't staffing levels, talent, or capabilities; it came down to whether a leader created a shared vision of success and alignment around the collaboration needed to achieve it.

As we saw at Gate C24, leaders have three options when facing organizational chaos:

One can be a Consensus Mode Manager like Tony Hsieh, embracing the chaos, prioritizing everyone's feelings and input, creating incredible psychological safety while somehow never actually getting the plane off the ground.

One can be a Founder Mode Manager like Brian Chesky, taking systematic control, making decisive improvements, achieving impressive short-term results while damaging the relationships and systems needed for long-term success.

Or one can be a 3rd Leader (Deliver Mode), engineering solutions that get everyone to Chicago while building the capabilities that make future flights run smoothly.

The choice between Founder Mode and Consensus Mode is a false choice. Both approaches have passionate advocates who can point to research and success stories, addressing real problems that the other mode struggles to solve. Both contain the seeds of their own destruction.

The Third Leader rejects this choice entirely.

DELIVER

The Leader Operating System

Instead of choosing between control and collaboration, speed and consensus, results and relationships, we will show you how to transcend these limitations entirely.

Your smartphone contains dozens of apps designed by different companies, serving various purposes, with different interfaces. Photography apps, social media platforms, productivity tools, navigation systems, each sophisticated enough to be a standalone business.

Yet they all work together seamlessly. You can take a photo, edit it, share it via text, post it to social media, and back it up to cloud storage without compatibility issues.

This coordination isn't magic; it's the result of an operating system that enables different applications to communicate and coordinate functions without conflict.

Leadership works the same way. Every leader develops individual capabilities, communication skills, strategic thinking, technical expertise, relationship building. These are like apps: powerful tools that serve specific functions. But without an operating system to coordinate these capabilities, even talented leaders struggle to deliver consistent results at scale.

The Leader Operating System consists of three integrated components that work together to transform Gate C24 chaos into sustained high performance:

Clarity provides the shared vision and definition of success that enables distributed decision-making without chaos. **Alignment** transforms individual awareness into collective ownership. **Movement** generates

DELIVER

sustainable progress through systematic execution and focus on High-Leverage Activities toward the metrics we must hit.

When all three function together, they create what we call "institutional ability," organizational capabilities that can deliver results consistently, even when circumstances change or when a leader isn't present to manage every detail.

This is how Third Leaders engineer success rather than hope for it. This is how they transcend the false choice between Founder Mode and Consensus Mode. This is how they build careers that accelerate while developing organizations that sustain excellence over time.

So, let's get to it. In the next sections of this book, we'll first make the case for each of these three elements of the Leader Operating System. We'll share examples of where leaders are doing it well and where they fall short, and we'll guide you through how to install LeaderOS in the way you lead. What you're about to read will change how you define effective leadership for the rest of your career.

DELIVER

Chapter 4: Gate C24
– Quick Start –

Key Points:

- Every team starts in Gate C24 chaos—individuals optimizing without coordination
- Founder Mode = controlling the chaos but damaging relationships
- Consensus Mode = embracing the chaos but never boarding the plane
- Third Leaders engineer solutions that get everyone to the destination together

Gate C24 Reality Check:

- Your team IS chaotic until you create systems for coordination
- Chaos isn't the problem—it's your starting point
- MIT research: High-performing teams have 89% alignment on top 3 priorities

Action Steps:

- **Consider:** Think about situations where you see the Gate C24 chaos. Is it trying to pick a movie to watch as a family or a restaurant to go to as a group of friends? Consider where you've seen it most recently in your career.
- **Seek Feedback:** Ask a team member, "What is a recent example where you felt like things were chaotic in our organization or on our team? On a scale of 1 to 10, how efficiently and effectively do you feel our team operates?"
- **Start Doing:** Realize that your job is to solve the natural chaos, or gravitational pull to ineffectiveness that the teams

DELIVER

you lead feel constantly. Commit to helping any team you lead be a high-performing team.

Third Leader Solution:

LeaderOS provides the operating system that transforms chaos into coordinated excellence.

PART THREE

INSTALLING LEADEROS: CREATE CLARITY

CHAPTER 5

THE CLARITY CRISIS

FEBRUARY 28, 2017. MANHATTAN.

The elevator climbed silently through the glass tower, each floor marker blinking past as Brian Cornell prepared for one of the most challenging presentations of his career. The weight of what he was about to propose felt heavier with each passing floor. In just a few minutes, Brian would walk into a room full of analysts who had serious doubts about his organization's future. They had done the math. Their biggest competitor, Amazon, had grown to thirteen times his company's value. Just yesterday, another competitor, Macy's, announced another 100 store closures.

The conversation inside quieted as Brian came through the door. Two hundred pairs of eyes tracked his movement to the podium. Brian Cornell cleared his throat and began to speak about the future of Target.

Target had just reported comparable sales down 1.5%, triggering a 13% stock plunge, the worst drop in nearly two decades. More than $5 billion in shareholder value had evaporated overnight. Across the industry, in just a period of months, retailers had shuttered a record-breaking 8,600 stores across America. The challenges facing brick-and-mortar retail seemed insurmountable.

Cornell stood before that skeptical audience and did something revolutionary. While every other retailer was trapped in the false choice between "stores" or "digital," Cornell rejected the premise entirely. He wasn't there to announce store closures or digital pivots. He was there to explain why Target's 1,800 stores weren't liabilities to be managed; they were competitive advantages waiting to be unleashed. He was there to announce the company wasn't cutting expenses but rather investing a stunning $7 billion in a strategy he believed would transform his organization and position it for growth.

Three Numbers That Defined Success

Behind Target's transformation lay something most business leaders miss entirely: the power of defining success through specific, measurable outcomes that every employee could understand and influence.

Cornell and his team distilled their entire $7 billion strategy into three crystal-clear metrics:

Metric 1: Fulfillment Cost Per Unit

Shipping an order from a store's existing inventory delivered substantial cost savings compared to traditional warehouse fulfillment. When customers used Drive Up or in-store pickup services, eliminated shipping costs created significant competitive advantages. Every store employee understood this because they lived it daily; picking an online order from their store's inventory instead of shipping it from a distant warehouse directly impacted profitability.

Metric 2: Speed and "Ready on Time" Percentage

Orders placed for Drive Up service had to be ready within two hours. Success wasn't measured by customer satisfaction surveys; it was measured by a binary outcome every team member could track in real time. Store managers across the country began their daily huddles with the same question: "What's our Ready on Time percentage?"

Metric 3: Digital Orders Fulfilled by Stores

Cornell's team tracked the percentage of digital orders fulfilled by stores rather than traditional warehouses. As this number climbed from under 50% to over 95%, it proved that Target had successfully transformed their greatest perceived liability into their most powerful competitive weapon.

These metrics forced a radical shift in mindset. Stores were no longer just showrooms; they became active fulfillment hubs. By focusing on these specific numbers, leadership removed any ambiguity about the store's evolving role. Every employee, from the backroom to the checkout lane, understood that moving inventory was now a dual-purpose mandate.

This wasn't just about logistics; it was about changing the scorecard. When you change how you score the game, players change how they play. Managers stopped viewing online orders as a distraction and started treating them as essential volume. This singular focus allowed Target to bypass the paralysis that gripped other retailers who were continually debating complex omnichannel theories without acting. Instead of drowning in data, they focused on the one lever that unlocked their massive physical footprint's latent potential and ultimately saved the company.

DELIVER

The Clarity Advantage

What made Target's transformation legendary wasn't the technology they deployed or the money they invested; it was the clarity with which they defined success. While competitors held strategy sessions about "omnichannel retail" and "customer experience optimization," Target's 350,000 employees knew exactly which numbers they were trying to move and how their daily work contributed to those numbers.

This clarity created something that money can't buy: organizational alignment at scale. From the C-suite to the stockroom, everyone understood what winning looked like. A store director in Minneapolis and a team member in Phoenix were optimizing for the same outcomes, measured by the same metrics, pursuing the same definition of success.

The results speak for themselves. By 2019, Target's digital sales had crossed $8 billion, with over 80% of that growth being fulfilled by their stores. Today, over 95% of Target's total sales, both in-store and digital, are fulfilled by a store. Their stores aren't just part of the system; they are the system.

What Cornell saw clearly in that New York hotel room, that 1,800 stores located within 10 miles of 75% of the U.S. population represented an insurmountable competitive advantage, became reality because clarity enabled execution.

Target's breakthrough reveals something that every leader needs to understand about the relationship between clarity and execution. To grasp this concept, consider the most transformative app on your smartphone, one that has fundamentally changed how we navigate our daily lives. It's the app that none of us think about anymore.

The Most Used App on Your Phone

Google Maps represents one of the most dramatic productivity transformations we've experienced in our careers consulting organizations around the world. Twenty years ago, our assistants would spend hours preparing for client meetings, printing MapQuest directions, highlighting routes, and placing carefully folded pages in envelopes marked "Boston Meeting" or "Kansas City Keynote." We'd collect these packets before traveling, hoping the printed directions were accurate and praying the meeting location wouldn't change.

Then came Google Maps.

Suddenly, our ability to get to meetings in New Zealand, Malaysia, Budapest, Florida, or Texas became incredibly simple. You don't need help appreciating the value of this app. But perhaps you've never considered the crucial insight that applies directly to leadership: Google Maps is useless until you type in your destination.

Think about it. The app contains incredibly sophisticated technology, satellite imagery, real-time traffic data, machine learning algorithms that optimize routes, integration with local business information, and access to millions of user reviews. It represents billions of dollars in development and some of the most advanced engineering on the planet.

Yet none of that sophisticated capability matters until you type in where you want to go.

Without a destination, Google Maps is just a pretty interface displaying your current location. All that powerful technology sits dormant, waiting for the one piece of information that makes everything else valuable: where are you trying to go?

DELIVER

The moment you enter a destination, everything changes. The app instantly calculates multiple route options, estimates travel times, identifies potential obstacles, and begins guiding you step-by-step toward your goal. The same technology that was useless without direction becomes incredibly powerful with clear destination clarity.

This is exactly what leaders do, or should do, for their organizations.

Your team is like that sophisticated Google Maps technology. They have incredible capabilities, valuable experience, creative problem-solving skills, and the desire to contribute meaningfully. Without clarity on where we're trying to go, all that capability either sits idle or spins its wheels on busywork that fails to move us in the needed direction.

When you define the destination clearly, like Cornell did with his three specific metrics, suddenly all that latent capability activates. Your team doesn't just understand where they're going; they can see how their daily work contributes to getting there. They can make smart decisions about priorities, trade-offs, and resource allocation because they have a shared definition of success. Silos exist due to the lack of a shared scoreboard.

This is why clarity must be the first foundational element of LeaderOS. Leadership training that starts with soft skills and doesn't connect to delivering results is entertainment or academic but not useful for organizations where failure is not an option.

What the Research Shows

While Cornell was creating competitive advantage at Target by defining the three results that matter most, most organizations were hemorrhaging value through the lack of clarity. We've seen it repeatedly, but here are a few headlines from lengthy studies that verify what we know from experience.

The $62 million problem: Research from the Economist Intelligence Unit reveals that the average organization loses $62.4 million annually due to poor communication. The primary culprit isn't technology failures or language barriers; it's the lack of clarity about priorities and expectations.

The Productivity Drain: Harvard Business School found that knowledge workers spend 41% of their time on discretionary activities that provide little value to their organizations and could be handled by others. Nearly half of your payroll is wasted because employees don't know what truly matters.

The Execution Gap: McKinsey discovered that 70% of strategic initiatives fail during execution, primarily due to employees being unclear about their roles in the strategy. Conversely, companies with clear strategic communication are five times more likely to be high-performing.

Perhaps the most telling statistic comes from Gallup: only 40% of employees strongly agree that they know what's expected of them at work. Six out of ten people arrive at work each day without understanding what success looks like.

The Neuroscience Reality: When we lack clarity about expectations, our brains trigger the same threat response as physical danger. Stress hormones flood our systems, impairing decision-making and creativity. We literally can't perform at our best when we're confused about what matters most.

The competitive implications are devastating. While one organization wastes 41% of their employees' time on unclear priorities, their competitor with crystal-clear focus channels at least 90% of their energy toward results. That's not a marginal advantage; it's a compounding competitive moat.

DELIVER

When Lives Hang in the Balance

Sometimes the most profound lessons about clarity come from the highest stakes imaginable—literally life and death.

March 23, 2018. Northern Thailand.

Twelve boys and their soccer coach are trapped two and a half miles inside a flooded cave system. The world is watching, and failure means thirteen people die.

Standing in the makeshift command center outside Tham Luang cave, surrounded by the world's best cave divers and rescue experts, you witness something remarkable about human behavior under extreme pressure. For the first twelve days, despite having hundreds of skilled professionals working around the clock, the rescue operation remains chaotic.

Monsoon rains continue to fall, pushing more water into the cave system with each passing hour. The cave is a nightmare of narrow passages, zero visibility, and powerful currents. The boys are trapped nearly three miles from the entrance, through passages so narrow that divers must remove their oxygen tanks to squeeze through.

Multiple rescue strategies are pursued simultaneously. Some teams focus on pumping water out of the cave. Others attempt to drill alternative access shafts from above. Military divers explore underwater routes while engineers study the cave's geological structure. Everyone is working hard, but their efforts aren't coordinated or successful.

Without a clear plan and strategy, it remained an urgent disaster without direction.

Then British cave diver Rick Stanton does something that changes everything. He looks at the impossible complexity and begins stripping it down to its essence: "We need to get those boys out, and we need to do it now. Everything else is noise."

Instead of continuing to pursue multiple approaches simultaneously, Stanton and his team define the destination with brutal clarity: extract all thirteen people alive within the next 72 hours, before the next storm system arrives and makes rescue impossible.

The solution becomes simple once the destination is clear: sedate the boys to prevent panic, have expert divers guide them through one by one, and stage support teams at critical points. They took the most complex rescue operation in modern history and reduced it to its essential elements. Get in. Get them. Get out.

Thirteen days after they went missing, all twelve boys and their coach were brought out alive. The rescue that experts called impossible succeeded because leaders took overwhelming complexity and made it simple.

This principle of stripping complexity down to essential elements applies equally in business settings, as we discovered when working with a hospital CEO.

The Scorecard That Wasn't

The setting was less dramatic, but it was a place where life begins and ends for some people each day. Elaine, a smart, experienced CEO of a hospital in the northeastern U.S., asked us to work with her executive team. Their hospital was struggling with the metrics that matter most. On our first call with her, we asked Elaine if the team had clarity around the most important outcomes.

DELIVER

"Absolutely," she said. "We have a balanced scorecard."

"Oh great, can you tell us what's on it?"

She told us she needed to retrieve it from her desk. Once she did, she began reading the scorecard to us.

She started to list several metrics, and we wrote them down as quickly as possible to keep up. By the time she reached the twentieth metric, we asked, "Is that all?"

"Oh no, that's the first bucket," she said.

"Oh... how many buckets are there?"

"Four."

"How many items are roughly under each one?"

"About the same amount."

"So basically you're asking the team to prioritize 80 things?" we asked.

"It doesn't sound very good when you say it like that," she replied.

We chuckled and said we didn't mean it harshly; we were just making sure we were counting right.

This might sound familiar to anyone who's worked in a large organization. The scorecard was thorough, meticulously so. But it was also overwhelming. And that's when the real clarity gap became apparent.

We began interviewing Elaine's direct reports, asking them the same question we'd asked her: "What are the most important results the hospital has to deliver this year?"

Their answers were startlingly similar: "We have a balanced scorecard."

Each person then said, "Let me pull it out." When we told them not to retrieve the document but to instead tell us from memory what was on it, every one of Elaine's direct reports did the same thing. They listed off three or four categories on the scorecard. But none of them provided the same three. The CFO focused on financial metrics. The Chief Nursing Officer talked about patient safety and satisfaction. They all defaulted to the results their department cared about most, and none of them could give us more than three or four things.

Clarity is not a balanced scorecard. Imagine typing in 80 destinations to Google Maps all at once. The idea is ridiculous. The app would force you to prioritize where you want to go first. Everything else becomes secondary.

To Elaine's credit, she recognized the problem and was open to our coaching. Working together, we helped her distill those 80 metrics into just three Key Results. These weren't arbitrary; they reflected the hospital's most pressing priorities, the outcomes that mattered most for patients, staff, and the bottom line.

And that's when things started to shift, and real progress toward the most important results began.

Suddenly, Elaine's team had a North Star, three outcomes that guided every decision and action. Meetings became more focused, and conversations more productive. People weren't just ticking boxes on a list of

DELIVER

metrics; they were working together toward meaningful, measurable results. Different departments started to coordinate their efforts because everyone was working toward the same clearly defined destination.

Clarity requires helping people focus and prioritize around a common destination that everyone can remember, understand, and influence through their daily work.

Installing LeaderOS requires you, as the manager, to define the destination. We'll walk you through how to do that effectively. But first, we need to issue a few watchouts. These are the most common mistakes we've seen in decades of conversations with executives and training sessions with managers who thought they were creating clarity but who actually spread confusion or, worse, resentment among their teams. Beware of the clarity extremes!

DELIVER

Chapter 5: The Clarity Crisis
– Quick Start –

Key Points:

- Clarity is your team's "destination" in Google Maps
- Target's success came from three clear metrics everyone knew and understood
- Most teams waste 41% of their time on unclear priorities
- 60% of employees don't know what's expected of them at work

Your Team Has Clarity When:

- Everyone can identify your Team Key Results without needing to pull up an email or find a PowerPoint slide
- Decisions get filtered through "does this advance our TKRs?"
- Meetings connect to shared outcomes, not just urgent tasks

Action Steps:

- **Consider:** Reflect on how vague definitions of success in your team might be creating confusion, and think about what three simple metrics, like Target's fulfillment costs or speed percentages, could make your daily work feel more focused and impactful.
- **Seek Feedback:** Ask a peer manager: "In our shared projects, do you think our teams have a clear, shared understanding of what success looks like, or are we operating under different assumptions?"
- **Start Doing:** Begin every team huddle by stating one key metric that defines success for the day, building a habit of

DELIVER

reinforcing clarity in small, consistent ways to align everyone's efforts

---

Third Leader Truth:

Most people measure their success by how busy they are every day. Successful people measure success by how much progress they made toward specific, prioritized results.

CHAPTER

6

THE CLARITY EXTREMES

THE NURSES AT BACKUS HOSPITAL in Connecticut had seen enough. Their "Code RED" campaign wasn't subtle; it was a public declaration that their workplace had become unsustainable. Seventy percent turnover over five years. Mandatory overtime that stretched shifts to seventeen hours. A nursing shortage so severe that the remaining staff were drowning.

But Backus wasn't unique. Walk into hospital break rooms across America, and you'll hear the same exhausted conversations. Experienced nurses leaving the profession entirely. New graduates burning out within months. Exit interviews revealed the same theme: caring for patients had been replaced by checking boxes on endless digital protocols.

In the relentless pursuit of patient satisfaction scores that determine Medicare reimbursements, hospital administrators believed they had provided clear direction. HCAHPS (shortened in hospital jargon

DELIVER

to 'H-Caps') surveys, which patients complete about their hospital experience, directly impact millions in government payments. Hospital leaders thought they were creating clarity around their most critical objective.

What they actually created was control masquerading as clarity.

This is the first extreme leaders fall into when trying to implement LeaderOS by creating clarity. Instead of making the complex simple, they make the simple complicated. Instead of fostering shared understanding, they engineer compliance through control. Hospital executives saw their most important outcome, patient satisfaction, and believed that more specification would create more clarity. They were mistaken.

The Checklist Trap

Jessica grabbed her iPad from the nurses' station in the surgery recovery unit and opened the CipherHealth app. It was time for her mandated morning round to check on all the patients. The screen flashed "Purposeful Rounding Protocol—Begin Now." She pushed the start button and walked into Room 417.

"Good morning, Mrs. Chen," she said with a smile as the iPad prompted her to complete Step 1: "Greet patient by name." Step 2: "Ask pain level; record on scale 0-10." Step 3: "Offer water." ... Step 17: "Update the whiteboard with your name as the nurse on duty." Step 18: "Inform patient when you'll return."

Each interaction would be tracked, timed, and fed into dashboards that hospital administrators would constantly monitor. This was what leadership called "evidence-based care delivery," and Jessica was growing tired of delivering evidence instead of actual care.

Mrs. Chen looked up expectantly as Jessica worked through the checklist. Tap, introductions completed. Tap, pain assessment recorded. "How are you feeling this morning, Mrs. Chen?"

"Much better, thank you. But I wanted to ask about—"

"That's wonderful," Jessica interrupted, checking off the response and moving to the next step.

Two minutes later, Jessica tapped "Round Complete" and headed for the door. Mrs. Chen's breakfast sat untouched, and she clearly wanted to discuss something important. But none of that appeared on the eighteen-step protocol.

In the hallway, Jessica muttered to her colleague, "Eighteen steps in two minutes." She headed into Room 418 next.

The hospital system's executive team called this "clarity." They had identified their most important outcome, patient satisfaction, and created comprehensive systems to achieve it. Every nurse knew exactly what to do, when to do it, and how success would be measured.

But the expensive solutions failed spectacularly: patient satisfaction scores flatlined while nurse engagement scores plummeted. Turnover increased. Exit interviews revealed a consistent theme: "I became a nurse to care for people, not to do checklists."

Jessica's hospital had fallen into the first extreme of the clarity trap. These are leaders who believe that more specification equals more clarity.

DELIVER

Why Too Much Detail Fails

In the effort to improve specific Key Results, some leaders decide the solution is to define every desired behavior. They think that if they can script every interaction and anticipate every scenario, their teams will execute flawlessly.

The logic seems unassailable: eliminate ambiguity, reduce variability, ensure consistency. But perfect specification isn't just impossible; it's toxic. These are humans on your team, not robots. When you treat them like machines, the outcome is predictable. They quit. And before they reach the breaking point, they become disengaged and stop caring. The result is entire departments or business units that feel like their opinions don't matter. Performance always drops, and turnover always increases. Leaders who try to perfectly engineer success fail to deliver sustained results. Ambitious, driven people just don't like working for them.

Let's illustrate this critical point with a bit of humor.

Consider Sarah's experience at Ultimate Fitness Revolution. The trainer approaching her had the kind of ponytail that could be trademarked and teeth so white that at least some of them had to be fake. Her name tag read "Brittany," and her entire existence seemed designed to make normal humans question their life choices.

"Welcome to your transformation journey!" Brittany chirped. "Are you ready to unlock your inner warrior goddess?"

Sarah looked around at equipment that appeared designed by aliens trying to torment humans. "I just want to, you know, get a little exercise and be a little more active."

"Perfect!" Brittany replied, reaching under the counter. "I have exactly what you need!"

What emerged was a three-ring binder so massive it required both hands to lift, a monument to the belief that more information equals better outcomes.

"Everything you could possibly need to know is in here," Brittany explained with obvious pride. "User manuals for every machine, anatomical diagrams, nutritional information organized by body type, fitness goals, and zodiac signs. There are workout routines for beginners, intermediate, and advanced levels, plus modifications for various physical limitations, weather conditions, and astrological compatibility."

Sarah stared at this encyclopedia of fitness doom. Around her, actual fit people were doing actual exercises while she clutched a manual that was probably more comprehensive than the instructions for building a satellite.

"Is there maybe a... simpler version?"

Brittany looked genuinely confused, as if Sarah had asked her to explain quantum physics using interpretive dance. "But why would you want less information? This has everything!"

The example might be a little cutesy, but the point is serious. One of the most frequent mistakes we see leaders make when trying to create clarity is over-complicating it. They wonder why their people seem confused and disengaged despite having access to "everything they need to know."

The problem isn't that people lack information; it's that they're drowning in it. When everything is documented, nothing stands out as truly

DELIVER

important. When every process is specified, no judgment is required. When every scenario is scripted, no thinking is necessary. When every decision is predetermined, no ownership is generated.

Over-specification doesn't create clarity; it demands compliance. And compliance without engagement or ownership produces exactly what hospitals with nurse burnout have discovered: this approach looks good on paper but feels burdensome and is demoralizing to your best employees.

Corporate Executive Board research exposes the damage: employees in over-documented workplaces waste 41% of their time on activities that could be eliminated entirely. Over-documented organizations kill engagement, scoring 23% lower than companies that trust people to think.

The over-specification trap is seductive because it feels like leadership. Creating comprehensive procedures, detailed training materials, and elaborate documentation systems requires significant effort and creates the illusion of thoroughness. Leaders point to their binders, process maps, and standard operating procedures as evidence of their commitment to excellence.

At the senior executive level, this over-specification doesn't come in the form of binders but instead in bloated PowerPoint decks. The well-intentioned executive thinks they're creating clarity for the organization as they define purpose, values, pillars, priorities, strategy, principles, and behaviors. Their well-designed decks look impressive and are greeted by applause, but what's missing is honest evaluation. Here's the truth: no one has a clue what you just said, and they intend to implement none of it. They're clapping because they like getting paid.

Clarity is simple. Not complicated. One slide. Not twenty.

The Opposite Extreme

While over-specification is destructive, the opposite extreme can be equally devastating. While hospitals discovered the repercussions of endless checklists, Jack Dorsey was learning the dangers of too little direction.

It was 2018, and Twitter's offices were covered with sticky notes that looked like a colorful explosion of possibilities. Twitter was experimenting with live video streaming through Periscope, testing disappearing tweets through Fleets, developing audio conversations through Spaces, exploring long-form content through Twitter Blue, integrating newsletters through Revue, building e-commerce features, developing professional networking capabilities, and pursuing at least a dozen other initiatives.

Dorsey genuinely believed Twitter could be everything to everyone. Each possibility seemed to intoxicate him and his team. They tried everything except focusing on what made people actually want to use Twitter in the first place: the simple, powerful ability to share thoughts and follow conversations in real time.

Engineering teams found themselves pulled in different directions simultaneously. Product managers couldn't secure resources for core platform improvements because budgets were spread across countless experimental features. The app became a confusing maze of half-implemented ideas rather than a refined tool for human communication.

While Twitter explored endless possibilities, competitors with laser focus captured entire market segments. TikTok concentrated exclusively on short-form video content and grabbed an entire generation's attention with algorithmic precision. Instagram perfected visual storytelling and dominated the creator economy. LinkedIn maintained its grip on professional networking by consistently improving instead of constantly pivoting.

Employee surveys revealed the human cost of endless exploration without decision-making. Teams reported feeling their work lacked impact because projects were continually deprioritized or abandoned for newer initiatives. The most talented engineers and product managers began leaving for companies where they could see clear connections between their daily work and meaningful outcomes. They left, and the stock kept dropping.

In October 2022, Elon Musk completed his acquisition of Twitter, and his initial moves were devastatingly simple: he eliminated 75% of the platform's features and focused on making the core functionality work reliably. Love him or hate him, Musk did what Dorsey couldn't; he chose focus over exploration, clarity over comprehensiveness, and decision-making over endless ideation. He let go of 50% of the workforce, and the app gained users while usage increased. We're not endorsing his tactics or commenting on his polarizing positions. We're simply pointing to evidence of an organization that suffered from a lack of clarity.

The Wall of Graffiti

This same pattern of exploration without execution plays out in organizations across every industry. We witnessed it firsthand in a second-floor conference room near San Diego.

The marketing executive who led us there was practically vibrating with excitement about her team's latest strategic breakthrough. "You have to see this," she said, her hand on the conference room door handle, eyes sparkling with pride. "My team is absolutely incredible. Wait until you see what they've created."

DELIVER

She pushed open the door, and we were hit by a visual assault that would have impressed a New York subway graffiti artist. An entire conference room wall was covered in colorful drawings, arrows pointing in every conceivable direction, mind maps that resembled neural networks, and business hieroglyphics that would have made ancient Egyptians jealous.

"This looks like an amazing brainstorming session," we said, and we meant it. The creative energy was palpable.

Her face lit up with the joy of a parent whose child had just performed beautifully at a school recital. "Right? I've never seen my team so engaged. The ideas just kept flowing."

"So which ideas did you decide to move forward with?" we asked.

The expression on her face shifted like weather changing.

"Well, it was such a productive session. Everyone left feeling so energized."

"But which specific ideas are you implementing?"

"You don't get it," she said, gesturing toward the wall of colorful chaos. "This is our plan."

We stood there looking at that beautiful wall of possibilities, thinking she'd done half her job brilliantly. She'd created psychological safety that enabled unfettered contribution. Her team felt heard, valued, respected, and energized about their collective potential.

But then she stopped right when leadership was most needed, when someone had to look at all that beautiful complexity and make it simple.

The Clarity Extremes

DELIVER

When someone had to take the graffiti wall of possibilities and translate it into three clear priorities her team could execute brilliantly. She'd fallen into the trap of prioritizing everything, which usually leads to accomplishing nothing.

Steve Jobs understood this principle better than most leaders. When his biographer Walter Isaacson asked what he was most proud of in the final months of his life, Jobs didn't mention the iPhone, iPad, or any revolutionary products that had changed the world. His answer was stunning: "I'm most proud of all the things we said no to."

The Second Extreme

This is the second mistake leaders make when trying to create clarity: they embrace vagueness in the name of progress. The result is teams that feel great about their inclusive process while delivering no meaningful results. They achieve perfect alignment around going nowhere. They create engagement without execution, enthusiasm without outcomes, collaboration without consequences, and creativity without focus.

These leaders often have the best intentions. But clarity isn't about having all the right conversations; it's about making the right choices. Teams need both psychological safety and clear direction. They need both creative exploration and decisive leadership. They need both collaboration and accountability.

McKinsey research reveals the organizational costs of this underspecification trap: companies that struggle with decision-making report 35% lower productivity compared to those with clear accountability structures. Teams in exploration-focused cultures spend 60% more time in meetings but deliver 40% fewer completed projects.

The marketing executive's graffiti wall was beautiful, but beauty without direction is just expensive decoration.

What Right Looks Like

So what does effective clarity actually look like? How do leaders avoid both the over-specification trap that creates compliance without engagement and the under-specification trap that creates enthusiasm without execution?

For that answer, we need to travel to a cramped conference room in New Jersey where a group of senior executives at one of the world's largest pharmaceutical companies was gathering for an afternoon meeting.

When we introduced the topic of clarity to this group, they responded the way almost all seasoned executives do. "We don't really need help with that," one member of the team said. As we stood at the head of the table in front of a couple of flip charts that we had asked an assistant to bring in, the body language on the leaders' faces communicated how they felt. They wanted us to skip ahead to get to what they perceived as the more important topics on the agenda.

We trust this process because we know how it plays out and how it affects performance across teams.

"Okay, so forgive our ignorance, but let's just quickly write down the clarity you all have created across the business. What's the first result we have to deliver?" we asked. Several people said, "financial." We wrote the word on the flipchart and then asked the group for the metric that defined success.

That's when this group of smart, seasoned, successful executives discovered what the thousands of people reporting to them already knew.

DELIVER

This team wasn't creating the level of clarity they believed they were for all the functions reporting up into them.

Our questions led to a discussion and debate that lasted for the next two hours. What was the actual number that represented the financial target for this part of the business? Was it gross revenue? Was it net profit? Was it the financial target handed to them by their global leadership team, or was it the number they had recently updated and discussed amongst themselves? Some executives in the room wanted to know where that new number had come from since they hadn't been involved in the recent discussions.

The reality was this group didn't have clarity amongst themselves, and no one below them on the org chart had it either. Our session with that leadership team ended later that afternoon with a flipchart page with three words and three metrics. The words represented different categories or objectives like growth, product, and people. The metrics were the targets the executives needed their collective teams to hit in the next 12 months.

Complexity doesn't scale. Simplicity does.

Whether you lead a team of 5 or 500,000, clarity always fits on a flipchart page. It's three words and three metrics. That's it. Annual operating plans or strategy documents require more detail, but the clarity your team is looking for comes in a much simpler form. That doesn't mean it's easy to create. In fact, that's why we're writing an entire section of this book about what clarity looks like and how to generate it for your team.

After those executives in New Jersey filed out of the conference room, their boss asked for a few days to sleep on what they had come up with

DELIVER

that day. She wanted to think about it more deeply. She wanted to get some additional data to make sure the numbers they came up with were solid and wouldn't need to be adjusted after they were rolled out. She wanted her team to have some time to reach out with any additional thoughts or hesitations over the next few days.

A few weeks later, on a townhall attended by thousands of people, the Key Results were shared with all employees. The senior executive talked about the process the leadership team went through to create what she was showing them. These were the three metrics that defined success. These were the outcomes that mattered most. This was the shared scoreboard that would demand new levels of collaboration, innovation, and execution to hit the targets.

The targets became the destination everyone was working towards. They became the battle cry that everyone knew and could recite without any need to search for an email, find a slide deck, or look through their notes. Clarity is top of mind. It is present constantly, guiding team members on what to focus on and prioritize. It informs all decisions. It determines what people say "yes" to and what they decide can wait until later.

When we say the phrase "create clarity" moving forward, we want you to visualize the flipchart page. Three words. Three metrics. We want you to think about all the complexity that exists and how a huge part of your role is to make it simple.

This is the type of clarity that transforms performance. It's the level of clarity that the research consistently shows 90% of teams don't have currently. It's the type of clarity we're going to help you create for your team. It's the level of clarity that most leaders never achieve but that you'll now be skilled at generating from now on.

DELIVER

The Third Way

Executives at hospital systems, Dorsey at Twitter, and the marketing executive with her graffiti wall represent the two extremes that well-intentioned leaders gravitate toward in their efforts to provide direction and vision.

Both approaches fail because they're based on the false assumption that leaders must choose between control and empowerment, direction and collaboration, and specificity and creative license.

The most effective leaders reject this false choice and adopt a third approach to mobilize teams to deliver. They create the type of clarity that emerged from that cramped conference room in New Jersey. How exactly do you do that with your team? We're glad you asked.

Chapter 6: The Clarity Extremes

– Quick Start –

Key Points:

- Extreme 1: Over-specification (hospital checklists) damages engagement
- Extreme 2: Under-specification (Twitter's endless features) creates confusion
- Third Leader approach: Simple, memorable, actionable TKRs (three results on a flip chart)

Avoid These Traps:

- Detailed procedures for every scenario (compliance without engagement)
- Vague aspirations without specific targets (collaboration without consequences)
- Balanced scorecards with 80+ metrics (paralysis by analysis)

Action Steps:

- **Consider:** Think about times when you've swung between micromanaging details or being too hands-off, and how that might be stifling engagement or causing confusion in your team.
- **Seek Feedback:** Ask a direct report: "Is my guidance on tasks and projects too prescriptive or too vague? Which one of those two do I lean more towards, and how are you seeing it affect motivation to contribute ideas?"
- **Start Doing:** In your next decision-making process, aim to define outcomes with just a few memorable measures of success, fostering a habit of balanced clarity that encourages both direction and creativity.

DELIVER

Third Leader Sweet Spot:

Three specific, measurable outcomes that fit on a flipchart and stick in people's minds. Resist the urge for tons of metrics!

CHAPTER

7

DEFINE THE DESTINATION

YOU UNDERSTAND WHY clarity matters and what undermines it. Now, it's time to create it.

When Brian Cornell transformed Target's results, he focused the entire organization on three numbers. When the pharma executives realized that the thousands of people who reported to them didn't have the clarity they needed they didn't start with a complex strategy. They prioritized three outcomes.

Leaders define the destination. Teams walk in circles until a leader steps forward and declares where we're headed. Think back to our Google Maps example—this is when you decide what destination to enter into the app.

DELIVER

Team Key Results (TKRs)

Team Key Results (TKRs) are three specific, measurable outcomes that define success for your team over the next twelve months. Not five outcomes, not seven priorities, not a balanced scorecard with dozens of metrics. Three. Period.

Almost every leader we meet believes they've created clarity. They act as if it already exists. Yet, 90% of the time, we find their teams disagree. Clarity isn't the revenue number you announced with great fanfare in January and then never mentioned again. Clarity isn't a list of projects your department is currently working on. Clarity isn't a set of principles or pillars. It's three metrics that everyone remembers without assistance and uses to navigate daily chaos and competing priorities.

Why Three?

The number isn't arbitrary. Cognitive research shows that humans can reliably track and prioritize no more than three to four items simultaneously without external aids. Marketing studies prove that consumers remember three-item lists far better than longer ones. Military leaders have known for centuries that soldiers execute simple, clear directives far more effectively than complex battle plans.

Three focuses attention. More than three creates confusion disguised as comprehensiveness. Some of you might try to be clever by picking three categories but then adding four sub-bullets under each one. You can do whatever you want, but don't deceive yourself into thinking you've created clarity. Some of our clients have insisted on that approach, and we've never seen it mobilize the masses.

Why Annual?

Unlike quarterly OKRs (Objectives and Key Results) that focus on specific projects, or monthly KPIs (Key Performance Indicators) that track operational metrics, TKRs define success for the entire year. They take the Annual Operating Plan (AOP) or Long Range Plan (LRP) and break it down into what each team needs to deliver over the next twelve months. Every team has a set of TKRs, and they all feed into each other as you climb through the org chart, creating a web of clarity that enhances focus and fosters collaboration.

TKRs become the filter for every decision: Does this advance our three prioritized outcomes or distract from them? They form the foundation for every meeting: How does today's discussion connect to what we're trying to achieve? They become the rallying cry in times of pressure: Remember, we're working toward [insert your memorable sequence here].

The Two Paths

Every manager finds themselves in one of two situations regarding organizational direction.

Path 1: You Have Some Clarity from Above

Your organization has provided direction, perhaps not in clear, memorable TKRs, but there are revenue targets, safety mandates, customer satisfaction goals, or operational efficiency requirements. It might resemble the guidelines of that biner at the gym or the app that nurses despise. Maybe it's overly complex and detailed, at least you have a starting point for crafting your TKRs.

If this describes your situation, begin by examining what your organization truly needs from your team. Look beyond the complexity to identify the core outcomes that matter most. What three categories would enable the broader strategic plan? Consider objectives and metrics that your team can directly influence.

Path 2: You Have No Clear Direction

The rest of you work for an organization or leader who provides vague aspirations, constantly shifting priorities, or no direction at all. You're operating in an organizational vacuum where everyone does their best, but no one knows what success looks like.

If this describes your situation, which is common in many companies when we start working with them, you become the leader who creates focus where none existed. Pay attention to the metrics, priorities, and initiatives most frequently discussed by your boss and other leaders. Are they consistently talking about safety goals? Revenue growth? Profitability? Market share? Product development?

Identify the three areas that generate the most executive attention and energy—not what the mission statement claims to value, but what actually drives decisions, resources, and conversations under pressure.

The TKR Process

Creating effective TKRs follows a systematic approach that avoids the endless debates that paralyze most teams. This isn't about finding perfect answers; it's about making good decisions quickly. What we're about to outline should be completed in the next day or week, not something that requires months of discussion or fine-tuning. The only exception is for those with thousands of people reporting up into you. In that case, this will require more effort due to the magnitude of your decision.

Start with Objectives

Begin by identifying three categories that define success for your team. These are broad areas like revenue, safety, customer satisfaction, operational efficiency, employee engagement, product launches, on-time delivery, quality, or market share. Think of one- or two-word answers that capture what matters most. This is where TKRs differ from other popular frameworks. TKRs force you to choose what matters most.

A word of caution: you'll feel pressure to perfect these three categories. There is no such thing as perfect TKRs. This debate could continue endlessly while your competitors gain ground. Ultimately, you need to decide on the three that most accurately define success and move forward.

Add Specific Metrics

You can't move what you don't measure. For each objective, identify a specific metric that captures progress. Sometimes you'll use existing measurements; other times, you'll need to create new ones.

For revenue growth, your metric might be the number of new customers. For operational efficiency, it could be the percentage of manufacturing defects. For a team-focused TKR, you might track retention rates or engagement survey scores.

You have flexibility in structuring these metrics: percentage increases (5% lift in revenue), raw numbers ($1 billion in sales), or rankings (top quartile performance). Choose what makes the most sense for your situation and creates the clearest definition of success. Pick a number that's ambitious yet achievable. This is where we must be by the end of the next 12 months.

DELIVER

Here are examples of how objectives become specific TKRs:

- **Revenue Growth Objective**: Add 10 new clients to core product sales compared to last year.
- **Operational Efficiency Objective**: Achieve a 15% reduction in manufacturing defects through new quality control processes.
- **Customer Satisfaction Objective**: Attain an 85% customer satisfaction rating on quarterly surveys.

Get Input, Make Decisions

Once you have a rough draft of your three TKRs, test them with those around you. This collaborative process enhances your TKRs while laying the groundwork for future alignment.

Start with your team. Meet with key members individually or set aside time in a team meeting. Explain why you're creating TKRs, present what you've developed, and request honest feedback. What stands out? What concerns them? What might be missing? What different metrics or targets would be more relevant?

Use whiteboards or flip charts if possible. Divide larger teams into groups of three or four and give them ten minutes to react and suggest changes. You're not seeking consensus—that's a mirage. You're gathering input to make informed decisions.

Next, discuss your proposed TKRs with your boss. Explain the process and share your drafts. Ideally, your entire organization is reading this book or going through the training associated with it, and your boss is eager for this discussion. If not, and your boss shows little interest in your effort to create clarity, you might be in the wrong department or organization. Incorporate any useful feedback they provide; their perspective is valuable.

DELIVER

This collaborative process should take one to two weeks at most. Move quickly. These TKRs are critical for focusing your team's efforts, and each day of delay gives competitors an advantage.

RPM: Making Them Memorable

Raw TKRs aren't enough. You need to transform them into something that becomes part of your team's DNA—a rallying cry that people can recite effortlessly and unite around under pressure. This is where the magic of memorable sequences fosters daily collective effort as you instill clarity in everyone's minds. You aren't creating a strategy deck or a list of projects and priorities; you're mobilizing the team.

The best TKR sequences share three characteristics captured by the acronym RPM:

- **Repeatable**: People don't focus their daily work on things they can't remember. Your TKRs need to be top-of-mind, requiring no effort to memorize. No one should need to pull out a balanced scorecard to know what matters most. The most effective sequences focus on the numbers: 95-5-100, 3-2-1, 85-5-100.
- **Purposeful**: Your three TKRs must reflect what your team truly cares about. If the metrics feel meaningless or disconnected from their daily work, people won't rally behind them. When one of the TKRs emphasizes employee retention or engagement, it shows that leadership prioritizes these issues. When nurses see patient safety or satisfaction in the TKRs, it connects to their reasons for choosing this profession. It communicates that you care about more than just revenue.
- **Measurable**: Each TKR needs clear, objective criteria for success. Is the target achievable yet challenging? Have you chosen the best metric? Remember, there's no perfect measurement; just select one that clearly defines success and move forward.

DELIVER

Creating memorable sequences takes creativity. Involve creative team members or friends who can help you find the flow that rolls off the tongue naturally. Test different arrangements of your numbers until you discover the combination that feels effortless to say and unforgettable.

When you achieve this, something powerful happens. Walk into any area of your organization and ask people what they're working toward; they'll respond with the same three numbers. It becomes more than metrics; it becomes identity.

Every Meeting, Every Time

Finalizing your TKRs is just the beginning. Without consistent reinforcement, even the most carefully crafted outcomes will fade into background noise, becoming just another forgotten announcement or topic in a past meeting.

Here's the rule that transforms TKRs from good intentions into a driving force: ***Every Meeting, Every Time.***

If it's worth holding a meeting, it's worth connecting it to your TKRs. This isn't bureaucracy; it ensures every conversation and decision aligns with what matters most.

In practice, this means your TKRs appear on every agenda. When discussing project updates, ask which TKR this advances. When reviewing budget requests, determine how this helps achieve your three outcomes. Before people leave meetings, identify what brings you closer to your TKRs.

Use them as decision filters. When new requests arise, ask whether they support the TKRs or distract from them. This consistent focus creates organizational alignment at scale; from the leadership team to individual contributors, everyone understands what success looks like.

These TKRs aren't something you roll out once with fanfare and then forget. They become embedded in annual reviews, one-on-one meetings, strategic planning sessions, and daily conversations. They're everywhere because focus requires constant reinforcement.

When TKRs Need to Change

Your TKRs are designed to provide focus for an entire year. The power of memorable sequences like "85-5-100" or "3-2-1" comes from consistency; people rally around outcomes that don't shift with every quarterly business review or monthly leadership mood swing.

But occasionally, market conditions or organizational realities may change so dramatically that maintaining your original TKRs becomes counterproductive. The key word is occasionally. Adjusting TKRs mid-year should be rare and reserved for significant shifts that render your current outcomes irrelevant or impossible.

When to Consider Changes

Major market disruptions that fundamentally alter your business model warrant TKR adjustments. A global pandemic that eliminates 40% of your customer base. A key competitor's bankruptcy that suddenly opens vast market opportunities. Regulatory changes that make your current approach illegal. Acquisition or merger activity that entirely changes your team's scope.

Notice what doesn't qualify: missing your targets for two months, discovering the work is harder than expected, or facing normal business challenges. These are execution issues, not TKR problems. Stick with your outcomes and address the underlying issues preventing achievement.

DELIVER

The Adjustment Process

When genuine circumstances require TKR changes, move quickly but deliberately. Gather your team and honestly assess what's changed in your environment. Are your current TKRs still relevant to organizational success? Can your team still influence these outcomes? Do the metrics still measure what matters most?

If you determine changes are necessary, follow the same collaborative process you used originally. Get team input, consult with your boss, and ensure your new TKRs remain memorable and motivating. Don't use this as an opportunity to perfect what was already working; fix only what the new circumstances require.

Annual Updates: The Norm

Most TKR changes occur annually as part of your regular planning cycle. This is when you evaluate what worked, what didn't, and what needs to shift for the coming year. Use the process outlined in this chapter: assess organizational priorities, gather team input, and create memorable sequences.

Ideally, your organization updates TKRs annually in a coordinated effort, starting with the executive team and cascading down through every level. Leadership provides clear priorities that inform team-level TKRs, creating alignment from top to bottom.

In the worst case, you might be the only Third Leader in your organization, creating focus where none exists. Even as a solo effort, annual TKR updates will significantly improve your team's performance and may eventually influence how your organization views clarity and focus.

Regardless, commit to the discipline of annual review and renewal. Your TKRs should evolve with your business while maintaining the consistency that drives exceptional results.

Wait, Don't Announce Them!

You have now completed the first step in installing LeaderOS: you've created clarity with three specific, measurable outcomes that define success for your team. You can see how these TKRs will enhance focus, decision-making, and performance. You're ready to roll them out to your team.

Stop!

Having clear TKRs is just the beginning. The real work, where most leaders fail, is creating genuine alignment around achieving them. It's the difference between people knowing your TKRs and feeling personally committed to making them happen.

You can't simply announce your three outcomes in a team meeting, send an email with the numbers, and expect everyone to feel the same urgency you do. Real alignment requires something more sophisticated: getting people to emotionally and operationally own the outcomes rather than just understand them intellectually.

Clarity about the destination enables everything else, but alignment around the destination determines whether you're on this journey alone or have your team ready to make it happen.

Don't present your TKRs to your team, whether it's 10 people or 10,000, until you understand how to create the alignment that drives movement. The destination is clear. Now let's get everyone on board.

Note: The next chapter is a tactical playbook providing step-by-step guidance for the process outlined here. Some of you may find it extremely helpful and should proceed to the next chapter. Others may view it as unnecessary since

DELIVER

you already have what you need to create your TKRs. If that's the case, skip the next chapter and move to the section on Alignment.

DELIVER

Chapter 7: Define the Destination

– Quick Start –

Key Points:

- TKRs = 3 specific, measurable outcomes defining success for 12 months
- Must be Repeatable, Purposeful, Measurable (RPM framework)
- Create memorable sequences like 85-5-100 or 3-2-1
- Third Leader discipline: Connect every meeting to TKRs

TKR Questions:

- Why 3? Cognitive limit for tracking without external aids
- Why annual? Longer than projects, shorter than strategy
- Why memorable? People focus on what they can easily remember

Action Steps:

- **Consider:** Reflect on the momentum you could generate if you could develop the skill set to get a group of people to collaboratively work on movement in the same direction. How would that affect your value as a leader and increase your ability to lead teams 2x or 10x larger than your current team?
- **Seek Feedback:** Ask your boss or a peer: "Given our organizational priorities, what three categories do you think my team should focus on to create the most impact this year?"
- **Start Doing:** Begin drafting TKRs using the process of objectives plus metrics. Seek informal feedback from team members on potential TKRs.

DELIVER

> **LeaderOS Foundation:**
>
> Don't announce TKRs until you understand how to build alignment around them. We'll show you how in the next section of this book.

CHAPTER

THE CLARITY PLAYBOOK

Note: This is your hands-on, roll-up-your-sleeves chapter. If you prefer to continue your journey and return to the tactical work later, feel free to skip ahead to Part 3 and Chapter 9. However, don't skip this entirely; you'll need this playbook to build your LeaderOS and establish the clarity that makes everything else possible.

We will guide you through the exact process we use with clients. Here's how we conducted an hour-long Zoom call with Maria, a Regional Manager overseeing 24 restaurant locations across three states in a mid-sized chain.

Follow along with Maria's responses, then answer the same questions for your situation. By the end of this chapter, you'll have your own memorable TKR sequence.

DELIVER

Question 1: What does current performance look like? What's going well and what's not?

Maria's Response: "Honestly? It's a mixed bag across my region. We're busy—busier than we've been in years, actually. Most locations are seeing strong traffic, especially on weekends. My management teams are hustling, and I'm proud of their hard work. Food quality is solid across the board, and service is generally good…"

She paused, then continued with a slight grimace. "But we're missing our revenue targets. Every month, when I look at the regional averages, it's the same story: we're close, but not quite there. And don't get me started on finding good managers. I have general manager and assistant manager positions open across multiple locations, and it feels like every good candidate gets poached before we can make an offer."

Our Follow-up: "Can you provide some numbers on that performance?"

Maria's Response: "Sure. Revenue-wise, we're averaging about 92% of our plan year-to-date across all 24 locations. Corporate keeps saying 'you're almost there,' but almost doesn't pay the bills, you know? Our guest satisfaction averages 64% on our GEM score—that's our Guest Engagement Metric from monthly surveys. Some locations are higher, some lower, but 64% is our regional average. I know that needs to improve, but at least it's trending up from where we were six months ago."

Your Turn—Question 1: What does your team's current performance look like? What's going well and what's not?

Now give us some numbers. Where are you ahead of plan, on target, or behind?

DELIVER

Question 2: What metrics has the company identified as most important for this year? What 3-4 categories come to mind, and are there specific metrics?

Maria's Response: "Corporate is focused on three main areas. Revenue is number one, obviously. They want us to hit our top-line targets across the region, period. Guest satisfaction is huge too; they talk about the GEM score constantly in our regional calls. Corporate expects us to average 75% across all locations, so we've got some work to do there. And then there's operational efficiency, which for us really means controlling labor costs and reducing management turnover. Those three come up in literally every conversation I have with my VP."

Your Turn—Question 2: What metrics has your organization identified as most important? What 3-4 categories come to mind?

Question 3: Is there anything missing? What other categories matter to you or keep you up at night?

Maria's Response: "You know what really keeps me up? Developing my team. As I mentioned, I can't find managers to save my life. The real issue is that I'm not building them from within my region. I have good people in my restaurants, but my GMs are so focused on day-to-day operations that we're not developing anyone for advancement."

Our Redirect: "Okay, but what specific outcome are you aiming for?"

Maria's Response: "I need a pipeline across all 24 locations. Each restaurant should identify potential managers—people who could step up if someone leaves or if we expand. Right now, we're reactive, scrambling to fill positions after they're vacant."

DELIVER

Us: "What would success look like?"

Maria: "Each location should spot about 5 people per month with management potential. That gives me around 120 candidates monthly across my region whom we can begin coaching and developing before we need them."

Our Follow-up: "That seems like a lot. What's realistic?"

Maria: "You're right. Let me think… If each restaurant identified just one solid candidate every two months, that's still 12 per month across my region. But honestly, 5 per month total across all 24 locations feels more realistic and would still address my pipeline issue."

Us: "So development is really about building regional bench strength?"

Maria: "Exactly. If I had that pipeline, my management turnover issues would likely resolve themselves, and my operations would run smoother because I'd have better people in key roles across the region."

Your Turn—Question 3: Is there anything missing from your list? What other categories matter to you or keep you up at night? What results or outcomes are affected?

Question 4: Now that you have your categories, what are the specific metrics and targets?

Maria's Response: "Alright, so I've got guest satisfaction, revenue, and development. For guest satisfaction, I want to raise our regional GEM score average from 64% to 75%; that's where corporate expects us to be. For revenue, it's straightforward: hit 100% of the plan on average across all locations. We're averaging 92%, so we need an 8-point improvement.

DELIVER

And for development, it's identifying 5 potential managers per month across my entire region."

Us: "So you're aiming for a 75% average GEM score, 100% of the revenue plan, and 5 manager candidates per month?"

Maria: "Right. Those three could transform my entire region if we could hit them consistently."

Your Turn—Question 4: Based on your categories, what are the specific metrics and targets?

Category 1: _____
Target: _____

Category 2: _____
Target: _____

Category 3: _____
Target: _____

Category 4: _____
Target: _____

Select your top 3 metrics:

_____
_____
_____

DELIVER

Question 5: Let's turn them into TKRs. What's your memorable sequence?

Us: "So we have a 75% average GEM score, 5 manager candidates per month, and 100% of the revenue plan. Let's see how these sound together. How about 75-5-100?"

Maria: "Seventy-five, five, one hundred…" She repeated it a couple of times. "You know what? That actually flows really well. It tells the whole story: guest satisfaction, people development, financial performance."

Us: "Let's test it against our criteria. Are these repeatable? Can you track them monthly?"

Maria: "Absolutely. GEM scores come monthly, I can track manager identification weekly across all locations, and revenue is daily if I want."

Us: "Are they purposeful? Do they connect directly to what matters most?"

Maria: "Yes. These three would transform my entire region."

Us: "And measurable, clear, objective criteria?"

Maria: "Completely. No gray area on any of them."

Us: "Congratulations. Your TKRs are 75-5-100."

Maria: "I love it. That's something I can share in regional calls, GM meetings, even with corporate. Seventy-five, five, one hundred. All my managers can remember that, and it works whether we're talking about individual restaurants or regional averages."

DELIVER

Your Turn—Question 5: Create your memorable TKR sequence. Take your top 3 metrics and arrange them into a sequence that flows well when you say it out loud:

My TKRs are: _____ — _____ — _____

Test your sequence:

Easy to say quickly?	☐ Yes ☐ No
Natural flow in conversation?	☐ Yes ☐ No
Memorable after hearing once?	☐ Yes ☐ No
Repeatable (easy for people to recall)?	☐ Yes ☐ No
Purposeful (connects to what matters)?	☐ Yes ☐ No
Measurable (clear, trackable)?	☐ Yes ☐ No

Congratulations! You now have your TKRs.

Every Meeting, Every Time:

Creating your TKRs is just the beginning. The real work starts now: keeping them alive and relevant in the daily rhythm of your organization. Without consistent reinforcement, even the most carefully crafted TKRs will fade into the background, becoming just another forgotten initiative gathering dust on a whiteboard.

Here's the rule that transforms TKRs from good intentions into a driving force: **Every meeting, every time.**

If it's worth holding a meeting, it's worth connecting it to your TKRs. This isn't about adding bureaucracy or slowing things down; it's about ensuring that every conversation, decision, and project aligns with what matters most.

DELIVER

The Power of Consistency: Lockheed Martin's "One More Hour"

A powerful example of consistent reinforcement comes from Lockheed Martin's "One More Hour" initiative. At a critical juncture in its history, the company set a bold target: increase aircraft production by adding just one extra hour of productivity to each shift. At first glance, it might seem like a simple or insignificant goal, but its brilliance lay in its clarity and consistency.

This single target, one more hour, was more than a metric; it became a rallying cry for the entire organization. Leaders didn't just announce the goal and leave it at that. They integrated it into every meeting, agenda, and conversation. Every department, from engineering to production to logistics, was asked, "What can we do to gain one more hour of productivity?"

The simplicity of the goal made it memorable and actionable. It sparked creative problem-solving across the organization. Teams brainstormed ways to optimize workflows, reduce bottlenecks, and eliminate inefficiencies. Small changes, such as rethinking equipment setups or adjusting shift schedules, began to accumulate. Every improvement, no matter how minor, was tied back to the overarching goal of "one more hour."

The consistent focus on this single target created a ripple effect. It fostered alignment, encouraged collaboration, and gave every employee a sense of ownership in achieving the goal. People weren't just working harder; they were working smarter, with a clear understanding of how their efforts contributed to the bigger picture. The results were extraordinary: record-breaking aircraft production, achieved not through sweeping changes or massive investments but through the power of clarity and consistent reinforcement.

Making It Practical

Here's how to implement "every meeting, every time" with your TKRs:

- **Start every team meeting** by briefly stating your TKRs. It takes 10 seconds: "Remember, we're working toward 75-5-100."
- **Connect agenda items** to your TKRs. When discussing a project update, ask: "How does this advance our goal of 75% guest satisfaction?" When reviewing a budget request, ask: "Will this help us achieve 100% of the revenue plan?"
- **End meetings with TKR relevance.** Before people leave, ask: "What's one takeaway from today's discussion that brings us closer to 75-5-100?"
- **Use TKRs as decision filters.** When new requests arise, ask: "Does this support our TKRs or distract from them?"

The goal isn't to become robotic about your TKRs; it's to integrate them into your team's thinking so they naturally shape every conversation and decision. By consistently reinforcing what matters most, your team stops wondering what success looks like and starts working systematically to achieve it.

What's Next?

Like Maria, you now have three specific outcomes that can transform your team's focus and performance. Your TKRs become the foundation for everything in your LeaderOS, the platform that fosters alignment and movement around what matters most.

In Part 3, we'll explore how to get everyone on your team aligned around achieving these outcomes. Having clear TKRs is just the beginning; the real challenge is ensuring everyone feels personal ownership in making them happen.

DELIVER

Chapter 8: The Clarity Playbook
– Quick Start –

Tactical Implementation:

- Assess current performance (what's working and what's not)
- Identify the company's top 3-4 priority categories
- Create specific metrics and targets for each
- Build a memorable sequence that flows naturally
- Test with RPM criteria: Repeatable, Purposeful, Measurable

Maria's Third Leader Example:

75-5-100 (75% guest satisfaction, 5 manager candidates monthly, 100% revenue plan)

Action Steps:

- **Consider:** Are your TKRs RPM? Are they Repeatable, Purposeful, and Measurable
- **Seek Feedback:** Ask family members, friends, or creative types you know: "How do I make my TKRs more Repeatable?"
- **Start Doing:** Finalize your TKRs and get ready to roll them out after we show you how to create alignment around them. Plan to start using the TKRs in Every Meeting, Every Time!

DELIVER

Third Leader Watchout:

Quit trying to make the TKRs perfect! There's no such thing. And don't put sub-bullets under each TKR with additional metrics or categories! Take the complex and make it simple!

PART FOUR

INSTALLING LEADEROS: BUILD ALIGNMENT

CHAPTER

THE ALIGNMENT GAP

THE SILENCE WAS SUFFOCATING.

Twenty thousand people sat in stunned disbelief, their collective breath creating an eerie vacuum where deafening cheers should have been. The air hung thick with the smell of spilled beer and abandoned popcorn, the stench of dreams dying in real time. Somewhere in the upper deck, a child was crying.

On the court below, confetti cannons that had been loaded hours earlier sat silent and useless. Security guards who had practiced victory protocols stood frozen, wondering whether they were supposed to go home since the place was emptying out fast.

The coach stood motionless on the sideline in his street clothes, hands buried deep in his pockets, watching the impossible unfold before him. His team, his perfect, record-breaking, historically dominant team, had just done something that had never been done before. The wrong kind of something.

DELIVER

The scoreboard told a story that would be replayed in sports documentaries for decades: Game 7. Final score. Season over. Championship lost.

But the numbers didn't capture what he was really witnessing. This wasn't just a loss. This was a collapse. This was one of the greatest teams ever assembled forgetting how to be a team when it mattered most.

The coach could hear the celebration beginning in the visiting locker. Champagne bottles popped. Grown men sobbed with joy.

And all he could think about was a single, haunting realization: *His team knew exactly what to do. They just stopped doing it together.*

The Awareness Trap

Steve Kerr had seen basketball teams fall apart before, but never like this. Never when they were this good. Never when the stakes were this high. Never when everything had seemed so perfectly aligned.

The Golden State Warriors had just blown a 3-1 lead in the 2016 NBA Finals, something that had never happened in the seventy-year history of the championship series. This wasn't just any team. This was the squad that had posted the greatest regular season record in basketball history, going 73-9. This was the team with the first-ever unanimous MVP, the team that had revolutionized how the game was played.

They had run the same offensive sets for two years. They had practiced the same defensive rotations thousands of times. Every player could recite their roles with military precision. Steph Curry knew when to shoot and when to pass. Klay Thompson knew his spots on the floor. Draymond Green knew how to anchor the defense while facilitating the offense.

They had awareness. Perfect, crystal-clear awareness of what it took to win basketball games at the highest level.

But they didn't have alignment when they needed it most.

Over the course of those Finals games, Kerr watched his players gradually revert to playing individual basketball instead of Warriors basketball. Curry started forcing shots instead of trusting the offense. Green let his emotions override team priorities. Even Thompson began hunting for his own shots instead of taking what the defense gave him.

They all knew better. They were aware of how they were supposed to play. But they weren't aligned anymore.

"The hardest thing to watch," Kerr would later reflect, "was seeing them play basketball instead of playing *our* basketball. They knew every play. They just weren't playing them together."

This is the awareness trap that destroys more teams, more companies, and more initiatives than any competitor ever could. Leaders create what they believe is perfect clarity: detailed strategic plans, comprehensive presentations, clear metrics, and targets. They share this information through carefully crafted communications and elaborate town halls.

Then they sit back and wait for the magic to happen.

Because they've confused nodding heads with genuine commitment, silent agreement with active ownership, knowledge transfer with emotional investment. They've fallen into the dangerous assumption that if people understand something, they're automatically aligned around it.

DELIVER

You might even have MVPs on your team, franchise players, the best performers in your industry. But talent without teamwork is just an overpaid roster.

Awareness is not alignment.

Awareness is passive. It lives entirely in people's heads, invisible and unverifiable. You can't look into someone's mind and determine whether they truly understand something, let alone whether they feel personally committed to acting on it. Awareness is private, individual, and, most dangerously, gives no indication of whether people will actually do anything different when they leave the room.

Alignment is something else entirely.

Rock Bottom in a Basement

Two months after the Warriors' collapse, we found ourselves in a windowless meeting room in the basement of a Park City resort. No natural light. No inspiring views. Just fluorescent bulbs humming overhead and the faint smell of industrial carpet.

It seemed like the perfect metaphor for where this company had landed.

When Tom returned to the company he co-founded, he walked into a storm. Revenue was down, morale was even lower, and the fractures in the company's foundation were growing deeper by the day. The numbers told a devastating story: halfway through the year, they were at only 15% of their revenue target. Six months in a row of missing their plan. Not even close.

Nobody wanted to be in that basement room. People walked in with heads down, shoulders slumped. The kind of body language that screams defeat before anyone says a word.

Tom stood in front of that room and displayed a PowerPoint slide containing just four words: "Optimism is a choice."

The room fell silent. Then he put up another slide: "Optimism is a choice especially when you don't have evidence to justify it."

Then he did something most leaders never have the courage to do. He invited the mess.

"Let's talk about all the evidence you brought to Park City for why we shouldn't choose optimism."

Alignment Is Messy and It Happens Out Loud

What happened next wasn't pretty. People complained about marketing. They pointed fingers at the executive team. They blamed the new private equity owners. Tom didn't minimize any of it. He validated it all.

He let the room vent for thirty minutes. Every complaint, every frustration, every piece of evidence for why optimism seemed impossible, he let it all pour out in that windowless basement room.

Because alignment is messy and it happens out loud. It's not a polite, orderly process where everyone nods in agreement. Alignment is the work of taking individual perspectives, concerns, and agendas and forging them into shared commitment. It requires people to voice their real thoughts, not their diplomatic ones. It demands that leaders address actual concerns, not imaginary ones.

Most importantly, alignment happens in the open, where everyone can see it, hear it, and participate in creating it.

DELIVER

When the venting finally subsided, Tom asked the group to make a choice: spend the rest of their time together creating evidence to justify optimism instead of cataloging reasons for pessimism. He pointed out that you don't have to look long or hard to find evidence to justify pessimism in any area of your life. There's nothing special or noteworthy about choosing pessimism. It's generally the default soundtrack of crowds. But optimism requires leaning into the possibility that you can affect your future.

Tom's team finished their season differently than Kerr's. It took enormous work and discipline, but they chose optimism repeatedly and actually broke thirty years of company revenue records. No one would tell you the path was flat or easy. But the accomplishment was remarkable.

Tom came to Park City that week in July not to create awareness of his team's TKRs; he already had that. What he was missing was alignment. And in that basement, through the mess, honesty, and individual involvement he pursued, he achieved it.

The Neuroscience of Commitment

Here's why Tom's approach worked and why so many leadership initiatives fail: awareness and alignment activate completely different parts of the human brain.

Awareness activates the prefrontal cortex, the analytical, logical centers that process information and understand concepts. This is where strategic plans live, where people nod in meetings, where knowledge gets filed away for future reference.

But alignment requires the limbic system, the emotional centers that drive motivation, trust, and commitment. This is where people feel personally invested, where they develop genuine buy-in, where they choose to act even when it's difficult.

The gap between these two systems is where most leadership fails. You can fill someone's prefrontal cortex with perfect information while their limbic system remains completely disengaged. They understand everything and feel committed to nothing.

Tom's messy conversation created the bridge. By giving people space to voice real concerns and participate in shaping the path forward, he helped his team leap from understanding problems to feeling invested in solving them together. The venting wasn't just therapeutic; it was neurologically necessary. You can't reach emotional commitment without first processing emotional resistance.

This is why companies that master this transition consistently outperform their competitors, not by small margins, but by dramatic ones. They've learned to activate both systems simultaneously.

The Rapids That Don't Forgive

You don't need a laboratory to witness this transformation. Sometimes the most profound lessons about alignment come from unexpected places, like the middle of one of Colorado's most unforgiving rivers.

The Animas River doesn't care about your plans.

It rushes down from the Rocky Mountains in a relentless torrent of snowmelt, forty-degree water that hits your face like liquid ice and tastes of granite and high-altitude storms. There are no lazy pools here, no gentle eddies where you can catch your breath and regroup. This is water with purpose, gravity's most urgent resource, carrying the weight

DELIVER

of Colorado's highest peaks toward the desert in an unbroken rush that has carved red rock canyons and humbled river guides for generations.

Fifty people, mostly teenage boys and their dads (including Russ, coincidentally during the very month we were finalizing this chapter), stood on the rocky and tiny launch point near Durango that summer morning, pulling on thick neoprene that clung to their skin like a second layer of protection they'd desperately need. Wetsuits, booties, helmets—gear that announced the seriousness of what they were about to attempt. The rafts themselves looked almost comically inadequate for the task ahead, rubber boats that would carry six people each into water that could kill them.

Russ found himself assigned to the lead boat. The guide, weathered by years of reading this river's moods, gathered them close. His voice carried the authority of someone who had seen what the Animas could do to those who didn't take it seriously.

"Listen carefully," he said, scanning the faces around him. "This water is frigid. Even in these wetsuits, you've got just a few minutes before hypothermia sets in if you go overboard. We're the lead boat, which means we are the last defense."

He pointed downstream where the water disappeared around a bend marked by towering red cliffs. "Humans float faster than rafts in rapids like these. If someone falls out behind us, our job is to pull them out. Follow my instructions and keep an eye out for floaters."

The group's excitement for their adventure now had a layer of stress.

Into the Rapids

The first few minutes felt almost peaceful. They pushed off from the rocky launch point, and the raft found the main current with a gentle lurch that sent spray across their faces. Russ turned on his GoPro camera to capture the scenes you're about to read about.

"Forward two!" the guide called, his voice cutting through the noisy current below. Six paddles hit the water in unison. The raft responded instantly, cutting through the current with purpose. They rounded the first bend, and Russ wondered how he had waited so many years to check this off his list.

For the next hour, they found their rhythm. The guide's commands became a cadence that drove their movements: "Forward two, back one, forward three!" Whether the rapids were moderate or intense, his voice carried the same authority and expectation of instant, unified response.

And it worked. The raft danced through obstacles that could have destroyed them, responding to their synchronized effort like a single organism. When they needed to dodge left around a fallen tree, six paddles drove them sideways with precision. When they needed to power through a hydraulic that wanted to hold them back or send them sideways, their collective force propelled them to safety.

Three Sisters

"Alright, listen up!" the guide shouted, his voice cutting through the roar of approaching rapids. "We're coming up on Three Sisters, three boulders the size of cars sitting right in the main channel."

Russ strained to see what the guide meant. All he could make out was more white water ahead, the same churning chaos they'd been navigating

DELIVER

all day. Only the seasoned leader on their raft had any idea what massive obstacles lurked beyond the next bend. Russ and everyone else had to trust that the guide knew what he was talking about.

"These rapids are the most intense we'll experience today," the guide continued, his voice taking on the tone of a drill sergeant. "When I say paddle, I mean paddle! When I say down, I mean get down! Put your head beneath your knees and don't pull it back up until I say back up. I don't care if water gets in your eyes; when I say forward two, you give me two. Do you understand?"

No one sat back. No one slouched. All of them, including Russ's youngest son, gripped their paddles with white knuckles, trusting completely in their guide's vision of danger they couldn't yet see. This was the moment when alignment wasn't optional; it was critical for survival.

Suddenly, as they swept around a curve in the canyon, the first Sister revealed herself: a massive mound of granite with sharp edges rising from the churning water like an ancient monument, water pounding around her bulk in explosions of spray that sent freezing droplets across their faces. Nobody flinched. Everyone awaited every word from the leader of their team.

"Forward two!" the guide yelled. "Two more!"

They shot past the first boulder, so close Russ could have reached out and touched it had they not sped past at full throttle. The team thought they'd made it, but now they stared directly at Sister number two, the current pulling them toward her sharp, unforgiving edges that could easily slice the raft in half.

"Forward two! Back three!"

The raft lurched and pivoted; it turned sideways and threw everyone off balance. "Duck!" the guide yelled as sprays of ice water blinded them. The raft avoided the boulder but nearly got caught in massive branches just a few feet above the water line. Without hesitation, all six heads went down to their feet, no one looking up even though the third Sister waited ahead like a final judgment.

"Up! Up! Up!" the guide yelled. All six heads shot back up from the bottom of the raft in perfect unison, eyes immediately locking onto the river ahead and ears tuning out all the sounds of nature, searching for commands from the guide.

"Forward three! Forward two!"

The rapids pushed them toward the third Sister, the largest and most menacing of all. No one in the group doubted their ability to avoid her. Their trust in the guide could not have been higher. At this point, anything he asked them to do, all six would have done without question or argument. He was their leader, and he had created a team with unmistakable alignment. His leadership, combined with their unified effort, produced speed, precise movement, and cut a path through obstacles that would have destroyed any other group lacking what existed at that moment in this raft.

As they cleared the final obstacle, everyone erupted in screams of exhilaration, everyone except the guide.

Beyond Individual Success

The guide stayed focused, immediately turned the raft backward in the barely calmer water below, and called everyone to attention. He silenced the celebration. Behind them, the other rafts were still maneuvering through the Sisters, still facing the same life-or-death challenges they'd just navigated.

DELIVER

"We're not done," he said firmly. "We have to make sure everyone else makes it through safely!"

They watched as boat after boat approached the three granite giants, the guides calling out warnings and commands to their attentive teams. One by one, the rafts emerged from the Sisters, each crew erupting in their own celebration as they realized what they'd just accomplished together. But Russ noticed that every guide maintained the same focus, the same commitment to the collective success of the entire group.

As they continued downstream through gentler rapids, Russ found his mind racing with implications that went far beyond whitewater rafting. The guide had seen danger that none of them could see. He'd demanded alignment before they even understood why it was necessary. What if there had been no guide? What if they hadn't trusted his direction? What if someone had shirked their responsibility or hadn't done their part? The Three Sisters demanded alignment and required leadership.

That night back at camp, as teenagers recounted their triumph and fathers shared stories of synchronized precision under pressure, Russ sat by the fire determined that his experience would make it into this chapter. He had helped hundreds of executive teams create greater alignment, but he had never experienced its value like he did that day in one of the most breathtaking places in the world.

The Science of Synchronization

Researchers have studied team synchronization on waterways and in laboratories for years, and their findings validate what every river guide knows instinctively: when it comes to performance under pressure, awareness and alignment are completely different things.

At the University of Groningen in the Netherlands, researchers studied fifteen rowing crews navigating the precise coordination required for optimal performance. Their findings were unequivocal: "crew members need to mutually synchronize their movements to achieve optimal crew performance" and that "better crew synchronization was related to less roll of the boat." We've all read the books or seen the movies about the lessons from winning rowing teams.

But the most compelling research comes from an unlikely source: Harvard Business School's analysis of Army crew teams. In what became known as the Army Crew Case Study, researchers documented a phenomenon familiar to anyone who has watched talented individuals fail to perform as a team.

The study featured two rowing teams: one made up of the top eight individual rowers and another consisting of the bottom eight. Despite their superior individual expertise and skills, the varsity team with the top performers was consistently beaten by the junior varsity crew, which was considered the less skilled team.

The reason? The elite team lacked alignment despite their superior talent. They were divided solely based on physical capabilities, without considering their mental and teamwork abilities. The varsity team suffered from ineffective leadership, resulting in disorganization and a lack of cohesion.

This issue extended beyond rowing technique or physical conditioning. Even the most exceptional individuals cannot thrive if their goals remain individualistic and they lack the ability to collaborate. The study revealed that a team can be much less than the sum of its parts when alignment breaks down.

In other words, you can have perfect awareness of what needs to happen and still fail spectacularly if your people aren't truly aligned around doing it together.

The Alignment Process™

What separates teams that achieve synchronization from those that remain collections of talented individuals? After studying hundreds of organizations, from Silicon Valley startups to Fortune 500 companies to world-class athletic teams, we've identified a three-step process that consistently shifts awareness to alignment.

This isn't theoretical. It's the same process Tom used in that basement in Park City. It's what Steve Kerr implemented after the Warriors' collapse. It's what the river guide demanded before they entered the Three Sisters. And it's what distinguishes organizations that thrive under pressure from those that fall apart when the stakes are highest.

The Alignment Process™

Step One: Make the Case
Alignment begins with something more compelling than information transfer. It requires leaders to sell the vision in a way that fosters emotional investment, not just intellectual understanding. This isn't about having the best PowerPoint presentation or the most comprehensive strategic plan. It's about helping people feel personally connected to the outcome.

Tom didn't start his Park City session with charts and graphs about revenue targets. He started with a choice: "Optimism is a choice, especially when you don't have evidence to justify it." That simple statement created an emotional decision point that no amount of data could achieve.

Steve Kerr didn't change his team's offensive schemes after their Finals collapse. Instead, he helped his players understand that they weren't just running plays; they were embodying a way of being together that would determine their success.

The river guide didn't explain the physics of hydraulics or the thermodynamics of forty-degree water. He made the case for why their lives depended on moving as one. Making the case is not just about what needs to be done but about the stakes involved.

Step Two: Gauge and Discuss
This is where most leadership efforts fail. After making their case, leaders assume that awareness equals commitment and move directly to defining execution. But real alignment requires something messier: honest conversations about concerns, resistance, and competing priorities.

Tom understood this instinctively. After presenting his choice about optimism, he didn't ask for commitment. Instead, he did something most leaders never have the courage to do: he invited people to voice evidence that had persuaded them to choose pessimism. For thirty minutes, he let the room vent every frustration, every legitimate concern, and every reason for skepticism.

Because alignment is messy and happens out loud. You can't achieve genuine commitment without first processing real resistance. The people in that basement couldn't get to optimism until they cleared their system

DELIVER

of pessimism. This step of The Alignment Process requires the leader to stop talking and start listening.

Gauging and discussing ensures that when people commit, they're doing so with full awareness of what they're signing up for.

Step Three: Get Involved

True alignment occurs only when people stop being passive observers and become active participants. This is where awareness transforms into ownership, where understanding becomes commitment.

Tom achieved this by changing the question. Instead of asking his team to execute someone else's plan for optimism, he asked them to create evidence to justify it. They weren't just responding to his request; they were co-creating the solution. When they broke revenue records by the end of the year, it wasn't because they'd complied with Tom's vision. It was because they'd made his vision their own.

The river guide achieved this by making everyone responsible not just for their own safety but for the collective success of the entire group. After navigating the Three Sisters, he didn't let them celebrate their individual triumphs. Instead, he turned the raft around and focused their attention on helping the boats behind them succeed.

Involvement is the ultimate measure of alignment.

These three steps: Make the Case, Gauge & Discuss, and Get Involved create The Alignment Process™.

DELIVER

The Twelve-Month Redemption

Steve Kerr's devastating lesson led to one of the most remarkable transformations in sports history.

The following season, he didn't change the X's and O's; those were already perfect. Instead, he made a different choice: he would rebuild the emotional foundation of his team.

Kerr established an environment where every voice mattered, from superstars to video coordinators. When a 24-year-old staff member named Nick U'Ren suggested a crucial lineup change during a championship run, Kerr didn't dismiss it because of the messenger's age. He listened, implemented the idea, and they won the title. "It didn't matter where the idea came from," Kerr explained, "but everybody feeling like they had a say and were empowered to speak their minds was part of what we wanted to build."

The Warriors also added Kevin Durant that summer, but not just for his talent. Durant had observed their culture from afar and was drawn to it. "One of the reasons we got Kevin Durant," Kerr said, "was that he had seen our culture from afar. He saw our desire to get better and work together."

When the 2017 Warriors faced adversity, they didn't collapse. They went 16-1 through the postseason, the best playoff record in NBA history. In crucial moments, players chose team success over individual achievement. They had moved from knowing what to do to being aligned around doing it together.

"I think the first championship just kind of came out of nowhere," Kerr reflected on the difference. "Deep down, I think we weren't really sure

DELIVER

in 2015 that we could win it. We were trying to convince ourselves that we could, but we didn't really know. And whereas in '17 we knew we were the best team in the world, and we knew we were going to win the championship."

That's the difference between awareness and alignment. In 2015, they hoped. In 2017, they knew. Same players, same system, different commitment.

Clarity + Alignment Is Game Changing

Alignment is the second step of LeaderOS. It sits right between clarity and movement. Most leaders have never been trained in how to create it. It's why they struggle to lead teams that consistently deliver. Now that you understand the difference between making your team aware of your Team Key Results (TKRs) and getting them aligned to them, it's time to walk through how to do it.

Some of you will be tempted to skip these next few chapters or not install this part of the Leader Operating System in how you manage teams. You may view this as unnecessary or something you don't have time for due to the urgent demands of your job or your company's unique circumstances. Trust us, we've seen the facial expressions, the body language, and heard the arguments hundreds of times. You think once you create clarity it's time to jump to execution.

Go try it. But first, bookmark this page. Because when your raft gets destroyed by that first boulder in the rapids due to the dynamics you've created on your crew, you'll want to return to this spot and study a different approach. The one that creates synchronized movement that delivers unthinkable results.

DELIVER

Chapter 9: The Alignment Gap

– Quick Start –

Key Points:

- A team's performance collapses when it lacks alignment (2016 Warrriors).
- Awareness = knowing what to do (lives in the head).
- Alignment = choosing to do it together (lives in the heart) — the second pillar of LeaderOS.
- Tom's basement conversation: alignment is messy and happens out loud.

The Alignment Process:

1. Make the Case (why this matters).
2. Gauge & Discuss (surface real concerns).
3. Get Involved (recruit ownership).

Action Steps:

- **Consider:** Think about the most aligned team you've ever been a part of in your career or personal life. How did it feel to be on the team?
- **Seek Feedback:** Ask several team members privately: "On a scale of 1 to 10, how aligned do you think we are as a team?"
- **Start Doing:** During meetings and discussions with colleagues, get in the habit of considering in your mind "do we have awareness or alignment on this issue?"

DELIVER

> **Third Leader Quote:**
>
> Optimism is a choice. Especially when you can't find evidence to justify it.

The Alignment Process™

CHAPTER 10

MAKE THE CASE

AT 3:47 AM ON TUESDAY, February 17, 2023, the first delivery van of the day hummed to life in Amazon's fulfillment center in Kent, Washington. The tall, silent blue box on wheels opened its eyes, ready for its daily voyage, one of over 250,000 Rivian trucks Amazon had ordered at $78,000 each. Before sunset, this single truck would navigate 160 stops across the Seattle metro area, delivering packages to front porches, apartment lobbies, and office buildings. It's just one small part of Amazon's relentless pursuit: getting more than 20 million brown boxes and white and blue plastic bags to customers every day.

Inside the warehouse, the night shift was reaching peak velocity. Hundreds of workers moved like a choreographed army. Yellow robots glided silently between towering shelves. This scene unfolded simultaneously across 1,000 fulfillment centers in 50 countries. Amazon's 1.5 million employees powered an unstoppable machine generating wealth at an almost incomprehensible scale: $514 billion in revenue the previous year. Put another way, that's a staggering $58 million flowing in every hour. Around the clock. Never stopping.

DELIVER

But forty miles north, in the gleaming towers of Amazon's Seattle headquarters, something unexpected was about to happen. The very people who designed and directed this global empire were about to discover that moving mountains of merchandise was different from moving people.

The Decision That Detonated

The Amazon Spheres sat nearly empty that Tuesday morning. The iconic glass domes, designed to inspire creativity and collaboration, had been largely vacant for three years. Across the campus, tens of thousands of desks waited for employees who might never return.

Andy Jassy had been grappling with this reality since replacing Jeff Bezos as CEO in 2021. For months, Amazon's S-Team debated different approaches to bringing people back. But Jassy reached a conclusion that would reverberate through the lives of 350,000 corporate employees worldwide: Amazon needed its people back in the office. Starting May 1st, every corporate employee would be required to work from the office at least three days per week.

At exactly 12:00 PM Pacific Time, Amazon's corporate employees received an email with the subject line "Strengthening Our Culture and Teams." The message began with Jassy acknowledging the complexity of the past three years. Then came the paragraph that would ignite a firestorm: "And ultimately, they've led us to conclude that we should go back to being in the office together the majority of the time (at least three days per week)... We plan to implement this change effective May 1."

What the memo didn't mention was crucial context: Just eighteen months earlier, Amazon had launched recruiting campaigns built on the promise of flexibility. Job postings had advertised remote positions. New hires had been told they could work from anywhere.

The Backlash

Within thirty minutes, an internal Slack channel called "Remote Advocacy" exploded with activity. By the end of the day, 5,000 employees had joined. By the end of the week, 16,000 Amazon workers had gathered in the largest digital rebellion in the company's history.

The responses revealed the human cost: "I moved 800 miles away during the pandemic because I was told I could work remotely indefinitely. Now I have to choose between my job and being near my family."

The Slack channel comments turned into a formal petition signed by 30,000 employees. The document challenged Amazon's arguments using the company's own internal data, showing that teams had maintained productivity while working remotely and that only 31% of employees actually wanted to return to the office.

Amazon's S-Team remained unmovable. The policy would be implemented exactly as outlined. The decision had been made, and compliance was expected.

The Science Behind the Resistance

Why did Amazon's approach create such fierce resistance? The answer lies in how human brains process information and make decisions about commitment versus compliance.

Wharton Professor Adam Grant's research reveals why Amazon's communication strategy was neurologically destined to fail. When people receive unexplained demands, their brains activate a "threat response"—the amygdala triggers stress hormones that impair decision-making and fuel resistance. But when people understand the reasoning behind requests,

DELIVER

they engage brain regions associated with voluntary cooperation and intrinsic motivation.

Grant demonstrated this principle with employees at a fundraising call center. Half the employees met and talked with an actual scholarship recipient for just five minutes. The other half never met anyone. The results were extraordinary: Employees who met the scholarship student worked twice as hard and raised 170% more money than their colleagues who never saw the impact of their work.

The insight was profound: People aren't motivated by being told their work matters. They're motivated by understanding how it matters and to whom.

David Rock's neuroleadership research explains why this pattern is so consistent. When people lack certainty about decisions affecting them, the brain uses dramatically more resources to process the experience, creating neurological stress that impairs performance. When Amazon employees received Jassy's memo, their brains literally interpreted the mandate as a threat. The resistance that followed was neurological.

Step One: Making the Case

What Amazon experienced reveals how critical the first step is in creating alignment. Alignment begins when leaders take time to make the case. Jassy's email was designed to inform employees of the policy, but it was not designed to create alignment.

The Alignment Process™

1 Make the Case → **2** Gauge & Discuss → **3** Get Involved

We're frankly surprised Amazon's S-Team chose to send an email rather than hold a town hall to communicate such an emotionally charged pivot. Imagine if Jassy had appeared on stage in front of hundreds of employees while the discussion was streamed to all corporate employees. Imagine if he had said something like this:

"Over the past six months, our customer satisfaction scores have dropped 20%, primarily driven by integration issues between our returns processing and order fulfillment teams working from different locations. Our cross-functional response time during last Prime Day increased by 47 minutes when issues arose—the kind of delay that directly impacts the customer experience we've built our reputation on.

I know many of you planned your lives around our previous commitment to flexible work, and I understand this feels like we're changing the rules. That concern is completely valid; we shouldn't have made commitments about permanent remote work without being clearer about the conditions that might require us to adjust. I own that and regret the experience we created for many of you.

Because we recognize our role in this situation, we're extending the transition timeline to September 1st instead of May 1st. For anyone who genuinely can't make this work due to family or housing situations resulting from our previous guidance, we'll provide additional support.

Returning to the office will give us what we've been missing: the organic collaboration that has fueled our greatest products and features. My primary role is to ensure our company maintains its obsession with customers, and I'm convinced this change will help us uphold that commitment."

Can you see the difference? When a leader seeks to create alignment rather than just awareness, they take the time to make the case.

DELIVER

Sharing the Backstory

Effectively making the case requires leaders to reveal their decision-making process. People want to understand not just what was decided, but how the decision was reached and what alternatives were considered.

This level of transparency can feel risky to some leaders. What if people disagree with the logic? What if they propose alternatives that seem impractical? What if sharing uncertainty makes you appear indecisive?

But research consistently shows that people are far more likely to support decisions they've seen develop, even when they disagree with the final outcome. The key is helping them understand the factors you considered and the constraints you faced.

When leaders say, "We decided to restructure the sales organization," employees perceive it as an arbitrary decision made by those disconnected from day-to-day reality.

When leaders explain, "We spent three months analyzing why our customer acquisition costs have tripled while our conversion rates have stayed flat. We examined everything from our marketing mix to our sales processes to our competitor strategies. What we discovered is that our current structure optimizes for activity rather than results. Here's what we found, and here's why we believe this change will enhance our service to customers," employees see a thoughtful process they can evaluate and potentially support.

The backstory doesn't need to reveal confidential information or proprietary strategies. It simply needs to show that decisions were made thoughtfully, with good intentions, based on real data rather than arbitrary preferences.

Connecting to the Bigger Picture

The most compelling cases link individual effort to organizational purpose in personal and meaningful ways. This isn't about manipulative messaging; it's about helping people see how their daily work contributes to Team Key Results they genuinely care about.

When making the case, help people see four levels of connection:

1. **Personal Impact**: How does this decision affect my daily work, career development, and quality of life? Leaders who overlook these personal considerations come across as tone-deaf, even when their organizational logic is sound. Validate their concerns about any potential negative impact to them personally while focusing on the benefits this change unlocks for them individually.
2. **Team Impact**: How does this change help our team deliver better results for those we serve? This is where the rubber meets the road; people need to see concrete ways that changes will enhance their ability to do work they're proud of. How will this increase collaboration or lead to a more unified effort?
3. **Organizational Impact**: How does this decision advance our mission in ways that wouldn't happen otherwise? This is where purpose comes alive, allowing people to trace a clear line from temporary inconvenience to meaningful progress on problems they care about solving. How do these TKRs, or whatever you're seeking alignment around, enable us to focus on the work our organization was built to do?
4. **Customer Impact**: Finally, connect to the group that matters most: customers, patients, or members. What's the ultimate impact on them? How will this help us serve them better or lead to the outcomes they care about most?

DELIVER

When leaders address all four levels, they make a strong argument for why this change or these results have been chosen and why team members should be involved in helping implement or achieve them.

Creating Alignment About Decisions

Our primary focus, as you work to install LeaderOS in the way you manage others, is to help you create alignment around your TKRs. That's no small feat and requires implementing each step of the The Alignment Process we're teaching you right now.

You'll also create alignment around other areas in the future. Frequently, you'll make decisions that impact your team members and other departments. This process is what we hope you'll consistently and intentionally use to create alignment around new policies, priorities, projects, and all decisions. To assist you, we're going even more granular and detailed on things to consider as you build alignment in common situations.

Before Announcing Major Decisions

Ask yourself three questions that will shape how you communicate the reasons to your team as you seek their alignment around new initiatives, priorities, or projects:

1. **What specific Key Results does this decision impact?** If you can't articulate this clearly, you're not ready to announce a decision. Generic benefits like "improved efficiency" or "better collaboration" aren't specific enough. How will this impact the TKRs? How does this decision help clear obstacles or set us up for greater success?
2. **What alternatives did you consider, and why did we choose this path?** People need to understand that you've evaluated options, not just picked the first solution. This doesn't mean sharing every detail of your analysis, but it does mean acknowledging that you weighed

trade-offs and considered the challenges or contradictions in what you're rolling out.

3. **What commitments or expectations are we changing, and how will we support people through that transition?** Every significant change requires people to give up something: time, convenience, familiar processes, or previous promises. Acknowledging these costs honestly builds trust and demonstrates that you understand the real impact of your decisions as you ask them to align with what you've decided.

Making It Routine

The most effective leaders don't just make the case during major changes; they incorporate case-making into their regular communication. This creates a culture where understanding drives action rather than authority driving compliance.

In Team Meetings: Before discussing what needs to happen, briefly remind people why these activities matter to the Key Results the team cares about achieving. This doesn't mean delivering a speech every time you assign a task, but it does mean regularly connecting routine work to larger purposes so that people never lose sight of how their daily efforts serve meaningful goals.

In One-on-Ones: When assigning new responsibilities or changing priorities, take time to connect those changes to the person's development goals and the team's Key Results. Help people see how new challenges serve their professional growth and the organization's success.

In Project Planning: Help people understand not just their role in a project, but how project success connects to customer value, organizational learning, or strategic progress. This transforms routine execution into purposeful contribution.

DELIVER

In Performance Reviews: Connect individual goals and expectations to team and organizational Key Results, helping people see their daily work as part of something larger and more meaningful than task completion.

This isn't about over-communicating or being repetitive. It's about creating clarity that enables ownership rather than just awareness.

Preparing to Listen

Making the case is the first step in building genuine alignment within the LeaderOS framework. When you skip this step, assuming that clarity should automatically lead to commitment, you risk encountering situations like Amazon's: smart people who understand your Key Results but don't see why they matter enough to invest their best effort in achieving them.

Now we'll move on to the next step of The Alignment Process, where you stop talking and start listening.

DELIVER

Chapter 10: Make the Case

– Quick Start –

Key Points:

- Step 1 of Third Leader Alignment Process: Help people understand WHY these TKRs matter.
- Amazon's RTO failure shows the consequences of skipping this step.
- People need a connection to purpose, not just understanding of tasks.
- Share your reasoning process, not just your conclusions.

Making the Case Means:

- Connecting TKRs to outcomes people personally care about.
- Explaining the backstory behind your decisions.
- Acknowledging what commitments are changing and why.

Action Steps:

- **Consider:** What's 'the why' behind your TKRs? Journal what the cost of not achieving them would be. Write down what the benefit would be if the team did accomplish them. What's the pain and the gain associated with the TKRs.
- **Seek Feedback:** Ask a couple team members privately: "Why does it matter if our team accomplishes these TKRs? Help me craft 'the why' behind them."
- **Start Doing:** Make it a habit to 'Make the Case" when you ask people to start a new project, follow a new policy, or take on a new assignment.

Make the Case > 157

DELIVER

Founder Mode Reality:

Most leaders operating in Founder Mode think 'the why' is a waste of time. They just want people to put their head down, stop asking questions, and go execute. That approach doesn't scale.

The Alignment Process™

CHAPTER

11

GAUGE & DISCUSS

TWO HOSPITALS. SAME COMPANY. Same challenge. Same resources. But two very different results.

Drive down Midlothian Turnpike in Richmond, Virginia, and within a few minutes, you'll encounter two hospitals that are more alike than different. Chippenham Hospital sits on busy Jahnke Road, its brick and glass facade housing 466 beds and one of Virginia's premier Level 1 Trauma Centers. Just four miles away via the Turnpike, Johnston-Willis Hospital rises from its quieter perch on Johnston Willis Drive, its 292 beds serving the community since 1909. Both are part of HCA's CJW Medical Center, their emergency room signs glowing the same reassuring blue against the Virginia sky.

Inside, the similarities are even more striking. Same nurse-to-patient ratios mandated by corporate policy. Same electronic health records system humming on identical workstations. Same motivational posters about patient care excellence hanging in break rooms that smell of burnt coffee and hand sanitizer. Same everything, really, except for one critical

DELIVER

difference that would soon separate them by a chasm as wide as the James River that flows between Richmond's downtown towers.

Both hospitals received the same directive from HCA corporate in Nashville: improve patient satisfaction scores. It wasn't a suggestion. In the complex world of healthcare economics, patient satisfaction isn't just about being nice; it's about survival. Medicare doesn't just pay hospitals for performing procedures anymore. If a patient rates their experience poorly, the hospital receives less money from the government. A satisfied patient walking out those sliding glass doors could be worth thousands more in reimbursements than a dissatisfied one leaving with the same medical outcome.

The stakes were clear. The goal was identical. What happened next at Chippenham and Johnston-Willis would reveal everything about the difference between awareness and alignment, highlighting why the next step of The Alignment Process is so critical.

Chippenham Hospital: The Bulletin Board Directive

Enter Chippenham's main entrance on Jahnke Road on a Tuesday morning in March, and you'd notice them on every bulletin board: signs showing the hospital's TKRs, with the first one about Patient Satisfaction Scores and the target of top quartile.

The nursing station on the cardiac unit buzzed with its usual controlled chaos. Monitors beeped while nurses moved between rooms with practiced efficiency. But if you looked closely as staff passed those bulletin boards, you'd see something telling: their eyes barely registered the TKR announcements. The signs had become part of the wallpaper.

During monthly staff meetings, unit directors explained that corporate wanted their patient satisfaction scores in the top quartile by June.

DELIVER

The rooms were quiet. Nurses sat listening, some checking their phones, others staring ahead with the kind of attention usually reserved for safety presentations.

When directors asked for questions, there were none.

The meetings ended, and people returned to their shifts. If you'd asked any of them about the patient satisfaction initiative, you might have gotten a polite nod or a generic response about doing their best.

But in real conversations during breaks and shift changes, you'd hear a different story. Staff would tell you there was no way anything would change until more nurses were hired. They all complained about staffing.

Three months later, when the patient satisfaction scores came back, Chippenham's numbers were virtually unchanged. All those bulletin boards, all those meetings, all those PowerPoint slides, and nothing had moved. The needle hadn't budged at all.

Johnston-Willis Hospital: The Hour That Changed Everything

Drive those four miles down Midlothian Turnpike to Johnston-Willis Hospital, and from the outside, you'd see the same HCA branding, the same emergency room entrance, the same parking lots filled with cars of people having the worst or best days of their lives. But this hospital, serving the community since 1909, was about to show how a different approach could yield dramatically different results.

Over two weeks, Johnston-Willis held a series of meetings in the same big, nondescript conference room. The meetings were spaced out to cover all shifts. Each session brought together diverse groups of staff members: nurses from different units, lab technicians, dietitians, custodial staff, and cafeteria workers. Hospital administrators presented

DELIVER

the TKRs, including the patient satisfaction score target of top quartile. Then they did something that no one did at Chippenham.

They asked questions. They got the group talking. What did staff think stood in the way of a better patient experience? The question wasn't rhetorical. Administrators had notepads open, pens ready. Staff members raised their hands, and real conversations began. Staff explained that patients complained most about waiting—for discharge paperwork, medication, or someone to answer their call button. But they were already stretched thin. If they were expected to spend more time with each patient, something else had to give.

Instead of defending the initiative, administrators asked what specifically took the most time that patients didn't see as valuable. Lab staff mentioned documentation, explaining how they spent significant time entering the same information into multiple systems while patients watched them type instead of engaging with them.

Cafeteria workers described how the meal delivery system created delays, with food sitting under heat lamps before reaching patient rooms. Patients thought staff didn't care about their experience, but it was the system that was failing them.

Custodial staff spoke about patients asking them questions—where's the bathroom, when will the doctor come, why is it so noisy at night? They wanted to help but had never been told what they should or shouldn't say to patients.

Administrators kept writing, kept asking follow-up questions about what would need to change for people to feel confident about hitting the goals.

The conversations continued for nearly an hour. People weren't just raising problems; they were building solutions together. Staff suggested cross-training so custodial workers could answer basic questions. Lab technicians proposed streamlining documentation. Cafeteria workers had ideas about meal timing that would require coordination between departments.

These hour-long sessions occurred with every department: Environmental Services, Pharmacy, Physical Therapy, Registration. Each group brought their piece of the patient experience puzzle, and each conversation revealed problems that the bulletin boards and PowerPoint slides had never addressed.

Three months later, when the patient satisfaction scores arrived, Johnston-Willis had rocketed into the top quartile of all HCA facilities nationwide.

The Science Behind Step Two

What Johnston-Willis stumbled onto wasn't luck; it was Step Two of The Alignment Process, a systematic approach to turning awareness into alignment through the incredibly simple yet often unused tactic of listening. While Chippenham stopped after making their case (Step One), Johnston-Willis moved into the critical second phase: gauge and discuss.

The Alignment Process™

DELIVER

The difference between these hospitals reveals why so many well-intentioned initiatives fail. MIT researchers discovered that 70% of strategic failures stem not from poor strategy but from inadequate alignment between leadership vision and team understanding. When Johnston-Willis administrators asked "What questions do you have?" instead of "Any questions?", they triggered a neurological shift in their staff.

The brain science is revealing: when people feel genuinely heard, oxytocin levels increase by 25%, activating trust and cooperation centers. Cornell research shows that this simple reframing—from "Do you have questions?" to "What questions do you have?"—generates 300% more meaningful responses. The difference isn't semantic; it's neurological.

But here's what most leaders miss: alignment isn't about getting people to agree with your vision. It's about creating space for them to make your vision their own. Stanford's research on goal co-creation proves that teams who help shape objectives achieve 40% higher performance than those simply assigned targets.

This requires a fundamental shift from broadcasting to listening, from certainty to curiosity. As one executive put it after experiencing this process: "I thought leadership meant having all the answers. It actually means creating space for others in the room."

This is where most leaders stumble. They make some effort at Step One, presenting compelling cases for the Team Key Results or a new policy. But Step Two requires a different skill set entirely. It demands that leaders stop talking and start asking questions, gauge where people actually stand, and engage in the messy, unpredictable process of real dialogue.

Alignment, as we say, is messy and happens out loud.

Jeff's Four-Hour Masterclass

Jeff was discovering this lesson the hard way. As CEO of a $500 million food manufacturing subsidiary, he'd spent eighteen months traveling to facilities across Texas and Mexico, consistently reinforcing one message: "We're going to hit $1 billion in revenue." The goal had become his constant refrain in leadership meetings, town halls, and visits to the plants.

But despite all this repetition, we started picking up troubling signals. In private conversations, we sensed noticeable doubt—not outright resistance, but a lack of genuine buy-in or at least hesitation among mid-level managers. People were concerned about how the organization would actually reach this ambitious target. The goal felt distant, maybe even unrealistic.

As we prepared for an offsite meeting with the expanded leadership team in Orange County, California, we suggested dedicating time to gauge alignment on the billion-dollar TKR. Jeff was open to it but unsure it was a good use of time. "I think we've got alignment," he said. "But if you feel it's important, we can go there."

During our portion of the offsite, we did something we call "Score It." The instruction was simple: take out a sheet of paper and write down a number between 1 and 10 that scores your alignment to the $1 billion revenue target. One meant "I'm not aligned at all," and 10 meant "I have no concerns or questions, just certainty we're going to hit it."

Once everyone had written their numbers, we asked them to raise their hands in segments. "Who's at a 1-3?" No hands went up; nobody wanted to admit a complete lack of alignment. "Okay, who's at 4-6?"

Half the room raised their hands.

DELIVER

Jeff was stunned. After months of emphasizing this goal, half his leadership team had mediocre alignment levels. That moment triggered what became a four-hour conversation that Jeff later called "one of the most valuable discussions my leadership team ever had."

But here's what made it a masterclass: Jeff didn't defend his goal or explain why people should align more. Instead, he asked a simple question: "What would get you to an 8 or 9?"

Knowing that a room full of 10s was impossible, Jeff focused on moving people toward strong alignment. Then he did something remarkable as CEO: he listened.

Hands went up around the room. People raised concerns about issues at the Dallas plant that hadn't been discussed openly. Others questioned whether the product innovation pipeline was robust enough to support such aggressive growth. Marketing resources became a topic of conversation. Talent challenges surfaced.

Jeff's response to each concern was consistent: validate, don't minimize. He didn't immediately jump to solutions. Instead, he asked, "Help me understand what that means for hitting our target," and "What would need to change for you to feel confident about this?"

Jeff facilitated without dominating. He kept asking questions, taking notes, and creating space for dialogue. People left feeling empowered to solve challenges collectively rather than relying on Jeff to be the solution to everything.

The transformation was immediate and measurable. The level of alignment shifted before lunch. It was tangible. While the conversation didn't solve everything and revealed many issues the senior team needed to address, it absolutely moved the needle.

Why Smart Leaders Skip This Step

Jeff's experience raises an obvious question: if gauging and discussing is so powerful, why don't more leaders use it? The answer lies in three costly assumptions that even experienced executives make.

Assumption 1: "If I explained it well, they got it."
This is perhaps the most dangerous assumption in leadership. Leaders mistake their own clear thinking for universal comprehension. The average Fortune 500 company loses millions annually on misaligned initiatives, not because the strategies were wrong, but because leaders assume explanation equals involvement. Jeff had been making this mistake for eighteen months, interpreting his team's polite attention or even applause as genuine buy-in.

Assumption 2: "Silence means agreement."
Neuroscience reveals that the brain's default response to uncertainty is threat detection, not cooperation. When people don't understand something or have concerns about feasibility, they often default to silence rather than risk appearing uninformed or resistant to change.

Cultural conditioning compounds this problem. Most organizational cultures inadvertently punish challenging authority, even when that challenge would be constructive. So leaders interpret politeness as alignment, quiet rooms as consensus, and a lack of questions as understanding.

Chippenham Hospital fell into this trap completely. Their managers asked for questions, got silence, and assumed everyone was on board. Meanwhile, the real conversations about staffing concerns and impossible expectations happened in break rooms and hallways.

DELIVER

Assumption 3: "We don't have time for all this discussion."

This assumption is particularly ironic given the research. Harvard Business Review data shows that alignment conversations save 40% of implementation time. The upfront investment in dialogue prevents the endless rework that comes from misaligned execution.

Jeff's four-hour conversation would have saved his company twelve months of spinning wheels on a goal that half his leadership team didn't believe was achievable. Time spent in gauging and discussing isn't time lost; it's time invested in preventing failure.

But there's a deeper reason leaders avoid this step: ego.

The Ego Factor

Asking "What questions do you have?" requires vulnerability. It opens the possibility that people aren't as aligned as hoped. It risks discovering that your brilliant strategy has holes you didn't see. It threatens the illusion of control that many leaders find comforting.

Research on leadership vulnerability shows that leaders who regularly ask "What am I missing?" achieve 23% better team performance than those who project certainty. But the human tendency is to avoid information that might challenge our competence.

The Real Cost of Skipping Step Two

The consequences of avoiding gauging and discussing extend far beyond missed targets. McKinsey research indicates that companies with high alignment achieve 2.3 times the revenue growth of their misaligned competitors. Teams with strong psychological safety generate 35% more breakthrough ideas. The correlation between alignment and performance is undeniable.

But the human cost may be even greater. When people feel unheard, when their concerns are dismissed or ignored, and when they're held accountable for goals they had no part in shaping, engagement plummets. The very people you need to execute your vision begin questioning whether you care about their perspective at all. Alignment isn't a nice-to-have; it's a competitive advantage.

The Three Levels of Psychological Safety

For gauge and discuss to work effectively, leaders must create an environment where people feel safe expressing their real thoughts. Our experience reveals that psychological safety operates at three distinct levels, each building on the previous one.

Understanding these levels helps leaders diagnose where their teams stand and what kind of dialogue they can expect when they start asking questions. The most basic, core human need is for safety. We are constantly in threat detection mode. Our brains are continuously receiving signals from our senses and using that data to determine if there is any danger or discomfort we should be concerned about. It's why, when there's a loud noise, you jump without thinking. It's why, when you smell even a faint bit of smoke, your brain goes into panic mode.

When you're asking your team to share their opinions and thoughts, they are subconsciously in threat detection mode. They are looking for any sign that saying what they really think will lead to danger or discomfort. A leader's job is to create an environment where people feel comfortable—or safe enough—to challenge what's being said. But that requires work and is the highest level of psychological safety people experience. They certainly don't start there when introduced to a team or leader for the first time.

DELIVER

Level 1: Observe

At this level, team members feel safe listening and observing conversations without immediate pressure to contribute. They're present, paying attention, but not yet comfortable engaging directly.

This is where a new team member typically starts. They come to a meeting or workplace and generally just listen and observe without saying much. They are in full threat detection mode, getting a sense of how things work.

To inexperienced leaders, a silent team can feel like success; after all, no one's arguing or creating conflict. But Level 1 safety is actually a warning sign. When rooms full of intelligent, experienced people have nothing to say about important initiatives or proposals, it usually means they don't feel safe speaking up. Alignment is undetectable at this level. There is no way to know if they're with you until they start speaking.

Level 2: Contribute

Individuals and teams operating at Level 2 feel safe voicing supportive thoughts and adding to discussions, but they avoid challenging ideas or raising significant concerns. You'll hear comments like "I like the focus on transparency" or "Good point about efficiency," but rarely will someone say, "I think this approach has serious flaws."

Level 2 safety is better than Level 1, but it's still insufficient for true alignment. People participate but self-censor anything that may be perceived as negative or resistant. They contribute to the conversation only in ways that feel socially safe. This level often exists in organizations or teams where leadership fosters the belief that they want agreement and compliance rather than dialogue and debate.

Many leaders observe individuals or teams operating at Level 2 and mistake it for healthy dialogue. They point to participation and discussion as evidence of engagement, not realizing that the most important voices—the concerns, doubts, and alternative perspectives—are still being withheld. Alignment may be starting at this level, but it's more about people going through the motions to maintain peace than fully committing to the pursuit of Team Key Results.

Level 3: Challenge

This is the gold standard: team members feel safe engaging in constructive challenge, even when it means questioning leadership decisions or raising difficult concerns. At Level 3, you hear comments like "I'm worried this timeline is unrealistic given our current capacity" or "Have we considered how this might impact our lowest-performing teams?"

Level 3 safety is what Johnston-Willis achieved in their department meetings. Staff felt comfortable raising genuine concerns about documentation systems, meal delivery issues, and resource constraints. They weren't just identifying problems; they were challenging existing approaches and proposing solutions.

This is also what Jeff's manufacturing team reached during their four-hour conversation. People felt safe questioning whether the billion-dollar target was achievable and raising specific barriers they saw in the way. Level 3 safety never occurs without intentional effort from the leader.

Some employees instinctively jump to this level. They possess unusual confidence or extroverted personalities that enable them to speak their minds regardless of their team or boss. The presence of one or two individuals on a team who feel comfortable respectfully pushing back or questioning what's being said should not be interpreted as a sign of widespread Level 3 safety. When the majority of a team engages in rigorous debate, then you know you have a leader where deep alignment is possible. With our consulting clients, this is always our goal. It leads to greater innovation, more buy-in, enhanced collaboration, distributed decision-making, and faster speed to market.

The Progression Isn't Automatic

Teams don't naturally evolve from Level 1 to Level 3. The progression requires intentional leadership behavior. Leaders must actively demonstrate that they value input, even when it's challenging or uncomfortable.

The fastest way to move teams toward Level 3 is to reward the first person who raises a genuine concern or challenges an assumption. Thank them publicly. Ask follow-up questions. Show that you value their input rather than see it as a problem.

Jeff exemplified this beautifully when the first person questioned the billion-dollar target. Instead of defending the goal or explaining why it was achievable, he thanked them for their honesty and asked what would need to change to make them feel more confident. That response signaled to others in the room that authentic input was not only welcome but valued.

Implementation: Gauge and Discuss in Action

Understanding gauge and discuss as Step Two of The Alignment Process is one thing. Implementing it effectively across different settings is another. Within the LeaderOS framework, gauge and discuss serves as the bridge between making your case and achieving genuine involvement. It's where awareness transforms into alignment, and compliance becomes ownership.

In Meetings: The Art of Strategic Silence

The most powerful tool in meeting-based gauge and discuss is silence. After presenting your TKRs or announcing an initiative, execution is everything.

DELIVER

DO:

- ✓ Ask "What questions do you have?" (not "Do you have questions?")
- ✓ Wait a full 10-15 seconds after asking, even if it feels uncomfortable.
- ✓ Take visible notes when people speak to show their input matters.
- ✓ Ask follow-up questions: "Can you say more about that?" or "What would need to change?"
- ✓ Thank people for raising concerns: "I'm glad you brought that up."

DON'T:

- ✗ Fill silence after 2-3 seconds with more explanation.
- ✗ Ask rhetorical questions when you really want to move on.
- ✗ Immediately defend or solve every concern raised.
- ✗ Rush through the Q&A portion to get to "more important" topics.
- ✗ Interpret silence as agreement or alignment.

In One-on-Ones: Reaching the Introverts

Individual conversations are where you reach thoughtful processors who won't speak up in groups but have crucial insights from their specific roles.

DO:

- ✓ Ask role-specific questions: "From your position in [department], how do you see this TKR?"
- ✓ Probe for unspoken concerns: "What are you worried about that we haven't discussed?"
- ✓ Give people time to think: "You don't need to answer now, but I'd love your thoughts on…"
- ✓ Focus on their unique perspective: "What am I missing from the [operations/sales/finance] angle?"
- ✓ Schedule follow-up conversations to continue the dialogue.

DELIVER

DON'T:

- ✘ Seek confirmation: "So you're all good with this, right?"
- ✘ Rush through a checklist of topics.
- ✘ Make it feel like an interrogation with rapid-fire questions.
- ✘ Assume introverts have nothing to contribute if they don't speak immediately.
- ✘ Use one-on-ones solely to deliver information that could be shared elsewhere.

In Slack and Teams: Creating Dialogue Channels

Digital platforms excel at fostering ongoing dialogue about initiatives, but only if structured for conversation rather than broadcast.

DO:

- ✓ Post specific questions about obstacles: "We're struggling with [TKR]. What barriers are you seeing?"
- ✓ Ask for ideas and solutions: "What would need to change to make this work better?"
- ✓ Engage with responses by asking follow-up questions in threads.
- ✓ Pin important discussions so they don't get buried.
- ✓ Use @channel sparingly and only for genuine dialogue requests.

DON'T:

- ✘ Post TKR updates expecting only emoji reactions.
- ✘ Broadcast directives without creating space for response.
- ✘ Let important conversations die after one round of comments.
- ✘ Use these channels primarily for announcements rather than discussion.
- ✘ Ignore or dismiss concerns raised in digital channels.

Now, It's All About Involvement

We've explored how to create robust discussion and debate that leads to alignment. You've made the case for your Team Key Results. You've sought your team members' perspectives and facilitated productive discussions, listening as they challenged and questioned. There's one final step in creating alignment that is arguably the most important: you need to secure their involvement. You need them to see the connection between their work and the TKRs. As we'll soon discover, not all involvement is created equal, and it doesn't automatically follow steps one and two of creating alignment. Let's complete the task of building alignment!

DELIVER

Chapter 11: Gauge & Discuss
– Quick Start –

Key Points:

- Step 2 of The Alignment Process: Create real dialogue about concerns, obstacles, and resistance.
- Two hospitals, same challenge: one asked "Any questions?" vs. "What questions do you have?"
- 3 Levels of Psychological Safety: Observe → Contribute → Challenge.
- Jeff's 4-hour conversation moved the team from awareness to ownership.

Watch Outs:

- **Founder Mode:** Creating no safe space for people to voice concerns, doubts, fears, and questions. Minimizing people's perspectives or data when they actually do push back or raise their hand.
- **Consensus Mode:** Having an endless discussion about concerns and endorsing all excuses for lack of movement. Empathy is powerful. Excusing lack of performance is not.

Action Steps:

- **Consider:** Reflect on how often your team pushes back on you. How does it make you feel? How do you react when they do? How can you adjust the emotion you might feel in those moments?
- **Seek Feedback:** Ask team members, peers, and your boss: "On a scale of 1 to 10, how movable am I generally on topics and issues that come up on our team."

DELIVER

- **Start Doing:** Use phrases like, "I'm movable on this," "What questions do you have?" "Maybe I'm wrong on this," "Who sees it differently and would be willing to help me consider a different option?"

> **LeaderOS Reality:**
>
> Many leaders skip this step thinking they don't have time for the team to weigh in. They skip taking time to create alignment and then waste months of time trying to fix the fact that they don't have it.

The Alignment Process™

CHAPTER 12

GET INVOLVED

AT THIS POINT IN OUR BOOK, we've portrayed ourselves as quite remarkable. We've shared our experiences with amazing Fortune 500 companies, stories about executives at the highest levels of major corporations, and glimpses into boardrooms and leadership meetings where billion-dollar decisions are made.

We've positioned ourselves as the consultants who help these exceptional leaders create clarity, build alignment, and generate movement toward their most important objectives.

But here's the truth we haven't revealed: we've hit rock bottom.

We went through a period lasting over two years when none of us were terribly excited to get out of bed. During the day, we played the role of consultants, assisting incredible executives at well-known companies. But in reality, we were part of the problem at our own company. We had become completely uninvolved.

DELIVER

Actually, that might be too strong. We were still showing up and putting in effort. However, our level of involvement in helping the company progress had declined dramatically. We were disengaged, frustrated, and no longer looking forward to each day.

We were going through the motions and barely showing up.

We're not proud of that time. In fact, we look back not with regret, but with a wish it had played out differently, that the valley wouldn't have been so deep, and that we wouldn't have let our involvement fade as it did.

The Chamber of Creativity

To understand how far we fell, you need to know where we started.

We were all employees of a consulting team at a boutique firm in Southern California. Each of us joined at different times: Tanner right out of college, Jared after a successful stint as a sales executive in Boston, and Russ last, after nearly two decades in the media industry, rising from street reporter covering school board meetings to traveling the world reporting from places like Banda Aceh, Indonesia, the site of one of history's worst natural disasters.

We joined that firm because of its two founders: Tom Smith and Roger Connors, men we profoundly respect, authors of bestselling books like *The Oz Principle* and *Change the Culture, Change the Game*. What they created was remarkable.

Our favorite meetings were at Tom's house. We'd arrive as a consulting team, immediately having fun, playing games, decompressing from our travels, and reconnecting as colleagues who had become genuine friends. Then we'd settle into Tom's living room while he set up two flip charts at the front of the room, markers scattered like art supplies waiting for inspiration.

Everything about the environment signaled: This is where creativity happens.

Tom would officially start the meetings, and then something magical occurred: total involvement. If you walked into that room, it looked like we were all running the meeting, a group of friends sharing insights from around the world: Singapore, Budapest, Prague, Kansas City, New York, Chicago, Orlando, Dallas, Sydney. We were observing, learning from our clients, and adjusting our content in real-time.

The energy was electric. You had to fight to get a word in because of the excitement, with so many people eager to share their observations. We were in create mode, brainstorming, ideating, and building something together that was bigger than any of us could have produced alone.

Those sessions weren't just meetings; they were laboratories for breakthrough thinking. We felt part of something meaningful, something that was changing how organizations operated globally.

The Slow Fade

Then came the moment Tom and Roger decided to sell.

What had been a client-focused culture shifted to one centered on bank reporting. The long-term approach we were used to was replaced by constant pressure to close deals. The purpose of our company, helping the organizations we worked with achieve their missions, fulfill their purpose, and deliver their Key Results, disappeared.

DELIVER

The creative sessions at Tom's house were canceled. Our meetings turned into phone calls from home offices, staring at computer screens in isolation. The corporate headquarters was mostly empty due to cost-cutting measures to meet EBITDA numbers.

The first two steps we taught you in the previous chapters—making the case and giving people the opportunity to gauge and discuss—were gone. And that's when our involvement vanished too.

The Personal Toll

As a result, the company's revenue declined, and so did everyone's compensation. Our pride in what we were part of disappeared. People around us started noticing; our spouses and kids could see it, and our friends commented on it.

Some of us hit that wall sooner, surrendering involvement earlier, while others tried to push through, stay optimistic, and keep our hearts in the work. Ultimately, we all reached the same place: disengagement.

We realized something had to change, leading us to create our own firm. But the lesson from that period isn't about leaving or staying; it's about understanding what happens when involvement fades and how leaders can prevent it from happening to their teams.

The ultimate measure of alignment is involvement. That's the whole point. That's why we make the case, gauge, and discuss. We put intentional effort into these steps because we're ultimately seeking involvement.

We want the people working with us, for us, and around us to get involved in achieving the Team Key Results we've created clarity around. Involvement is the ultimate outcome of alignment, and we know how

DELIVER

empowering and energizing it is. We understand the impact leaders can have in fostering it.

Most leaders think involvement is just about role clarity—helping people understand their responsibilities and how their work connects to company targets. But there are three distinct levels of involvement that work together. Our story illustrates what happens when one or all disappear.

Alignment Builds Up to This

The final step of creating alignment is arguably the most critical. Without emotional and operational buy-in from the people you lead, your Team Key Results are just dreams.

The Alignment Process™

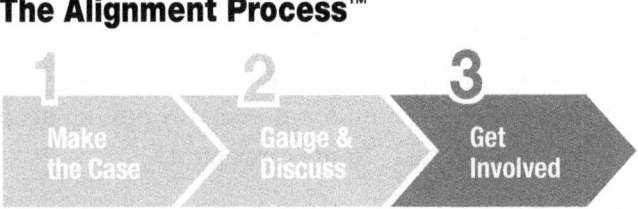

Right now, some of you are flying solo. You feel it every day; your team isn't with you. When you call out "forward two!" like that river guide on the Animas River, no one's paddling. You're headed straight for those huge boulders, steering the raft alone while everyone else just watches the scenery go by.

Without genuine involvement, you're not leading a team toward Team Key Results. You're dragging dead weight toward an impossible goal. Here's where many leaders let themselves off the hook, and it's where we need to have a real conversation about your career.

Get Involved > 183

DELIVER

"Nobody's ever helped me get bought in," you might think. "My boss isn't doing this alignment work with me. Why should I be expected to do it with my team?"

Fair point. But here's the thing: you want a different career trajectory than your boss, don't you? Our aim in this book isn't just to help you in this moment, in this role, at this company. We're upgrading you as a leader. If you let yourself off the hook here, your potential flatlines. Focus on what you can control with your team, not what others are or aren't doing for you.

"But I'm way too busy," you say. "I don't have time to recruit involvement. I just need people to execute."

Good luck with that.

Here's what happens when you skip the involvement step: You either raise your voice to get people moving, threaten consequences to create urgency, or offer large cash bonuses, essentially bribing people to get involved in work they should already care about.

None of these approaches work long-term in today's market. Your people will leave. The best talent has options, and they're not sticking around for leaders who manage through volume, fear, or occasional bribes.

You have a choice: invest time now to cultivate genuine involvement or spend exponentially more time later managing disengaged people merely going through the motions. The market's too competitive, and your people are too valuable to settle for compliance when you could have commitment.

And here's the measurement reality: involvement isn't just a nice-to-have cultural element; it directly impacts your ability to track progress toward your Team Key Results. When people are truly involved, emotionally and operationally, you see the activity needed to move the needle on results.

There are three levels of involvement that team members choose as they consider their connection between their work and the accomplishment of the TKRs. Every team member is at one of these three levels. Which level the majority of your team is at determines the speed at which the defined metrics will be achieved.

Level 0: No Involvement ("Good Luck With That")
The first level is No Involvement, or Level 0, where individuals provide no progress or contribution toward the Team Key Results (TKRs). These are the people who sit through alignment discussions, thinking, "I hope things go well for you all." They mentally distance themselves from product launches, quality metrics, customer experience, or revenue targets.

In large organizations, this group can be substantial. We grow weary when executives label parts of the company as "support functions," leading to disconnection from the organization's Key Results. This also occurs on teams when individuals see themselves as separate or in unique roles that aren't really responsible for the TKRs presented. When policies or initiatives are rolled out, some people instantly define their involvement as zero, thinking, "This has nothing to do with me, but I'm glad they invited me to be aware of this new development."

Level 1: Operational Involvement ("I'll Do My Part")
The next level is Operational Involvement. This group recognizes the connection between their work and the TKRs, understanding they have an important role in the overall effort. They link their daily tasks to the team's purpose and actively contribute to achieving the TKRs.

DELIVER

You can rely on these people to show up daily and fulfill their responsibilities. They consistently contribute, helping get tasks done.

However, something is missing from this group. They leave on time—or even early. They do what is asked but nothing more. Their primary satisfaction seems to come from their paycheck, focusing on money and stability.

This group rarely contributes new ideas or innovative approaches. It's not that they lack the ability; they simply don't care enough. For them, this is just a job—nothing more, nothing less. These employees are important to the current performance of the team. But they aren't the future, and they're not going to help you advance far beyond your current output.

Level 2: Emotional Involvement ("I'm All In")

The highest level is Emotional Involvement. At this level, individuals are not just going through the motions. Their connection to the team's goals runs deep. When you introduced the TKRs, these are the folks who spoke up the most. They asked the most probing questions. They instantly started figuring out ways the obstacles could be overcome.

This part of your team is eager to succeed. Their motivation extends beyond a paycheck; they align their purpose with the team's purpose. When they come to a meeting or discussion, they bring their full selves, contributing ideas and feeling emotionally invested in the work. They offer ideas. They almost shed a tear when there are setbacks or potential customers say no.

The success of your team in achieving TKRs largely depends on the number of people at this level of involvement. While it's impossible to get everyone to Level 2, having a majority here is crucial; otherwise, success will be limited.

The Harvard Diary Revelation

Dr. Teresa Amabile analyzed 12,000 diary entries from knowledge workers across seven companies, revealing a surprising reality: people felt meaningful progress toward something important on fewer than 25% of their working days.

"We discovered that people's motivation, creativity, and performance peaked on days when they felt they were making meaningful progress toward a clear goal," Amabile wrote.

What fosters emotional involvement? A personal connection to purpose, a clear understanding of the work's significance, feeling valued and heard, and being part of something bigger than yourself.

What undermines it? Treating people as interchangeable parts, focusing solely on tasks rather than outcomes, removing the human element from work, and making individuals feel their input doesn't matter—exactly what happens when creative collaboration is replaced by dashboard compliance. This is why we emphasized Making the Case and leading discussions to Gauge and Discuss? You're working toward creating Emotional Involvement on your team.

Damon and the Twelve-Minute Turnaround

We've worked with Southwest Airlines over the years, training hundreds of their managers and observing their distinctive culture. One person we met during those visits was a baggage handler named Damon.

We watched Damon approach the Boeing 737 that had just landed from Phoenix. The operations manager said over the radio: "Team, you gotta be tight; this one is literally 12 minutes, and we need to board."

DELIVER

Twelve minutes. That's the difference between Southwest Airlines' industry-leading on-time performance and being just another airline struggling with delays and complaints.

As we spoke with Damon during a break, we discovered something remarkable: he didn't view himself as just someone who loads bags. He saw his role as helping families spend time together, getting business travelers to their meetings, and maintaining Southwest's reputation for reliability.

"When I'm loading bags," Damon explained, "I think about my girls. When I travel with them to see their Nana, I want that plane on time. Every bag I load means someone is getting home to their kids."

This is Emotional Involvement in action. Damon understood how his work contributed to Southwest's TKRs and had personal reasons for caring about those results. He could draw a direct line from his individual actions to outcomes that mattered to him personally. He wasn't just going through the motions; he genuinely cared.

The Sequential Reality

Here's what happens when you get the sequence wrong:

- **Operational without Emotional = Compliance:** People do what they're told because they have to, not because they want to. Performance is adequate but not exceptional. When pressure increases or obstacles arise, they do the minimum required instead of going above and beyond.
- **Emotional without Operational = Frustration:** People care about outcomes but can't figure out how to contribute meaningfully. They want to help but don't know how, leading to busy work, misdirected effort, and disengagement when they realize their energy isn't generating impact.

- **Both Levels Together = Ownership:** People understand why the work matters and how they can contribute to success. This combination creates conditions for exceptional performance, creative problem-solving, and sustained engagement, even in challenging circumstances.

When leaders grasp this sequential relationship, they can build involvement systematically rather than hoping it emerges naturally.

Making It Practical: The Recruitment Conversation

Involvement doesn't happen automatically, even with a compelling case and dialogue. It's an individual, binary moment that occurs one person at a time, not team by team. Leaders must actively recruit both levels of involvement through individual conversations.

This is what alignment in action looks like—not just team announcements or group sessions, but personal recruitment conversations where leaders invite specific individuals to choose involvement over mere awareness.

Recruiting Operational Involvement

The operational involvement conversation helps individuals see their connection to the Team Key Results. This requires curiosity and patience as leaders work together to clarify connections that may not be immediately obvious.

The recruitment conversation for operational involvement includes:

- "How do you think you affect our financial growth TKR?"
- "What's the connection between your function and our quality TKR?"
- "Walk me through how your daily work contributes to customer satisfaction."
- "If you were explaining how your role impacts our success, what would you say?"

DELIVER

Recruiting Emotional Involvement

The emotional involvement conversation encourages people to choose to be "all in" rather than just going through the motions. This requires vulnerability and directness from the leader.

The recruitment conversation for emotional involvement includes:

- "What's holding you back from being fully committed to this?"
- "I need to know if you're genuinely on board or just going along."
- "What would need to change for you to feel excited about this direction?"
- "Are you willing to choose optimism about our ability to hit these goals?"

This is personal, individual, and binary. People must choose their level of emotional investment. Leaders can't assume that compliance equals commitment.

Some connections will be direct, like Damon loading bags to maintain on-time performance. Others will be indirect, like the hospital custodian preventing infections to reduce mortality rates. Both matter but require different conversations to make them visible.

The key is helping people see their fingerprints on the results rather than just completing assigned tasks. When people can trace a clear line from their daily activities to meaningful outcomes, they naturally develop operational involvement.

The Reality of Direct vs. Indirect Involvement

Not every role connects to every Team Key Result the same way. Leaders need to acknowledge this while helping people find their specific connection points.

Direct Involvement Examples:

- Sales representative → revenue TKR
- Customer service agent → satisfaction TKR
- Quality control specialist → defect reduction TKR

Indirect Involvement Examples:

- Dietitian → patient satisfaction TKR (through meal quality and nutrition)
- IT support → all TKRs (through system reliability and efficiency)
- Facilities management → employee engagement TKR (through work environment)

The goal isn't to force artificial connections but to help people discover real connections they might not have considered. Everyone in an organization affects outcomes, but those connections vary in directness and visibility.

Leaders who try to make every connection seem equally direct lose credibility. Leaders who acknowledge the spectrum while helping people find their place on it build trust and genuine involvement.

Involvement Is Up To You

Every leader faces the same fundamental choice we encountered during our rock-bottom period: Will you focus on compliance or involvement? Will you settle for people showing up with their hands and feet, or will you do the harder work of recruiting their hearts and minds?

Compliance is easier in the short term. You can mandate attendance, assign tasks, and measure completion. You can create systems that function adequately without genuine investment from the people operating them.

DELIVER

But involvement creates sustainable excellence. When people choose to be emotionally invested and operationally clear about their contributions, they bring discretionary effort that transforms adequate performance into exceptional results.

The recruitment conversations we've outlined require more time and vulnerability than simply issuing directives. They require leaders to engage with individuals rather than just manage groups. They require acknowledging that involvement is a choice people make rather than a response you can command.

Organizations that master this approach consistently outperform those that rely on compliance alone. They develop capabilities that can't be copied because they're based on human commitment rather than just systematic processes.

Involvement isn't something that happens to people; it's something they choose. Leaders who understand how to inspire that choice are the ones who deliver.

DELIVER

Chapter 12: Get Involved
– Quick Start –

Key Points:

- Step 3 of Third Leader Alignment: Two levels needed for ownership
- Emotional Involvement: "I'm in" (heart commitment)
- Operational Involvement: "I see my part" (clear connection to TKRs)
- Both levels required—sequence matters (emotional first, then operational)

Our Rock Bottom Story:

- We experienced disengagement when involvement disappeared
- Lost emotional connection to meaningful work
- Lost operational clarity about impact
- Result: showing up with hands and feet but not hearts and minds

Action Steps:

- **Consider:** Think about how you're showing up in the organization right now. How much operational involvement are you demonstrating toward the organization's Key Results? How much emotional involvement do you feel?
- **Seek Feedback:** Ask your team: "What would it look like if someone was operationally involved in achieving our TKRs? What would you see if they were emotionally involved in delivering them?"

DELIVER

- **Start Doing:** Stop using words like "agreement" and "consensus." They don't describe what great leaders seek. Start asking, "are you aligned?"

Third Leader Approach:

Routinely ask people if they see their specific role in helping accomplish the TKRs, priorities, projects, and policies. If they say "yes," ask them to describe how they view their involvement.

The Alignment Process™

1. Make the Case
2. Gauge & Discuss
3. Get Involved

CHAPTER

13

THE ALIGNMENT PLAYBOOK

Note: This is your hands-on, roll-up-your-sleeves chapter. If you want to continue the journey and return to the tactical work later, feel free to skip ahead to Part 4 and Chapter 14. But don't skip this completely; you'll need this playbook to build alignment around the TKRs created in the Clarity Playbook.

We're going to walk you through the exact process we use with actual clients. Here's how we did it in a follow-up call with Bob, a Plant Manager overseeing tankless water heater manufacturing in Peachtree City, Georgia, just outside Atlanta.

Three weeks after our initial clarity session, where Bob established his TKRs of 85-95-100 (85% employee engagement, 95% fulfillment rate, 100% quality), he reached out for guidance on rolling them out to his team.

DELIVER

Question 1: When and where are you planning to have the TKR alignment conversation with your team?

Bob's Response: "I've got it mapped out. Next Tuesday, I'm meeting with my 14 plant supervisors in our main conference room here at the facility. These are my shift leaders, quality supervisors, and department heads, the people who really run this place day-to-day. I need them bought in first before we take this to the factory floor."

Our Follow-up: "That sounds like a smart approach. What's your plan after the supervisor meeting?"

Bob's Response: "Once I get the supervisors aligned, we'll cascade it to the entire plant. I'm thinking we do it by shift over the next two weeks, day shift first, then evening, then night shift. Each supervisor will lead the conversation with their teams, but I want to be there for all of them. We've got about 300 people total, so it's going to take some coordination."

Our Follow-up: "Why start with the supervisors first?"

Bob's Response: "These supervisors have been with us for years. They know the plant, they know the people, and honestly, they know where the bodies are buried. If I can't get them aligned on 85-95-100, I'll never get the factory floor aligned. Plus, they're the ones who'll have to live with these numbers every day."

Your Turn—Question 1: When and where are you planning to have the TKR alignment conversation with your team?

DELIVER

Meeting Details:

Date/Time: _____
Location: _____
Who will be there: _____
Duration planned: _____

Rollout Strategy:

Will you do it all at once or in phases? _____
If phases, what's the sequence? _____
Who else needs to be aligned first? _____

Question 2: Why do these specific TKRs matter to your team and organization? (Make the Case)

Bob's Response: "Look, we're not just making widgets here. These tankless water heaters go into people's homes, their showers, their kitchens, their daily lives. When we ship a defective unit to Home Depot, it's not just a number on a spreadsheet. It's a family in Marietta who can't get hot water for their kids' baths."

Our Follow-up: "That's powerful. What about the other two numbers?"

Bob's Response: "The 95% fulfillment rate is about keeping our word. When Home Depot places an order, they're counting on us. If we're late, they've got empty shelves and angry customers. We're not just another supplier to them; we're a partner. And the 85% engagement is about our people. We've had way too much turnover this past year. People are working Saturdays, sometimes unpredictably, and it's wearing them down. If we can't engage our workforce, we'll never hit the other two numbers anyway."

DELIVER

Our Follow-up: "How will you connect this to what your supervisors care about personally?"

Bob's Response: "Every one of my supervisors has been promoted from the line. They know what it's like to work mandatory overtime, deal with quality issues, and watch good people leave because they're burned out. The 85% engagement isn't just a corporate metric to them; it's about creating the kind of workplace where they'd want their own kids to work someday. And the fulfillment and quality numbers? Those are what keep us competitive and secure their jobs."

Your Turn—Question 2: Why do these specific TKRs matter to your team and organization? (Make the Case)

Business Impact:

TKR #1: Why does this matter to the business? _____

TKR #2: Why does this matter to the business? _____

TKR #3: Why does this matter to the business? _____

Personal Connection:

How do these TKRs connect to what your team members care about personally? _____

What's at stake if you don't achieve them? _____

DELIVER

What becomes possible if you do achieve them? _____
_____

Question 3: What resistance or concerns do you anticipate about these TKRs? (Gauge & Discuss)

Bob's Response: "The engagement number will be the hardest sell. People will say, 'How can you expect us to be 85% engaged when you're making us work Saturdays?' And honestly, they have a point. We've been reactive about overtime; sometimes people find out on Friday afternoon that they're working Saturday. That's not sustainable if we want engagement."

Our Follow-up: "What about the other numbers?"

Bob's Response: "The 100% quality will be the easiest. We're already at 98%, and quality is the foundation of this company. Everyone understands that. The 95% fulfillment is trickier. We just installed new monitors throughout the plant that track our fill rate in real-time, with red, yellow, and green indicators everywhere. Some people are excited about the visibility, but others feel like we're monitoring them too closely. There's also pressure from sales to promise aggressive delivery dates."

Our Follow-up: "Any other concerns?"

Bob's Response: "Supervisors will want to know what support they'll receive. They'll ask about staffing, equipment maintenance, and whether we're providing the tools to achieve these numbers or just holding them accountable for results beyond their control. They'll also want to know about the Saturday shifts: do we eliminate them, make them predictable, or just hope for the best?"

DELIVER

Your Turn—Question 3: What resistance or concerns do you anticipate about these TKRs? (Gauge & Discuss)

Expected Resistance:

TKR #1: What pushback do you expect? _____

TKR #2: What pushback do you expect? _____

TKR #3: What pushback do you expect? _____

Underlying Concerns:

What are people really worried about? _____

What past experiences might make them skeptical? _____

What do they need to feel confident about success? _____

Your Responses:

How will you address the most common concerns? _____

What support can you offer to address their worries? _____

Question 4: How will you help your team get emotional and operational involvement with these TKRs? (Get Involved)

Bob's Response: "For emotional involvement, I need them to see these aren't just my numbers; they're our numbers. Regarding engagement, I'll be honest about the Saturday shift issue and ask for their input on solutions. Maybe we implement a rotating Saturday schedule so people can plan ahead, or we increase staffing to reduce overtime. I want them to help design the solution."

Our Follow-up: "What about operational involvement?"

Bob's Response: "Each supervisor needs to see their impact on these results. For fulfillment, every department plays a role; if maintenance doesn't keep equipment running, if quality holds up a batch, if shipping makes an error. I want each supervisor to outline exactly how their area affects the 95% target. The same goes for engagement; each will own the engagement score for their team and have monthly check-ins with their staff."

Our Follow-up: "How will you make it feel personal to them?"

Bob's Response: "I'll ask each supervisor to reflect on the best job they ever had before this one. What made it great? Then, I'll ask what they want this plant to be known for when they retire. Do they want to be remembered as the place that burned people out or as the place that set the standard for manufacturing? These numbers are how we build the legacy they want to leave."

DELIVER

Your Turn—Question 4: How will you help your team get emotional and operational involvement with these TKRs? (Get Involved)

Emotional Involvement ("I'm In"):

How will you help people feel personally connected to these results? _____

What vision will inspire them? _____

How will you show that you value their input? _____

Operational Involvement ("I See My Part"):

TKR #1: How does each person/role impact this result? _____

TKR #2: How does each person/role impact this result? _____

TKR #3: How does each person/role impact this result? _____

Making It Personal:

What questions will you ask to connect these TKRs to their values? _____

How will you invite them to shape the solution? _____

DELIVER

Question 5: What obstacles in the coming weeks or months could knock your team out of alignment?

Bob's Response: "The biggest risk is if sales continues to promise delivery dates we can't meet. We may be making progress on engagement and quality, but if fulfillment becomes impossible due to unrealistic commitments, people will lose faith in the whole system. I need to talk to our VP of Sales about realistic lead times."

Our Follow-up: "What other obstacles do you see?"

Bob's Response: "Equipment breakdowns. Some of our aging machinery could fail and disrupt our fulfillment numbers. Also, if we don't resolve the Saturday shift issue soon, engagement will drop even if people initially buy into the 85% target. And if Home Depot changes their quality standards or delivery requirements, that could throw everything off."

Our Follow-up: "How will you stay ahead of these challenges?"

Bob's Response: "Monthly alignment check-ins with the supervisors. Not just 'how are the numbers?' but 'what's threatening our alignment?' I want to catch problems before they escalate. I'm also going to establish a direct line with sales and our maintenance team. If something is going to impact our ability to hit 85-95-100, I want to know early so we can adjust expectations or find solutions."

Your Turn—Question 5: What obstacles in the coming weeks or months could knock your team out of alignment?

DELIVER

External Threats:

What outside pressures could undermine these TKRs? _____

What changes in the business could affect alignment? _____

What's outside your control that you need to monitor? _____

Internal Risks:

What internal dynamics could cause alignment to fade? _____

What competing priorities might emerge? _____

What resource constraints could become problems? _____

Early Warning System:

How will you detect alignment problems early? _____

How often will you check in on alignment? _____

Who else needs to be part of maintaining alignment? _____

Contingency Planning:

If alignment starts to slip, what will you do? _____
_____

How will you communicate adjustments to the team? _____
_____

What's Next?

Just like Bob, you now have a systematic approach to building alignment around your TKRs. Your alignment work becomes the bridge between the clarity you've created and the movement you need to generate.

In Part 4, we'll explore how to convert alignment into sustained movement—the disciplined execution that ensures your TKRs not only inspire but are achieved. Because alignment without movement is just costly enthusiasm.

The Alignment Process transforms the relationship between leader and team from director-actor to co-creator. People aren't just following your vision; they're contributing to a shared mission they understand, believe in, and feel ownership for achieving.

This is how leaders engineer success rather than hope for it. This is how you build sustainable engagement that enables teams to deliver extraordinary results consistently, not just when everything goes according to plan.

Your TKRs are clear. You're about to create alignment. Next, it's time to move!

DELIVER

Chapter 13: The Alignment Playbook

– Quick Start –

Tactical Implementation:

- Plan your TKR alignment conversation (when, where, who)
- Prepare to make the case (why these TKRs matter personally/professionally)
- Anticipate resistance and concerns (what pushback do you expect?)
- Design involvement recruitment (emotional + operational ownership)
- Plan for obstacles that could derail alignment

Bob's Third Leader Example:

Plant manager rolling out 85-95-100 to supervisors first, then cascading to 300 factory workers with clear support for Saturday shift concerns.

Action Steps:

- **Consider:** Ponder potential threats to your team's alignment and how anticipating them could keep everyone invested in TKRs.
- **Seek Feedback:** Have the Gauge & Discuss conversation with your team about your TKRs. Roll them out!
- **Start Doing:** Schedule monthly alignment check-ins to discuss risks to alignment and asking individual team members what their involvement in helping achieve the TKRs looks for the next 30 days.

DELIVER

Install LeaderOS:

Use the 5-question framework to systematically build alignment around your TKRs.

The Alignment Process™

PART FIVE

INSTALLING LEADEROS: GENERATE MOVEMENT

CHAPTER 14

MOVEMENT, NOT MOTION

WEEDS SPROUT FROM CRACKS in the asphalt like nature reclaiming what industry abandoned. Broken windows stare across the Mississippi Delta, reflecting nothing but emptiness. This parking lot once held thousands of cars belonging to workers who built America's washing machines and dishwashers. Now it hosts only wind-blown debris and the occasional scavenging bird.

Inside the cavernous facility, machinery sits frozen mid-assembly, as if workers vanished mid-shift, leaving behind the industrial archaeology of a more optimistic time.

A single figure walks across the cracked pavement, boots crunching on broken glass and years of accumulated debris. He's not seeing the decay or mourning what was lost. He's seeing the future of AI.

His phone buzzes with an incoming text: "Timeline?"

DELIVER

He types back without breaking stride: "We'll figure it out."

The AI Super Computer

Our journey to this point has focused on creating clarity and building alignment. Now we shift to movement. Everything we've done so far is designed to harness the power of collaboration. To showcase what's possible, we chose Brent Mayo because what he and his team accomplished in just 122 days at that abandoned Memphis compound happened quietly, yet the whole world needs to know about it.

When discussions stop, excuses die, and waiting for perfect conditions ends, disciplined execution becomes unstoppable. The scale defied comprehension. It wasn't just that they built the most powerful computer the world had ever seen. It was that they did it with a speed that highlights just how painfully slow the rest of us have become, weighed down by discussion, meetings, planning, coordination, more meetings, additional discussion, and an endless swirl that obstructs the very thing we as leaders were hired to create: Movement!

The War for Silicon

The first obstacle wasn't engineering or construction; it was supply chain warfare. xAI needed 100,000 specialized computer chips, each more powerful than the computers that sent humans to the moon, cured diseases, and decoded the human genome. But these weren't just any chips; they were NVIDIA H100 GPUs, the most coveted piece of technology on Earth.

The global demand was so intense that tech giants like Google, Microsoft, and Meta had essentially declared economic war on each other, with billion-dollar purchase orders used as weapons in a battle for computational supremacy. Every major AI company needed these chips, but

NVIDIA's fabrication capacity was finite. Securing 100,000 of them meant acquiring roughly 20% of the world's entire annual supply.

The mathematics were staggering. Each server rack containing just eight of these processors cost over $300,000, more than most people's homes. A single row of racks could cost $10 million. The total hardware bill would exceed $7 billion, representing one of the largest technology purchase orders in business history.

Most companies would approach this challenge through established protocols: form procurement committees, analyze vendor relationships, negotiate phased delivery schedules spanning multiple years, secure board approval for capital expenditures, and build risk mitigation strategies for supply chain disruptions.

xAI gave themselves sixteen weeks.

The Challenge In Memphis

They chose the abandoned Tennessee warehouse because building the ideal facility would take too long. That would save them years of work. xAI was the underdog in the artificial intelligence industry. ChatGPT, Google, and China all had a massive head start. In AI, being six months behind might as well be six years. The first company to achieve artificial general intelligence wouldn't just win market share; they would fundamentally alter the balance of global power.

xAI's team searched every city in America for the largest existing empty structure they could find. Finding and securing the 785,000 square foot monster outside Memphis would have taken most companies more than a year to locate, form a committee to evaluate the pros and cons of purchasing it, interview dozens of firms to represent them in negotiations,

DELIVER

and then go back and forth with redlines on proposed contracts for months. xAI did it all in a couple of weeks.

Once they became the proud owners of the dilapidated compound, they had to figure out how to keep it cool. Engineers faced a problem that paralyzes most organizations: 100,000 processors running at full capacity would generate over 100 million watts of heat.

To put that in perspective: that's enough thermal energy to power a small city, concentrated in a single building. The heat density would be approximately 100 times greater than a typical office building. If you've ever noticed your laptop getting warm when working hard, imagine that problem multiplied by 100,000, where laptop overheating means slower performance, while data center overheating means millions of dollars of equipment literally melting.

Traditional data center air conditioning wouldn't just be inadequate; it was physically impossible. The volume of air required to cool this facility through conventional methods would create hurricane-force winds inside the building, with air velocities that would be dangerous to humans and destructive to equipment. They had to find a different way to keep their billions of dollars of the fastest chips on earth cool and functional.

The only solution was direct-to-chip liquid cooling on a scale never before attempted in human history. This wasn't just an engineering challenge; it was a physics problem that pushed the boundaries of thermal management science.

The system they designed resembled the cooling infrastructure of a nuclear power plant more than a typical computer facility. Miles of precision-welded, leak-proof piping would carry coolant directly to each processor. Thousands of sensors would monitor temperature and flow rates in real time. Automated shutoff systems would respond in milliseconds to prevent catastrophic failures.

Dr. Sarah Chen, leading the thermal engineering team, captured the challenge with brutal simplicity: "It turns out it's just really hard work."

The 24/7 War Machine

What followed was construction warfare unlike anything the industry had ever seen. The 785,000-square-foot Electrolux plant had been empty for years, a monument to American manufacturing's decline. But now it buzzed with activity that never stopped, a 24-hour-a-day, seven-day-a-week operation that transformed abandonment into cutting-edge technology infrastructure. Three shifts of electricians, plumbers, and technicians worked around the clock in a carefully choreographed dance of construction, installation, and testing.

The power requirements alone demanded infrastructure typically reserved for small cities. The local Tennessee Valley Authority grid, while robust, couldn't deliver the massive electrical load they needed fast enough to meet their timeline. Traditional utility infrastructure development takes years of planning, environmental review, and construction.

So they built their own power plant in the parking lot.

Thirty-five mobile gas turbines arrived on flatbed trucks like an invasion force, transforming the broken asphalt into an industrial power station. Each turbine was the size of a shipping container, capable of generating multiple megawatts of electricity. Together, they would push 72 megawatts of power, enough electricity to supply 60,000 homes, into a single building.

DELIVER

The sight was surreal and somehow prophetic: an abandoned appliance factory surrounded by a convoy of generators, humming day and night like mechanical insects, feeding enormous amounts of energy into a structure that would contain the world's most powerful supercomputer. It looked like a scene from a science fiction movie about humanity's technological future, except it was happening in real time in Memphis.

They Did The Impossible

Mayo's philosophy became the team's operational mantra: "Why spend 2-3 years engineering and planning... then 2-3 years building when you can do it all in less than one year?" While competitors around the world held planning meetings about data center requirements, xAI was retrofitting an appliance factory. While others formed committees to study cooling solutions and debate thermal management strategies, xAI was welding miles of precision piping. While others negotiated vendor partnerships over months and analyzed cost-benefit ratios, xAI was installing server racks and running tests.

The numbers that emerged were staggering and would have been dismissed as impossible just months earlier:

- 122 days from site selection to operational (industry standard: 18-24 months)
- 19 days from hardware arrival to AI training start
- 100,000 processors deployed initially, doubled to 200,000 within 92 additional days
- Miles of liquid cooling infrastructure installed with zero tolerance for failure
- $7+ billion in hardware deployed faster than any comparable project in history
- 785,000 square feet of abandoned factory space converted to cutting-edge technology infrastructure

DELIVER

In September 2024, history was made. The largest number of physically connected computer chips ever assembled drew their first collective breath. Cooling fluid began its endless circulation through miles of precisely welded pipes as the humans who had worked tirelessly to create the most powerful thinking machine in history stood by and watched. Temperature sensors throughout the facility registered numbers that would have seemed like science fiction just six months earlier, everything holding steady in optimal ranges. Everything held.

They had accomplished the unthinkable and, in that moment, pulled ahead—at least temporarily—in the global AI race, all because of one team led by one person who saw what was possible while standing on the broken pavement of the abandoned appliance plant.

Leaders who create movement within teams achieve remarkable results. They deliver while others dream, discuss, and debate. The Leader Operating System isn't just about creating clarity and alignment on teams; those are means to an end. None of it matters if you don't deliver. In the following pages, we'll break down the process and show you how to create movement. But first, we need to show you what you're up against.

Inside Microsoft's Command Center

While xAI was achieving the impossible in Memphis, teams at Microsoft were watching what was happening in every other organization around the world. Dr. Jaime Teevan, Chief Scientist at Microsoft, and Dr. Shamsi Iqbal, Principal Researcher in Microsoft's Productivity and Intelligence group, sit in a global command center in Redmond, Washington. Their screens display the activity of 250 million workers in real time through data streams that map every click, app switch, and moment of distraction occurring in offices and home offices globally.

DELIVER

They can see every meeting you schedule in Outlook, every Teams message you send at 10:47 PM, and every time you open Excel while your boss speaks during a Teams meeting. Teevan and Iqbal can see the productivity spiral that's been happening since work became virtual and hybrid.

The statistics are alarming! They know you're interrupted 275 times per day—not because you reported it in a survey, but because their algorithms tracked every notification ping, every "urgent" message, and every colleague who pulled you from focused work. Every 1.7 minutes during your workday, something demands your attention.

They watched your meetings explode by 153% since February 2020—not through estimates or self-reporting, but through direct monitoring of every Teams call scheduled, every Outlook invitation sent, and every conference room booking that multiplied like a virus across organizational calendars. They documented the catastrophic surge in real time as millions of workers, including you, became trapped in endless meetings, unaware of the toll on their actual productivity.

They discovered you spend 60% of your time on communication and only 40% on creation. Fifteen percent of your day is consumed by emails you barely read, 19% by chat messages, and 23% by meetings. Less than half your time is spent on the actual work you were hired to accomplish.

Most tellingly, they can see you checking email at 10:47 PM, then again at 11:23 PM, part of what they've termed the "triple peak day"—workers who are active not just at 9 AM and 2 PM, but diving back into inboxes by 10 PM. Twenty-nine percent of workers, quite possibly including you, are caught in this exhausting cycle.

Microsoft has inadvertently created the most comprehensive surveillance system of human productivity ever built. What they discovered is that millions of workers are trapped in patterns that systematically destroy organizational effectiveness, completely unaware they are caught in a low-leverage activity epidemic that diminishes their value daily.

Movement Isn't Just Motion

Here's the connection that should alarm you: while the xAI team built the future in Memphis, you were likely stuck in coordination theater that masquerades as productivity.

Right now, as you read this, you're probably stuck in the same patterns. While xAI completed the impossible in 122 days, you might struggle to complete meaningful projects in 122 weeks because you're trapped in activities that feel productive but don't actually advance any objectives critical to your organization's success.

Movement vs. Motion vs. Waiting

We've reached the part of the LeaderOS framework that transitions from discussion to action. The Team Key Results have been established. Everyone knows them. You've created not just awareness but have gotten the team aligned around what success looks like. Now, as the leader, it's your job to mobilize your team to do the things that will accomplish the TKRs.

But here's the challenge: all that noise Microsoft observes in their command center is hurting you more than helping you. Let's clarify what LeaderOS is not.

LeaderOS isn't Clarity + Alignment + Waiting. That occurs when leaders assume perfect conditions will eventually arrive—more resources, better market timing, fewer obstacles, additional staff, or clearer direction from above. Waiting is a trap many of your colleagues fall into. They believe execution can begin only when we hire more people, secure more funding, or the market shifts.

LeaderOS isn't Clarity + Alignment + Motion. Motion is activity without progress. It's staying busy without advancing toward objectives that matter. Motion is the productivity theater Microsoft documented across millions of workers. You weren't hired to respond to emails, schedule meetings, or send messages in Teams or Slack. Stop blaming others for your lack of productivity and block off time on your calendar to execute.

LeaderOS IS Clarity + Alignment + Movement. Movement is targeted progress toward your Team Key Results, regardless of obstacles, resource constraints, or market conditions. Movement is what the Third Leader creates, irrespective of the environment or circumstances they face. Movement is what's required to deliver.

Desire, Discipline, and Consistency

Movement is where you start to see real separation between those who truly implement LeaderOS and those who merely talk about it while remaining trapped in coordination theater. This is where desire, discipline, and consistency become the determining factors in leadership effectiveness.

Desire: Movement requires genuine commitment that exceeds preference or good intentions. When obstacles multiply and urgent distractions demand immediate attention, only leaders who truly desire the outcomes defined in their TKRs will stay focused on activities that advance those results. Desire distinguishes those who want results from those who want the appearance of progress. How badly do you really want to achieve those TKRs? Is failure an option for you? If you're not truly committed to achieving them, then you are not a leader who knows how to deliver.

Discipline: Movement demands systematic focus on High-Leverage Activities while eliminating low-leverage distractions that feel important but don't drive results. This isn't about working harder or longer hours; it's about having the discipline to identify the specific activities that directly impact your TKRs and the courage to say no to everything else. Discipline separates those who know what to do from those who consistently do it. We'll discuss HLAs in the next chapter and help you identify and accomplish them.

Consistency: Movement requires sustained execution over time, not sporadic bursts of effort or periodic campaigns. Teams that deliver exceptional results are led by those who maintain consistent focus on what matters most, week after week, month after month, regardless of changing circumstances or competing priorities. Consistency distinguishes those who start strong from those who finish successfully.

What Movement Actually Looks Like

The Memphis facility proves what becomes possible when leaders refuse to accept limitations others consider immutable laws of business physics.

While competitors held planning meetings about what might be possible given sufficient time and resources, xAI made the impossible real with the time they had.

While others debated timelines and feasibility through committee processes designed to minimize risk, xAI was operational and gaining competitive advantage daily.

No committees studying whether it could be done. No multi-year strategic planning processes. No waiting for perfect conditions or the ideal plant to build itself.

DELIVER

Just crystal-clear focus on an objective that mattered, complete alignment around making it happen, and systematic movement that turned impossible timelines into operational reality.

What they built in Memphis wasn't just impressive engineering or a triumph of project management. It was infrastructure for a future where artificial intelligence helps humans solve problems we can't tackle alone. But the real lesson from Memphis isn't about artificial intelligence, computer chips, or construction timelines.

It's about what becomes possible when clarity and alignment unlock pure movement toward objectives that matter.

Your Gate C24 is waiting to be transformed. Your team is prepared to shift from ineffective chaos to systematic execution toward objectives that matter. The question isn't whether you have the resources needed to make it happen.

The question is: Do you have the desire, discipline, and commitment to consistency to actually move the needle on your Team Key Results, and the courage to eliminate everything else?

It's time to focus you and your team on the High Leverage Activities that will achieve the TKRs.

DELIVER

Chapter 14: Movement Not Motion

– Quick Start –

Key Points:

- xAI built the world's most powerful supercomputer in 122 days compared to the industry standard of 18-24 months.
- Microsoft data: You're interrupted 275 times a day and spend 60% of your time communicating instead of creating.
- Movement = targeted progress toward TKRs despite obstacles (third pillar of LeaderOS).
- Motion = activity without progress (productivity theater).

The LeaderOS Difference:

- Waiting = hoping for perfect conditions.
- Motion = staying busy without advancing objectives.
- Movement = systematic progress despite circumstances.

Action Steps:

- **Consider:** Reflect on activities your team spends time on that feel productive but don't drive results, and how you could better model the urgency of the xAI team building a super computer in 122 days.
- **Seek Feedback:** Ask your boss: "Of all the activities my team does on a regular basis which ones have the highest ROI?"
- **Start Doing:** Reduce the noise on your team. Send fewer DMs, emails, and schedule fewer meetings. Create time and space for movement and reduce motion.

DELIVER

> **Third Leader Requirements:**
>
> Desire (genuine commitment), Discipline (focus on what matters), Consistency (sustained execution over time).

CHAPTER 15

HIGH-LEVERAGE ACTIVITIES

THE TENT SHUDDERS AGAINST the pre-dawn wind as Marcus unzips the flap and steps onto the rocky outcrop 14,000 feet above sea level. Mount Whitney's summit stretches endlessly in every direction, a landscape so remote that cell towers are just a memory from the valley below. He pulls a device the size of a sheet of paper from his pack, sleek, white, with a simple cable that connects to his laptop.

Sixty seconds later, he's video-calling his team in San Francisco, uploading cloud-based presentations, and running his marketing agency from a peak where previous generations would have been completely cut off from civilization. The internet connection is faster than what he gets at his downtown office.

How is this even possible?

DELIVER

The answer begins 340 miles above his head, where a constellation of over 7,000 satellites moves in perfect choreography, beaming connectivity to every corner of the planet at the speed of light.

Six Satellites A Day

The Falcon 9 rocket stands 230 feet tall against the Florida sky, its nine Merlin engines capable of generating 1.7 million pounds of thrust. In the pre-dawn darkness, floodlights illuminate the white-and-black vehicle that will, in the next eight minutes, deliver another piece of humanity's largest machine.

The countdown reaches zero.

The ignition is not an explosion; it's controlled violence that shakes the earth for miles. Orange flames erupt from the base as liquid oxygen and rocket-grade kerosene combust at temperatures exceeding 6,000 degrees Fahrenheit. The sound isn't just heard; it's felt in your chest, a physical force that vibrates through your bones as 1.3 million pounds of rocket and cargo lifts against gravity at three times the acceleration of a Formula 1 car.

Within two minutes and thirty seconds, the first stage has burned through most of its fuel and separates from the second stage, beginning its controlled descent back to Earth. While the second stage continues toward orbit, the first stage reignites its engines twice: once to slow its descent and once to land with mechanical precision on a floating platform named "Just Read The Instructions," bobbing in the Atlantic Ocean twenty miles offshore.

This particular booster is completing its 16th mission. Tomorrow, it will begin refurbishment for mission number 17.

Eight minutes and forty-six seconds after liftoff, the second stage releases its cargo: 23 Starlink satellites, each weighing 573 pounds and designed to operate for five years in low Earth orbit. They separate from their deployment mechanism like mechanical flowers blooming in the vacuum of space, solar panels unfurling as onboard computers start the systematic process of positioning themselves in the precise orbital slots that will maximize global coverage.

Within 24 hours, these satellites will be operational, their signals beaming down to devices like the one Marcus uses on Mount Whitney. This launch happens every two days on average—a cadence that makes NASA's entire annual launch manifest look leisurely.

The Woman Building Global WiFi

Gwynne Shotwell stands in the mission control room at SpaceX headquarters in Hawthorne, California, watching data stream across dozens of monitors. As President and COO, she's the operational architect behind this ambitious engineering project.

Shotwell, a 60-year-old Northwestern-trained mechanical engineer, didn't set out to revolutionize space flight. She spent years in the aerospace industry observing projects take decades to complete and cost billions to develop. When Elon Musk recruited her to SpaceX in 2008, she thought she was joining another rocket company. Instead, she helped build a manufacturing revolution disguised as a space program. SpaceX owns and operates the Starlink network of satellites that provide the most complex WiFi network in the world.

"We never intended to be a disruptor," Shotwell has said. "We just intended to do the work." But that work required rethinking everything about how spacecraft are built, tested, and deployed.

DELIVER

Walk through SpaceX's Hawthorne facility, and you'll see something unprecedented in aerospace: a factory that produces six satellites per day. Traditional satellite manufacturers might build six satellites per year. Each Starlink satellite costs approximately $250,000 to manufacture, a figure that would have been impossible for previous-generation spacecraft that cost tens of millions each.

The production line operates with automotive-industry precision. Components flow from station to station as teams of engineers and technicians assemble, test, and package satellites for launch. Quality control happens at every step, with each satellite undergoing over 200 individual tests before being certified for flight.

But the satellites are only one component of the system. The rockets themselves represent an even more dramatic departure from traditional aerospace manufacturing. Where NASA's Space Shuttle program required 9-12 months of refurbishment between flights, SpaceX can refurbish and refly a Falcon 9 booster in as little as 27 days.

The ground infrastructure spans the globe: tracking stations, gateway facilities, and laser communication links that enable the satellite constellation to function as a unified network rather than individual spacecraft. Each satellite can communicate with up to four others using optical inter-satellite links, essentially fiber optic cables made of light beams, creating redundancy and speed that earthbound networks cannot match.

The numbers are staggering: SpaceX has launched more payload mass to orbit in the past three years than the rest of the world combined. They operate 65% of all active satellites in space. One company that most people have never heard of owns nearly three out of four satellites floating above Earth.

The difference isn't just technical; it's managerial. SpaceX managers focus their teams on building things. Their competitors focus their teams on talking about building things. This systematic focus on High-Leverage Activities, the work that actually drives results, created their dominance.

He Cancelled All Meetings

January 2023. Shopify COO Kaz Nejatian stood before a screen displaying thousands of recurring meetings: weekly one-on-ones, department standups, cross-functional reviews—the digital embodiment of coordination theater that masquerades as productive work.

"We've been talking about meeting fatigue for months," Nejatian said. "But this isn't about giving people more time. It's about reorienting toward execution."

The mass deletion took exactly thirty-seven seconds. Every recurring meeting in the company: gone.

Within hours, leadership released three principles for rebuilding calendars: default to asynchronous communication, designate clear decision-makers for essential meetings, and protect large blocks of time for High-Leverage Activities that advance business outcomes.

The result? Project velocity increased as teams spent more time building and less time talking about building. Shopify had proven something radical: eliminating Low-Leverage Activities creates focus on work that actually drives results.

DELIVER

The Focus Problem Killing Results

As we learned in the last chapter from standing in Microsoft's command center, email overload and meeting fatigue are real problems that drain energy from important work. But even if you eliminated every distraction, most teams would still struggle because they can't distinguish between activities that feel important and activities that actually drive their Team Key Results.

Your people aren't lazy. They're working on the wrong things.

Reducing the noise matters, but choosing the right activities matters more. Your team needs both: fewer Low-Leverage Activities that consume time without creating value AND more focus on High-Leverage Activities that directly impact your TKRs.

What High-Leverage Activities Actually Look Like

So, how do you identify a High-Leverage Activity (HLA)? HLAs share two key characteristics that set them apart from the busy work that occupies most teams:

1. **Impact—It Directly Impacts a Team Key Result**: Every HLA must advance at least one of your three most important outcomes. If an activity doesn't move the needle on a TKR, it's consuming resources without adding value.
2. **Shared Value—Others Need It or Benefit from It**: If no one is requesting, relying on, or using it, it's not value; it's vanity. It's a pet project or an outdated priority.

The test is simple: if your team stopped this activity entirely, would progress toward your Team Key Results slow down? If yes, it's an HLA.

If no, it's consuming bandwidth that could be redirected to work that truly matters.

Is this something you think is important or worth your time, but no one else has asked for it? Then it likely offers little ROI. Abandon it, and most likely, no one will notice.

The Solution's In the Drive-Thru

What you're witnessing at SpaceX and Shopify isn't just technological achievement or organizational innovation; it's a systematic focus on High-Leverage Activities that deliver on Team Key Results. This same discipline applies whether you're launching satellites or serving chicken sandwiches.

In the spring and summer of 2020, every restaurant faced the same existential crisis: dining rooms closed overnight, foot traffic vanished, and revenue plummeted. While most chains scrambled to survive, Chick-fil-A discovered something that would reshape their entire strategy.

Drive-thru traffic surged to unprecedented levels. Cars wrapped around buildings, spilled into parking lots, and backed up onto public streets. Some locations served over 262 cars in a single hour—more than four cars per minute. But the real revelation came from the financial data: drive-thru customers delivered significantly higher ROI than dine-in customers. No tables to clean between parties, no bathrooms to maintain, no play areas to sanitize, no booth cushions to replace, and no dining room lighting or air conditioning costs. Drive-thru eliminated entire categories of operational overhead while maximizing revenue per square foot.

This wasn't just a pandemic trend; it was a fundamental business insight. Drive-thru traffic was the ultimate High-Leverage Activity.

DELIVER

Chick-fil-A leaned in hard, and the results were staggering. Average revenue per freestanding location jumped from approximately $7 million before the pandemic to $8.1 million in 2021, and then to $9.4 million in 2023. In contrast, McDonald's produced $4 million per location in 2023. Chick-fil-A expanded to two drive-thrus using cones from Home Depot and assigned employees in the parking lot to take orders, driving revenue to $9.4 million per location while McDonald's made no changes to how they took orders and pulled in $4 million per restaurant. This isn't about chicken and hamburgers; it's about movement versus complacency.

The Four-Step HLA Framework

A systematic focus on High-Leverage Activities requires a leader who helps their team develop the discipline to channel time and energy into the right work consistently amid endless distractions.

Step 1: Identify High-Leverage Activities

Start with your Team Key Results and work backward. Every HLA must connect directly to at least one of your three most important outcomes. This connection must be measurable, not theoretical.

Shotwell's team at SpaceX filters every decision through their mission clarity: "Does this advance global connectivity faster and more reliably than anyone else?"

When pandemic traffic revealed drive-thru's ROI advantage, Chick-fil-A managers didn't just say, "Let's improve drive-thru." They identified specific activities that directly advanced their key results: mobile order-takers with tablets taking customer orders while in line instead of at the window, allowing them to serve over 100 cars per hour while maintaining 94 percent order accuracy, the highest in their industry.

The diagnostic question isn't "Is this important work?" It's "Will this create compound momentum toward our TKRs?"

Managers help their teams choose HLAs while executives evaluate their organizations to identify low-ROI work. The more indirect the connection between a department's work and the organization's Key Results, the less vital that part of the business becomes. In our work with large organizations, we've seen that those with the highest tolerance for functions and departments indirectly contributing to Key Results have the slowest speed to market, the smallest growth year over year, and the most toxic cultures. You either focus on doing or enabling High-Leverage Activities, or you get cut. Leaders reward movement, not motion. We've established the difference.

Step 2: Establish Expectations

Clear expectations turn HLAs into tactical actions. This is where you create systems and routines. Shopify's calendar rebuild succeeded because they established specific principles around new meetings rather than vague aspirations.

Chick-fil-A's drive-thru success comes from specific standards rather than vague goals. Their HLA of getting cars through the drive-thru faster led to these tactical expectations: greet every car within 30 seconds with eye contact and enthusiasm, complete all orders within 90 seconds, and cross-train every team member for all roles to prevent bottlenecks regardless of who is on the schedule. HLAs should become expectations that include timelines, measurements, and clear owners.

Teams don't execute; individuals execute. Groups don't deliver results; people on teams deliver results. Assign clear ownership to specific individuals, not committees or departments. When everyone is responsible, no one is accountable.

DELIVER

People perform best when they understand what success looks like and can measure their progress against specific, observable outcomes that everyone recognizes. Movement results from clear expectations set by every manager in an organization.

Step 3: Schedule Check-Ins

HLAs require sustained focus over time, which means creating rhythms that maintain momentum even when distractions multiply. Most HLAs fail not because of a lack of capability, but because competing priorities gradually erode focus without course corrections. Check-Ins provide your guardrails.

Chick-fil-A achieves consistent performance through systematic monitoring: real-time tracking of cars per hour, order accuracy, and customer satisfaction scores throughout each shift, enabling immediate adjustments when performance drifts. Brief huddles at the start of each shift review previous performance and confirm role assignments for optimal coverage. Monthly innovation sessions allow teams to experiment with new approaches and implement improvements.

We suggest weekly planning to identify your top three HLAs for the coming week and schedule blocks of time to focus on them. Treat these blocks like client meetings—non-negotiable commitments that don't get rescheduled for convenience. This weekly discipline forces conscious choices about what deserves HLA designation and creates protected time for deep focus.

Daily reflection tracks what percentage of your time actually went to HLAs versus LLAs. Most leaders discover they're spending far less time on high-leverage work than they believe. This isn't about perfection; some days require more LLA attention due to genuine emergencies. But tracking reveals patterns that allow for conscious adjustments. Too much time spent on putting out fires either indicates resource challenges or undisciplined managers or team members.

Monthly reviews assess which activities are actually driving TKR progress versus those consuming energy without creating proportional value. Be ruthlessly honest about abandoning activities that aren't producing the leverage you expected, regardless of the effort invested in developing them.

SpaceX's systematic launch cadence results from this discipline. Each mission is evaluated against connectivity objectives. Each manufacturing improvement is measured against cost and quality targets. The rhythm of review prevents drift toward activities that feel productive but don't advance their mission.

Step 4: Adjust Accordingly

Maintain unwavering commitment to your Team Key Results while remaining flexible about the activities used to achieve them. When evidence suggests an activity isn't creating the expected leverage, pivot quickly to alternatives that might work better. You're working in a dynamic market where conditions and customer demands shift quickly. What was an HLA six months ago might not qualify today.

This requires intellectual honesty about what's working based on evidence rather than hope, tradition, or sunk costs. The activities that got you to your current performance level may not be the activities that will elevate you to the next level.

When Chick-fil-A discovered that drive-thru customers delivered higher ROI than dine-in customers, they didn't stick with traditional restaurant designs due to previous investments. They opened a revolutionary prototype in the suburbs of Atlanta featuring a second-floor kitchen, conveyor belts that sent orders down to four lanes of drive-thrus every six seconds, and no dine-in area at all.

SpaceX's evolution consistently illustrates this principle. Their original satellite designs were larger and more costly to manufacture. Upon discovering that smaller, cheaper satellites could provide equivalent coverage at a lower cost, they did not cling to their original approach due to prior investment. They pivoted to what was more effective, even if it meant abandoning significant previous work.

The adjustment discipline requires three capabilities: evidence-based assessment of which activities yield expected results, rapid abandonment of ineffective approaches regardless of effort invested, and an experimental mindset that treats new activities as tests to be evaluated rather than commitments to be sustained indefinitely.

This four-step framework enables the systematic discipline that distinguishes organizations like SpaceX and Chick-fil-A from competitors who remain busy without generating movement.

The compound effect is undeniable. SpaceX has reduced the cost of launching one kilogram into orbit from $10,000 to under $3,000 while launching more payload mass than the rest of the world combined. Chick-fil-A generates $9.4 million per location compared to McDonald's $4 million, more than double the industry leader, while maintaining the highest customer satisfaction scores in fast food.

This systematic advantage compounds year over year, creating competitive moats that become nearly impossible for competitors to breach.

DELIVER

Your Job is to Create Movement

Marcus connects to the internet from Mount Whitney because thousands of people made choices that enabled rockets to reach space at a rate no one thought possible. Your competitors are facing the same choice you confront right now. Some will continue expending energy discussing movement while others will develop the systematic discipline to actually create it.

The difference will be evident in quarterly results, market position, and organizational capability. But the choice is made daily, in small decisions about where to focus when urgent distractions multiply, inboxes overflow, meeting invites keep arriving, and low-leverage activities threaten to drown your teams.

You've created clarity about what matters most through your Team Key Results. You've built alignment with your team around achieving them. Now comes the moment that separates leaders who engineer extraordinary results from those who merely hope for them.

Your Team Key Results are waiting. It's time to generate movement!

DELIVER

Chapter 15: High-Leverage Activities
– Quick Start –

Key Points:

- HLAs have two characteristics: Impact (drives TKRs) + Shared Value (others need it)
- SpaceX's dominance came from systematic focus on HLAs versus competitors' motion
- Chick-fil-A generates $9.4M per location versus McDonald's $4M through in part due to HLAs
- Third Leader Framework: Identify HLAs, Establish Expectations, Schedule Check-ins, Adjust

Diagnostic Questions:

- If we stopped this activity completely, would TKR progress slow?
- Is this something others are requesting, or just something we believe is important?
- Are we building things, or merely discussing building things?

Action Steps:

- **Consider:** Think about how your team's time splits between High-Leverage Activities (HLAs) that drive TKRs and low-leverage distractions, and what shifts could mirror SpaceX's focus. What percentage is spent on each? What about you personally?
- **Seek Feedback:** Ask a direct report: "What tasks do you think we should stop or delegate to free up time for high-impact work?"

DELIVER

- **Start Doing:** Help your team identify HLAs, establish clear expectations round them, and develop a system of regular check-ins to create accountability.

Consensus Mode Watchout:

Talking about HLAs is not the same as adjusting your routine and systems to focus on them.

CHAPTER

16

REWRITE THE SCRIPT

THE ELEVATOR CLIMBED silently through the empty corporate tower, each floor marker blinking past like a countdown to disaster. It was 6:00 PM on a Tuesday in downtown Philadelphia, and the building that had buzzed with activity just hours earlier now felt like a mausoleum.

On the fourteenth floor, we walked past the employee cafeteria that had been bustling just two hours earlier. Now it sat dark, chairs stacked on tables, the salad bar covered with plastic wrap. The conference room we'd been directed to appeared abandoned midway through setup. Tables were pushed against walls, stacks of chairs scattered around, and ten seats arranged in a rough semicircle that resembled an intervention more than a leadership meeting.

This wasn't just any company. This was one of the world's largest healthcare organizations, a Fortune 50 company whose decisions affected millions of patients and generated billions in revenue. But tonight, their senior leadership team was on the brink of collapse.

DELIVER

The Explosion

By 6:15, ten executives filtered in, individuals who collectively controlled billions in revenue and made decisions that moved markets. None of them wanted to be there. All of them looked like defendants showing up for sentencing.

Then Ben walked in.

Ben was the head of revenue for the tenth-largest company in the world, closer to retirement than anyone else in the room. This wasn't your typical high-energy sales executive. Ben was an introvert who flew first class with his head down, hoping no one would interrupt his reading. He wore crisp suits and gold rings that caught the fluorescent light. This was a man who hadn't been born into wealth but had created it through decades of disciplined execution.

But tonight, Ben wasn't looking for advice. He was looking for a fight.

We stood at the front with our prepared presentation materials, suddenly realizing that PowerPoint slides weren't going to cut it. "Let's start with opening comments," we suggested. "Maybe the three most senior leaders could set the tone."

The first two executives mumbled diplomatic non-statements about hoping the discussion would be productive. Corporate speak that said nothing while confirming everything was wrong.

Then Ben stood up.

"This is an effing waste of time," Ben declared, his voice cutting through the silence. "Consultants are a waste of money. I have zero confidence this is going to be worth a damn. But I was told to be here, so here I am."

The temperature in the room dropped ten degrees. No one moved. No one breathed.

But Ben wasn't finished.

He pointed at the head of operations. "The problem isn't with my sales team. It's your department that's the issue. Your departments are the &@&# issue. Sorry, but the truth hurts."

Then came the flood. Month after month of accumulated frustration poured out as Ben detailed every broken promise, every missed deadline, and every time his sales team had to explain to customers why the company couldn't deliver on its commitments.

"My sales reps across North America have been filing complaints for months," Ben continued. "Every time operations promises a delivery date they can't meet. Every time we have to tell customers that what we sold them isn't actually available."

When he finished, Ben sat down hard, arms crossed, staring at the floor. The silence that followed was devastating. Ten intelligent, successful people who were supposed to be leading one of the world's most important organizations had ended up here, listening to their colleague enumerate all the ways they'd failed each other.

The Shift

We made a decision that avoided making matters worse. We turned off the projector, put away our slides, and abandoned our carefully crafted agenda. One of us walked to the front of the semicircle and sat down at their level.

"Ben," we said quietly, "tell us more about what your team has been experiencing."

DELIVER

What happened next was like watching a dam break in slow motion. Ben's rage transformed into detailed venting about specific problems. As he spoke, the other executives started listening, really listening.

The head of operations began to nod. "We've been so focused on optimizing our internal processes that we haven't been tracking how those changes affect customer promises."

The technology leader leaned forward. "I didn't realize our system maintenance windows were coinciding with your peak ordering times."

The conversation shifted from venting to lamenting to observing. People began acknowledging their own contributions instead of defending their territory. The finger-pointing gave way to something that looked almost like vulnerability.

By 9:30, we suggested wrapping up. Ben, who had initially called consultants (us) a waste of money, made the final comments.

"I guess you all know how I felt about this meeting," he said, allowing a slight smile. The room erupted in laughter. He turned to us: "I guess not all consultants are a complete waste of space."

Then Ben did something that nearly made us faint. "I think we started the right dialogue tonight. I'm offering to come back tomorrow and continue it if you all are willing too."

The Transformation

The next morning, everything felt different. Sunlight poured through the windows, the nearby cafeteria buzzed with activity, and that executive team did something remarkable: they identified the scripts that had been poisoning their relationships and sabotaging their results.

DELIVER

Ben's sales team had been burdened by scripts from other departments—scripts that claimed sales "overpromised to close deals" and "didn't understand operational constraints." Meanwhile, sales held scripts about operations "not caring about customer commitments" and technology "always failing when we need it most."

These weren't just personality conflicts; they were organizational scripts—deeply embedded beliefs that each department held about the others, shaping how they interpreted every interaction, decision, and request for help.

Within six months, the impact was enormous. Sales orders increased as internal cooperation translated into confident client relationships. Operations formed a committee that worked directly with sales representatives. Technology developed escalation procedures for sales-critical issues. They hit their revenue numbers for the first time in three years.

The transformation didn't happen because we provided them with new strategies. It happened because they identified and rewrote the scripts that other teams held about each other.

Movement Is Also About Boulders

At the pinnacle of his career, Tiger Woods drew crowds unrivaled in professional golf. That gallery typically just watched until one day he actually needed their physical help to compete.

Tiger's tee shot on the 13th hole of the Phoenix Open landed directly behind a giant boulder. After surveying the scene, Tiger approached a rules official and asked if the boulder qualified as a "loose impediment."

"It qualifies if you can move it," the official replied.

DELIVER

Tiger turned to the crowd and asked, "Anybody want to move a rock?"

About a dozen fans pushed the estimated 2,000-pound rock away from Tiger's ball, giving him a clear shot. Tiger birdied the hole.

Scripts work like Tiger's boulder. They seem to heavy to budge but they actually can be moved. Moving them usually requires help from your team.

You've learned to identify High-Leverage Activities, the critical work that drives results toward your Team Key Results. However, even the most disciplined focus on HLAs can be undermined by limiting beliefs others hold about your team. Scripts are the invisible barriers that make other departments say, "That won't work with them" or "They never follow through" before engaging with you.

The Science Behind Scripts

What we witnessed in Philadelphia wasn't just workplace dysfunction; it was neuroscience in action. Dr. Matthew Lieberman at UCLA recruited 200 employees from various companies for a study that revealed why scripts are so powerful and destructive.

Using fMRI brain imaging, Lieberman tracked neural activity while participants listened to different organizational narratives. Some reflected positive scripts ("Our team always finds creative solutions"), while others reflected negative scripts ("Management never follows through on commitments").

The discovery was remarkable: negative scripts activated the same neural pathways as physical threats.

When employees heard limiting beliefs about other teams, their brains responded as if they were in danger. The amygdala triggered stress responses that decreased cognitive function, reduced creative thinking, and impaired decision-making quality. These neural patterns persisted for hours after exposure, meaning toxic workplace scripts create physiological stress that extends beyond the office.

Even more striking: the brain processes organizational scripts using the same neural networks involved in personal identity formation. When someone challenges a deeply held script about another team, the brain reacts as if core aspects of identity are threatened.

Consider Ben's explosion. His brain wasn't just processing workplace frustration; it was responding to what his neural networks categorized as genuine threats to his team's survival. The scripts other departments held about sales, and that sales held about other departments, had become so embedded that every interaction triggered fight-or-flight responses.

"Organizational scripts aren't just beliefs; they're neurologically embedded patterns that shape how people perceive and respond to their work environment," Lieberman explained. "Changing these patterns requires more than providing new information. It requires creating new experiences that can override existing neural pathways."

This explains why logical arguments rarely change scripts that others hold about your team. You can't persuade people to abandon beliefs their brains categorize as essential for survival. You can only replace them by creating new experiences that demonstrate different outcomes are possible.

DELIVER

The Framework: Moving Your Boulders

Scripts about your team are loose impediments, but moving them requires a systematic approach. Here's the proven framework for script transformation:

Step 1: Identify Scripts About Your Team

The first step is uncovering the beliefs and perceptions that other teams, departments, or stakeholders hold about your team. These scripts often hide in casual comments, assumptions, and the language people use when discussing working with you.

Listen for patterns in how others describe your team:

- **In cross-functional meetings:** How do other departments talk about collaborating with you? Do they express skepticism about timelines, quality, or follow-through?
- **During project planning:** What assumptions do people make about your team's capabilities, priorities, or willingness to adapt?
- **In casual conversations:** What scripts emerge when people discuss past experiences working with your team?

Common scripts about teams include:

- "They always miss deadlines."
- "They don't understand the business side."
- "They're too focused on perfection and not speed."
- "They overpromise and underdeliver."
- "They don't listen to feedback."

In Philadelphia, Ben's outburst revealed scripts that other departments held about sales: that they "overpromised to close deals" and "didn't understand operational constraints." These weren't random accusations; they were deeply held beliefs based on real experiences that had solidified into limiting narratives.

Remember: scripts aren't fiction. They're based on actual interactions and outcomes that have been generalized into broader beliefs about how your team operates.

Step 2: Rewrite the Script

Once you've identified the limiting scripts others hold about your team, the next step is to define what you want them to believe instead. This isn't about denying past problems or pretending issues didn't occur. It's about creating a new narrative that fosters better collaboration and results.

Effective script rewriting focuses on behaviors and outcomes rather than intentions:

- Instead of "They always miss deadlines" → "They deliver when they commit."
- Instead of "They don't understand the business" → "They balance technical excellence with business needs."
- Instead of "They're too slow" → "They're thorough and reliable."

The key is choosing scripts that are:

- **Believable:** Based on capabilities your team can actually demonstrate.
- **Specific:** Clear enough that others know what to expect.
- **Valuable:** Focused on perceptions that will improve collaboration and results.

In Philadelphia, the sales team needed to rewrite scripts about "over-promising" to "making realistic commitments they could keep."

DELIVER

Operations needed to shift from being seen as "not caring about customers" to "balancing customer needs with operational realities."

Step 3: Create New Experiences for Other Teams

Scripts can only be changed through new experiences that prove different outcomes are possible. This is the most critical step because it requires your team to consistently demonstrate the new script through concrete actions that others can see and feel.

Creating new experiences means:

- **Proactive Communication:** Instead of waiting for others to ask for updates, provide regular status reports that demonstrate reliability and transparency.
- **Collaborative Problem-Solving:** When issues arise, invite other teams into solution development rather than trying to fix everything internally.
- **Consistent Follow-Through:** Meet every commitment you make, even small ones, to build evidence that the new script is real.
- **Visible Improvements:** Make changes to processes, systems, or approaches that others can observe directly.

The Philadelphia team created new experiences systematically. Sales established clearer communication with operations before making customer commitments. Operations formed a committee to work directly with sales representatives before implementing process changes. Technology developed escalation procedures that prioritized sales-critical issues.

Each new experience provided evidence that the old scripts, "sales overpromises," "operations doesn't care," and "technology always fails," weren't inevitable truths. They were changeable patterns that could be disrupted through intentional action.

Scripts in Action: The New Jersey Revelation

One of the most powerful script identification exercises we've ever facilitated occurred in a conference room in New Jersey with the leadership team of a global pharmaceutical company. The energy in the room was tense; these executives worked together daily but had never honestly discussed how they perceived each other's leadership styles and team effectiveness.

We ripped off flipchart paper and stuck sheets on all four walls of the conference room. At the top of each flipchart, we wrote an executive's name. After establishing trust and psychological safety, we sent each executive to the flipcharts, but not to their own. They moved around the room, writing feedback about their colleagues on the sheets.

The instructions were simple: write a couple of sentences of appreciative feedback and a couple of sentences of constructive feedback about challenges or areas for improvement. Be honest, specific, and helpful.

For thirty minutes, the executives rotated around the room, carefully writing their perceptions of each colleague's leadership approach, team management, and collaboration style. The room was quiet, except for the sound of markers on paper; everyone was taking this seriously.

Once the writing was complete, we invited each executive to take the sheet with their name on it and find a quiet space elsewhere in the building to read through all the feedback privately. "Take your time," we said. "Process what you're reading. Then come back, and we'll discuss what you learned."

Twenty minutes later, they returned to the conference room. The transformation was evident in their faces; some looked surprised, others thoughtful, and a few appeared uncomfortable but determined.

DELIVER

"Nothing here surprised me," one executive said, "but it's striking to see so many of you saying the same things about my approach."

Another executive nodded. "I thought I was managing my team well, but the way I handle decisions comes across very differently than I intended."

The head of U.S. Commercial spoke last: "That's the most impactful meeting we've ever had as an executive team."

What made this exercise so powerful wasn't just the feedback itself; it was the realization that perceptions of each team were shared beliefs, not individual opinions. When multiple colleagues identified the same patterns independently, it became impossible to dismiss them as misunderstandings or personality conflicts.

The executive who discovered that four different people saw him as "always negative" could no longer assume that one person was being unfair. The team leader who learned she was viewed as "micromanaging" by multiple departments had to confront the possibility that her leadership style was affecting collaboration across the organization.

This systematic approach to script identification revealed limiting beliefs that constrained team effectiveness and positive scripts that weren't fully leveraged. Some executives discovered strengths that others recognized but they themselves took for granted.

The power lay not just in identifying the scripts but in realizing they could be changed through new experiences and different approaches to leadership and team management.

Microsoft's Script Revolution

Microsoft under Satya Nadella exemplifies systematic script transformation at the enterprise level. When Nadella became CEO in 2014, Microsoft was hindered by limiting scripts held by customers, partners, and employees: "They're a Windows company in a mobile world," "Their culture is too competitive to innovate," and "They missed the cloud transition."

Nadella's script rewriting was both symbolic and practical, focusing on creating new experiences for external stakeholders. One of his first moves was to appear at an Apple event to announce Microsoft Office for iPad. For years, customers and partners operated under the script that Microsoft was Apple's enemy. By publicly embracing collaboration, Nadella demonstrated a new script for the entire industry: "Microsoft helps customers be productive on whatever platform they choose."

The internal reaction was skeptical, but when Office for iPad became one of the most successful app launches in App Store history, a new script began to emerge among customers and partners: "Microsoft's software can thrive everywhere."

Nadella continued creating experiences that challenged old scripts held by different stakeholder groups. He invested heavily in cloud computing to prove to enterprise customers that Microsoft could lead, not just follow, in emerging technologies. He acquired LinkedIn and GitHub to show developer communities that Microsoft valued rather than competed with their ecosystems. He instituted hackathons that resulted in customer-facing innovations, proving to the market that Microsoft's culture could drive breakthrough thinking.

Each action was designed to create new experiences for specific audiences—customers, partners, developers, and employees—that would rewrite their scripts about what Microsoft represented and what working with the company would be like.

The transformation was measurable across all stakeholder groups: customer satisfaction increased, the partner ecosystem expanded, developer adoption grew, and employee engagement reached all-time highs. Market capitalization grew from $300 billion to over $2 trillion as external scripts about Microsoft's potential shifted from limiting to enabling.

The Stakes

Scripts that others hold about your team directly impact your ability to achieve Team Key Results. No matter how clear your objectives or well-defined your High-Leverage Activities, limiting scripts can sabotage execution by hindering the cooperation and support you need from other departments.

The Philadelphia organization had clear revenue targets, sophisticated processes, and talented people. However, scripts between departments prevented the coordination necessary to achieve their goals. Sales struggled to work effectively with operations due to scripts about "overpromising." Operations couldn't support sales because of scripts regarding "unrealistic expectations." The transformation enabled business results by changing how teams perceived each other's capabilities and motivations.

The most dangerous scripts about teams sound reasonable but create invisible barriers to collaboration:

"They always miss deadlines" prevents others from including your team in time-sensitive projects. "They don't understand the business side" limits your involvement in strategic initiatives. "They're perfectionists who slow things down" excludes you from rapid-response opportunities. "They overpromise and underdeliver" makes partners hesitant to rely on your commitments.

Each script contains elements of truth based on past experiences, making them particularly insidious. However, when specific incidents solidify into unchangeable beliefs about your team's character or capabilities, they obstruct the collaboration and trust necessary for breakthrough results.

Organizations that consistently deliver exceptional outcomes are those whose teams have learned to identify and rewrite the scripts that limit their effectiveness. They don't ignore past problems or pretend challenges didn't occur. Instead, they systematically create new experiences that demonstrate different outcomes are possible when teams collaborate effectively.

Moving Forward

That Philadelphia team discovered something profound in their transformed conference room: the scripts that had blocked their coordination weren't immovable fixtures. They were loose impediments that could be removed through sustained effort to create new experiences for each other, much like Tiger's boulder that seemed permanent until a dozen fans proved it could be moved.

Your team faces the same choice. You can work around the limiting scripts that others hold about you, finding creative ways to succeed despite constrained relationships. Or you can systematically identify those scripts, define what you want others to believe instead, and create new experiences that validate the new narrative.

Script transformation is the final element that bridges your clarity and alignment with sustained movement toward your Team Key Results. If

DELIVER

you're ready to identify and rewrite the limiting beliefs that others hold about your team, move to Chapter 17 for the implementation playbook. If not, skip ahead to Part 5 and return to this work when you're ready to tackle this level of movement.

The boulder is waiting. Your team is ready. The only question is whether you're willing to challenge the beliefs others have about your capabilities and create new experiences that prove those beliefs wrong.

DELIVER

Chapter 16: Rewrite the Script

– Quick Start –

Key Points:

- Scripts = beliefs other teams hold about your team that limit collaboration
- Philadelphia executive team's breakthrough: Ben's explosion revealed toxic scripts between departments
- Scripts work like Tiger's boulder—seem immovable but qualify for removal
- Neuroscience: Negative scripts activate the same neural pathways as physical threats

Third Leader Framework:

1. Identify scripts others hold about your team
2. Rewrite the script (define what you want them to believe)
3. Create new experiences that prove different outcomes are possible

Action Steps:

- **Consider:** Reflect scripts that others hold about you right now. Identify one that you'd like to work on that is holding you back from future opportunities or promotions. Identify one you'd like to work on in your personal life that's held by your partner, children, or someone close to you.
- **Seek Feedback:** Ask a peer from another department: "What is a belief your team holds about mine that you think we ought to work on?"
- **Start Doing:** Develop the habit of listening for scripts that those you work with are developing about you or your team.

DELIVER

Create a "radar system" for detecting these in meetings, emails, and conversations.

Founder Mode:

Scripts are necessary friction in the system. Identifying them and working on shifting them is a waste of time.

Consensus Mode:

Scripts are something that are held but rarely shared due to fear how the other person would respond if they were vocalized.

Third Leader Mode:

Scripts are natural obstacles to movement. It's healthy to share beliefs you hold about others and to expect candor when you ask others to share them with you.

CHAPTER 17

THE MOVEMENT PLAYBOOK

Note: This is your hands-on, roll-up-your-sleeves chapter. If you want to continue the journey and return to the tactical work later, feel free to skip ahead to the final section. But don't skip this completely; you'll need this playbook to convert your clarity and alignment into sustained movement toward your Team Key Results.

We're going to walk you through the exact process we use with actual clients. Here's how we did it in a follow-up call with Sarah, a Regional Sales Director overseeing 12 area sales managers across the upper Midwest for a global pharmaceutical company based in Minneapolis.

Six weeks after our initial sessions, where Sarah established her TKRs of 3-1-5 (3 new sales clients per month per rep, 1 meaning everyone hits their sales number, 5% growth in team member engagement) and built alignment with her team, she reached out for guidance on sustaining movement toward these results.

DELIVER

Question 1: How are you doing on delivering your TKRs right now? How are you all tracking?

Sarah's Response: "We're slightly behind plan right now, but I have to say the plan is aggressive. We set these targets knowing they would stretch us. Some areas are doing better than others, my Minneapolis and St. Paul reps are actually ahead on new client acquisition, but my outstate territories are struggling. Overall, we're probably at about 85% of where we need to be across the board."

Our Follow-up: "How concerned are you about being behind?"

Sarah's Response: "I'm concerned, but not panicked. We definitely need to fix it, and we have runway to do so. The good news is we identified the gap early enough to course-correct. The concerning part is that if we don't adjust how we're working, being slightly behind now could become significantly behind by quarter-end. That's why I wanted to have this conversation about movement, we need to change our approach, not just work harder."

Your Turn—Question 1: How are you doing on delivering your TKRs right now? How are you all tracking?

Current Performance Assessment:

TKR #1 Status: _____ % of target
TKR #2 Status: _____ % of target
TKR #3 Status: _____ % of target

DELIVER

Performance by Area/Team:

Strongest performing area: _____
Most challenging area: _____
Overall trend: _____

Urgency Level:

How concerned are you (1-10 scale)? _____
What's your runway for correction? _____
What happens if trends continue? _____

Question 2: What are the Low-Leverage Activities creating noise and distraction right now?

Sarah's Response: "We've got too much of a 'wait and see' attitude. People are being reactive instead of strategic. We aren't targeting new clients effectively; reps are calling on anyone who will see them instead of researching which prospects fit our ideal client profile. Additionally, we spend too much time servicing low-margin accounts, which limits our bandwidth for new and key accounts."

Our Follow-up: "Can you be more specific about the low-margin servicing issue?"

Sarah's Response: "Perfect example: we have reps spending two hours a week on administrative follow-up for accounts that generate about 5% of their revenue. Meanwhile, they claim they don't have time to prospect for new business or deepen relationships with our top 20% accounts. It's classic busy work that feels productive but doesn't impact any of our TKRs."

DELIVER

Your Turn—Question 2: What Low-Leverage Activities are causing noise and distraction right now?

Time Wasters Identified:

Activity 1: _____
Activity 2: _____
Activity 3: _____

Impact Assessment:

How much time do these LLAs consume weekly? _____
_____

Which TKRs do they hinder progress on? _____
_____

What's the opportunity cost? _____
_____

Elimination Strategy:

Which LLAs can be stopped immediately? _____
_____

Which need to be delegated or automated? _____
_____

What will you say "no" to going forward? _____
_____

DELIVER

Question 3: What High-Leverage Activities should your team focus on?

Sarah's Response: "We need to be much more strategic. This means taking time to plan each week and month which clinics to visit, which relationships to leverage, and which referrals to request. It involves identifying real opportunities instead of just making activity-based calls. It also means managing their calendars to maintain strong relationships with key accounts while allowing focused time for new business development."

Our Follow-up: "How does this strategic approach connect to your specific TKRs?"

Sarah's Response: "For acquiring 3 new clients per month, strategic targeting ensures they engage with prospects who actually need our solutions and have the budget to buy. For those meeting their sales targets, it means spending time with accounts that can deliver revenue. And for engagement, it shows that people feel they are working smart rather than just hard; they can see the link between their daily activities and meaningful results."

Your Turn—Question 3: What High-Leverage Activities should your team focus on?

Strategic HLAs for Each TKR:

TKR #1 HLAs:
Primary activity: _____
Supporting activity: _____
Frequency/commitment: _____

DELIVER

TKR #2 HLAs:
Primary activity: _____
Supporting activity: _____
Frequency/commitment: _____

TKR #3 HLAs:
Primary activity: _____
Supporting activity: _____
Frequency/commitment: _____

Connection Validation:

How do these HLAs directly advance your TKRs? ___
_____

What stops happening when the team focuses on these? ___
_____

Question 4: What expectations will you establish with your team?

Sarah's Response: "I'm setting three clear expectations that everyone can track and I can measure. First, spend at least an hour each week managing your calendar to prioritize new business and key account activities, proactively planning your highest-value tasks. Second, visit one potential new client each week through a clinic visit, lunch, breakfast, or another meaningful appointment. Third, identify one activity this week to strengthen a key account relationship, and it can't be sending an email; it must be more meaningful than that."

Our Follow-up: "How will you know if people are meeting these expectations?"

Sarah's Response: "Calendar management will be reflected in their weekly planning; I can assess if they're being strategic with their time. New client visits will be tracked in our CRM with meeting notes and next steps. Strengthening key account activities will be documented with specific actions taken and outcomes achieved. These aren't just activity metrics; they're strategic behaviors that directly drive our TKRs."

Your Turn—Question 4: What expectations will you establish with your team?

Specific Behavioral Expectations:

Expectation #1:
What: _____
How often: _____
How measured: _____

Expectation #2:
What: _____
How often: _____
How measured: _____

Expectation #3:
What: _____
How often: _____
How measured: _____

Accountability Framework:

How will you track compliance? _____
_____

DELIVER

What support will you provide? _____

_____

How will you address non-compliance? _____

_____

Question 5: What will your check-ins look like? When and how will you do them?

Sarah's Response: "We'll post in Slack every Friday in our new HLA channel about how we've met these three expectations. People will share their wins, challenges, and best practices there. I plan to spend 30 minutes in that channel every Friday reviewing everyone's updates and another 30 minutes each Monday providing feedback and support. It's now blocked on my Outlook calendar to ensure I don't skip it."

Our Follow-up: "How will you structure the Friday posts?"

Sarah's Response: "Simple format: What's one win from your HLA focus this week? What's one challenge you faced? What's one best practice you can share with the team? Then, on Monday mornings, I'll respond to everyone with specific feedback, recognition for wins, and offers to help with challenges. It keeps the momentum going and fosters peer learning."

Your Turn—Question 5: What will your check-ins look like? When and how will you conduct them?

Check-in Structure:

Platform/method: _____
Frequency: _____
Format/template: _____

DELIVER

Your Commitment:

When will you review updates? _____

How much time will you spend? _____

How will you ensure consistency? _____

Team Sharing Framework:

What will people report on? _____

How will you encourage participation? _____

How will you facilitate peer learning? _____

Response Protocol:

How quickly will you respond? _____

What type of feedback will you provide? _____

How will you address challenges? _____

DELIVER

Remember: Movement is about systematic behavior change, not just goal setting. Focus on activities that drive results, eliminate those that create busy work, and maintain consistent rhythms that keep everyone focused on what matters most.

Your TKRs are clear. Your team is aligned. Now it's time to move with purpose, discipline, and the strategic focus that distinguishes high-performing teams from those that merely stay busy.

The path is defined. The expectations are set. Time to execute with excellence.

DELIVER

Chapter 17: The Movement Playbook
– Quick Start –

Tactical Implementation:

- Assess current TKR performance (where are you vs. targets?)
- Identify low-leverage activities consuming time/energy
- Define High-Leverage Activities that directly advance TKRs
- Establish specific behavioral expectations with measurement
- Schedule regular check-ins and feedback loops

> **Sarah's Third Leader Example:**
>
> Regional sales director implementing weekly planning, new client visits, and key account strengthening with Slack-based Friday updates and Monday feedback.

Action Steps:

- **Consider:** Ponder how clear expectations and regular check-ins, like Sarah's Slack updates, could turn your team's alignment into sustained progress toward TKRs.
- **Seek Feedback:** Ask a team member: "What are some low-leverage activities that you think our team gets caught up in?"
- **Start Doing:** Implement weekly HLA check-ins with a simple template, creating a habit of tracking and adjusting efforts to maintain momentum.

DELIVER

> **Install LeaderOS:**
>
> Success at scale requires you to create Clarity, Alignment, and Movement constantly. This isn't a one-time checklist. Make it your Leader Operating System for the rest of your career.

PART SIX

THE SEARCH FOR THE THIRD LEADER

CHAPTER 18

MENLO PARK VS. HIGHLAND PARK

WE BEGAN THIS BOOK in Mountain View, California, and Las Vegas, Nevada. Brian Chesky rejected the advice of consultants, coaches, and board members and chose Founder Mode. Tony Hsieh rejected corporate org charts and transformed a successful online shoe company into a bunch of circles.

The truth is Brian's Founder Mode Manifesto wasn't groundbreaking. Tony didn't invent Consensus Mode. And the current debate in organizations around the world over which leadership approach is most effective isn't new.

To understand how these two modes became the default and flawed choices in modern organizations, we must go back in time. This context will forever change how you view the decisions leaders make as they grapple with the chaos of Gate C24. It will also reveal that we didn't invent

DELIVER

LeaderOS—the Leader Operating System. It emerged in an unexpected place and from a person history has tragically forgotten. Until now.

Menlo Park, New Jersey

The train's whistle cuts through the crisp October air as you step onto the platform at Menlo Park, New Jersey. It's 1878, and the smell of coal smoke mingles with the electric scent of possibility. The Industrial Revolution is reshaping America, but here, just twenty-five miles from Manhattan, something different is happening. Something that will change the world.

The sign above the door reads simply "Edison's Invention Factory," but everyone calls it the Wizard's workshop. As you push through the heavy wooden door, you're hit by a wave of sensory overload. Gas flames flicker from workbenches scattered throughout the cavernous space, casting dancing shadows on walls lined with tools, wire, and half-finished contraptions. The air is thick with the smell of solder, sawdust, and the metallic tang of experimentation.

Twenty men move through the workshop with purposeful energy, but there's no rigid hierarchy here. A machinist argues good-naturedly with a physicist about the properties of carbon filaments. A glassblower demonstrates a new technique to a group gathered around his bench. And in the center of it all, sleeves rolled up and hands dirty, stands Thomas Edison himself.

"Boys, we're not here to make perfect things," Edison calls out to his team, his voice carrying over the noise. "We're here to make things perfect through trying." He's examining a light bulb prototype, holding it up to the flickering gas flame to study the delicate filament inside. "This one lasted six hours. What if we tried bamboo instead of cotton thread?"

The workshop operates on Edison's philosophy of productive failure. Every dead end is celebrated as a step closer to success. The walls are covered with diagrams, sketches, and notes. Charles Batchelor, Edison's right-hand man, approaches with a notebook full of test results. "We've tried over 300 different materials for the filament," he reports. "Platinum works, but it's too expensive. The carbon paper shows promise but burns out too quickly."

Edison grins. "**Then we've only got 700 more to try!**" The room erupts in laughter, but there's steel behind the humor. This is how breakthroughs happen, not through individual genius alone, but through collective determination to outlast the problem.

The Menlo Park laboratory operates like a creative commune. Ideas flow freely between the twenty inventors, scientists, and craftsmen who work here. There are no rigid job descriptions, no organizational charts. A machinist might suggest a solution to an electrical problem. A clerk might propose a new approach to marketing an invention. Edison has created something unprecedented: a factory for innovation itself.

John Kruesi, Edison's master machinist, waves you over to his workbench. "When Edison gets an idea, we can build it the same day," he says. This integration is Edison's secret weapon. When inspiration strikes, there's no delay, no bureaucracy. The idea moves immediately from mind to matter.

As evening falls, the workshop doesn't quiet down; it transforms. Edison often works through the night, fueled by coffee and curiosity. Tonight, he's wrestling with the practical challenges of electric lighting. Gas lamps dominate the market, but Edison sees a future powered by electricity. The technical hurdles are immense, but that's exactly the kind of challenge that energizes him.

DELIVER

"Gentlemen," Edison announces to the assembled team, "we're not just building a light bulb. We're building an entire system: generators, distribution, meters, everything. We're going to light up all of New York City."

It's an audacious vision, and everyone in the room knows it. But they also know Edison's track record: the telegraph improvements, the telephone enhancements, the phonograph that seemed like magic when he first demonstrated it. If anyone can electrify the world, it's the man they call the Wizard of Menlo Park.

Highland Park, Michigan

Three hundred miles west, in the bustling industrial heart of Detroit, a very different kind of innovation is taking shape. The year is 1913, and you're standing outside the Highland Park Plant, watching history in motion. Unlike the intimate workshops of Menlo Park, this is industry at scale, a brick cathedral to efficiency spanning sixty acres.

The sounds are different here. Not the improvisational jazz of Edison's lab, but the precise rhythm of a mechanical symphony. Henry Ford stands on the factory floor, stopwatch in hand, studying the movement of workers and parts with the intensity of a scientist. But where Edison experiments with possibility, Ford experiments with process. His laboratory is the assembly line itself, and his hypothesis is revolutionary: skilled craftsmen are unnecessary if you can perfect the system.

"Watch this," Ford says to his plant manager, Charles Sorensen, as they observe a worker installing an engine. "Yesterday it took him fourteen minutes to complete that task. Today, after repositioning his tools and adjusting the height of the work surface, it takes him eleven minutes. Tomorrow, we'll have it down to nine."

This is Ford's genius: the elimination of waste, delay, and variation. Where Edison's workshop celebrates creative chaos, Ford's factory demands ordered precision. Every movement is choreographed, every second accounted for. The result is breathtaking: a complete automobile rolls off the line every 93 minutes, compared to the 12.5 hours it took just five years earlier.

But Ford's genius extended beyond mechanical innovation to human organization itself. The Highland Park Plant represents more than manufacturing innovation; it's a new philosophy of human organization. Ford has taken the complex craft of automobile building and broken it down into hundreds of simple, repeatable tasks. A worker no longer needs years of training to build a car; he needs only the ability to perform one operation repeatedly, with mechanical precision.

Walking through the plant, you witness this philosophy in action. At Station 47, a worker installs wheels—only wheels, all day, every day. The conveyor belt carries the growing automobile from station to station, each worker adding their piece to the puzzle. No one worker builds a car, but together they produce thousands.

This systematic approach wasn't born from intuition alone; it was built on Frederick Winslow Taylor's revolutionary theory of Scientific Management. Taylor, a Philadelphia engineer, challenged America's approach to industrial work with a radical insight: traditional manufacturing was inefficient because it relied on workers' individual knowledge and discretion. His solution was to study every task scientifically, identify the single most efficient method, and standardize that approach. Factories implementing Taylor's methods saw productivity gains of 300-400%.

But Ford studied Taylor's writings and saw beyond their crucial limitation: Taylor focused on optimizing individual workers while leaving the broader production system unchanged. Where Taylor optimized the worker, Ford reimagined the entire system. His moving assembly line represented a philosophical departure from Taylorism; instead of perfecting individual tasks, Ford orchestrated the motion of people, parts, and products in synchronized flow.

This division of labor allows Ford to accomplish something no manufacturer has ever achieved: making automobiles affordable for the workers who build them. The Model T, once a luxury item for the wealthy, now costs less than half the average American's annual salary. Ford hasn't just built a better car; he's democratized mobility itself.

But the unprecedented $5-a-day wage comes with strings attached. Ford's "Sociological Department" sends investigators to workers' homes, ensuring they live according to company standards. They should be sober. The home should be orderly. The family's budget will be reviewed at the kitchen table. The result is a workforce that's simultaneously grateful and resentful: excellent pay, but mind-numbing work and intrusive oversight unheard of in the land of the free.

Ford has created prosperity through process, but at the cost of worker autonomy and creativity.

An Unlikely Friendship

Most people today would be surprised to learn that Thomas Edison and Henry Ford were not rivals but close friends. The two men, representing seemingly opposite approaches to innovation and industry, shared a mutual respect that lasted decades. Their relationship began in 1896 when Ford, a young engineer at the Edison Illuminating Company, attended a company dinner where Edison was the guest of honor.

Ford approached the famous inventor with sketches of his gasoline-powered "quadricycle," a crude but promising automobile he had built in his spare time. Most experts of the era believed electric vehicles were the future, and Ford expected Edison to dismiss his gas-powered contraption. Instead, Edison studied the drawings with interest, asking probing questions about the engine design and fuel efficiency.

Encouragement from the world's most famous inventor changed Ford's life. Years later, he would say, "The greatest satisfaction of my life was having Thomas Edison approve of my automobile."

Their friendship deepened over the years, built on mutual admiration despite their different approaches. Edison admired Ford's ability to transform an idea into a mass-market reality, while Ford respected Edison's genius for invention and his ability to inspire teams to achieve the impossible.

In 1914, when Edison's film studio and laboratory complex in West Orange, New Jersey, was destroyed by fire, Ford immediately offered financial assistance. "I'll give you whatever you need to rebuild," Ford told his friend. Edison, characteristically optimistic, replied, "All our mistakes are burned up. Thank God we can start anew."

Perhaps the most touching symbol of their friendship is preserved today at the Henry Ford Museum in Dearborn, Michigan. When Edison was dying in 1931, Ford asked his friend's son, Charles, to capture Edison's last breath in a test tube. That sealed tube, containing what Ford believed to be the essence of his mentor's final moment, remains on display, a testament to the deep bond between two very different but equally extraordinary men.

Their camping trips together in the 1910s and 1920s, along with tire magnate Harvey Firestone and naturalist John Burroughs, became legendary.

DELIVER

The press dubbed them "The Vagabonds," and their expeditions, complete with a convoy of cars, a professional chef, and a portable power plant, were anything but rustic. For Ford and Edison, these trips represented something precious: time to think and explore ideas. They were history's most consequential camping trips, a mastermind group that would electrify cities, motorize America, and ignite the industrial age.

The Collaborative Trap

Edison's workshop at Menlo Park resembled a leadership paradise, with brilliant minds working together, ideas flowing freely, and innovation occurring at unprecedented speed. But beneath this collaborative success lay a hidden weakness that would ultimately cost Edison his place in the very industry he created.

Edison's collaborative approach generated over 400 patents, roughly one every ten days. The phonograph, the incandescent light bulb, the carbon microphone—breakthrough after breakthrough flowed from his team's collective genius.

Edison and his team did something most people aren't aware of: they not only built the light bulb; they lit up New York City. In 1882, Edison's Pearl Street Station in Manhattan began providing electricity to 85 customers, illuminating 400 light bulbs in the process. Edison supplied the power that lit up the J.P. Morgan building at 23 Wall Street and the first newsroom of the New York Times.

But as his electrical business grew, Edison's collaborative instincts became a liability. While competitors embraced alternating current (AC) power systems, Edison's team remained emotionally attached to their direct current (DC) innovation. The same inclusive approach that had produced breakthrough thinking now created decision-making paralysis when swift action was required.

The result was devastating. In 1892, the company named Edison General Electric quietly dropped his name, rebranding itself as General Electric. The man who had pioneered the electrical age and powered America's first city found himself marginalized in the very industry he had founded.

Today, when people think of Edison, they remember the inventor of the light bulb, not the visionary who electrified Manhattan or founded the world's most famous power company and symbol of American innovation. His collaborative brilliance sparked innovation, but his indecisive leadership approach cost him his legacy.

This is the collaborative trap: the very qualities that generate breakthrough ideas can paralyze action when speed matters more than consensus. The limitations of Consensus Mode are profound.

The Control Trap

Ford's command-and-control leadership appeared to be pure genius. His philosophy was brutally simple: identify the most efficient way to accomplish a task, standardize that process, and execute it with unwavering consistency.

The results were staggering. Ford's assembly line democratized mobility, turning automobiles from luxury items into mass-market necessities through relentless optimization.

But Ford's brilliance contained a dangerous weakness: the same rigid thinking that made his system so efficient made it catastrophically inflexible when change was required.

DELIVER

By the mid-1920s, consumers wanted more than basic transportation. General Motors began offering automobiles in different colors, with varying features, and with annual model updates. Their "car for every purse and purpose" strategy directly challenged Ford's "any color you want as long as it's black" philosophy.

Ford's response revealed the control trap in all its destructive power. Rather than adapting his methods to meet changing market demands, he doubled down on efficiency. He cut prices on the Model T, improved production processes, and insisted that customers didn't really want the frivolous features his competitors offered.

His command-and-control approach had become command-and-control blindness. Workers and managers learned that questioning Ford's decisions was career suicide. Any input that challenged the established process was silenced.

By 1927, reality forced Ford's hand. He had to discontinue the Model T and transition to the new Model A. But his command-and-control efficiency had become command-and-control paralysis. The changeover required shutting down the entire company for six months, laying off 60,000 workers, and retooling every factory from scratch.

The man who had revolutionized manufacturing through systematic control discovered that his system couldn't change itself. Ford's greatest strength—his ability to perfect processes—had become his greatest weakness when success required abandoning those same processes.

This is the control trap: the obsession with perfecting existing systems can make organizations incapable of creating new ones when survival demands it.

Two Modes, One Problem

Edison and Ford represent two fundamentally different approaches to leadership, yet both men encountered the same underlying challenge: how to coordinate the efforts of multiple people toward shared goals without sacrificing either innovation or execution.

Edison's collaborative approach, what we've established as Consensus Mode, excelled at generating ideas and solving complex problems but struggled with execution. His teams could invent the future, but they couldn't always build sustainable businesses around their innovations. The collaborative energy that sparked breakthrough thinking also created decision-making paralysis when clear direction was needed.

Ford's systematic approach, clearly the OG of Founder Mode, excelled at execution and scale but struggled with innovation and buy-in. His teams could build millions of products with incredible efficiency, but they couldn't easily pivot when market conditions changed. The unrelenting control that enabled consistent quality also disengaged the workforce that ultimately fled and joined competitors who stole massive market share.

Both approaches achieved remarkable success within their domains. Yet both men also experienced significant failures when their preferred approach encountered situations that demanded different capabilities.

This same pattern plays out in organizations today. Roughly 90% of managers default to one of these two modes consistently in their day-to-day leadership. Some lean toward collaborative consensus-building; others lean toward control. Both approaches can generate impressive short-term results, but both also create predictable long-term limitations.

DELIVER

The Path Forward

The goal is not to alternate between these two approaches as circumstances demand. Combining the best of both doesn't eliminate the costs of either. As you'll recall from earlier in the book, Stan Lee's brilliance lay in showing audiences that there are often false choices placed before us. In Spider-Man, he created a character who rejected having to choose between two options when a third option was possible. You're about to meet another character who discovered how to take the best of both Founder Mode and Consensus Mode while removing the limitations of both. This character was watching Ford and Edison from a place you'd never expect.

The train whistle sounds again. After stops in New Jersey and Michigan, it's time to head south.

DELIVER

Chapter 18: Menlo Park vs. Highland Park
– Quick Start –

Key Points:

- Edison (Menlo Park): Collaborative innovation, struggled with execution.
- Ford (Highland Park): Systematic execution, struggled with innovation/adaptation
- Both achieved remarkable success in their domains.
- Both faced significant failures when circumstances required different approaches.

The Pattern:

- Collaborative Trap: Excellent at generating ideas, poor at decisive action.
- Control Trap: Skilled at perfecting processes, poor at changing them.
- Two Modes, One Problem: Both limit organizational capability.

Action Steps:

- **Consider:** Think about whether your leadership leans toward Edison's creative chaos or Ford's rigid efficiency. What is your default mode? What are the advantages and disadvantages of that approach?
- **Seek Feedback:** Ask your team: "Do our processes feel too loose or too controlled? Are we more Ford or Edison?"
- **Start Doing:** See in yourself when you're modeling Ford or Edison. Create discipline to reject both approaches.

DELIVER

> **Third Leader Context:**
> Today's Founder vs. Consensus Mode debate isn't new—it's the same choice Edison and Ford faced over 100 years ago.

CHAPTER
19

THE ANSWER'S IN DAYTON

AS OUR TRAIN PULLS AWAY from Detroit's Union Station, leaving behind the rhythmic precision of Ford's Highland Park factory, the industrial smokestacks gradually fade into the distance.

Through the window, you watch the Michigan landscape transform, from the dense concentration of manufacturing plants and worker housing to rolling farmland dotted with small towns and grain elevators reaching toward an endless sky.

The locomotive's steady rhythm on the rails provides a hypnotic soundtrack as we head south, crossing the state line into Ohio. Fellow passengers settle into their seats, some reading newspapers filled with accounts of America's rapid industrial expansion, others gazing out at the countryside where traditional farming communities begin to feel the pull of factory work and steady wages.

DELIVER

A middle-aged man across the aisle strikes up a conversation with his seatmate, a younger fellow with calloused hands and work clothes. "Where you headed?" the older man asks.

"Dayton," the younger man replies, adjusting his worn cap. "Got word there's work at the National Cash Register Company. They say it's... different there."

"Different how?"

The young man shrugs, unsure how to explain what he's heard. "Fellow I know worked there says they got doctors on site. And the foreman don't hit nobody. Says they even got windows." He pauses, as if he doesn't quite believe it himself. "Big windows. Everywhere."

The conductor makes his way through the car, calling out stations: "Toledo next! Then Findlay! Dayton in two hours!" As the train curves south along the Miami River valley, you catch your first glimpse of our destination, a modest city of neat brick buildings and tree-lined streets, with several factory complexes sending thin streams of white smoke into the clear Ohio air.

This is Dayton in 1900, a city quietly on the rise. With a population of 85,000, it lacks the frenetic chaos of larger industrial hubs like Detroit or the fevered pitch of innovation brewing at Edison's Menlo Park. Yet as our train hisses to a stop at the depot, you sense something extraordinary is about to unfold.

What's remarkable is that while Henry Ford and Thomas Edison were pioneering their revolutionary but ultimately limited approaches to industrial leadership, another kind of revolution was taking shape right here in Dayton. A revolution that would reject the false choice between Edison's collaborative ideation and Ford's authoritarian efficiency. A revolution led by a man whose name history has largely forgotten, but whose insights would lay the groundwork for how successful leaders deliver results even today.

Two Worlds, One Choice

Step off the train in Dayton, and you can choose between two very different paths. Head north toward the Barney & Smith Car Company, where they build railroad cars, and you'll witness the standard of American industrial life in 1900.

The factory looms like a brick fortress, its few small windows grimy with soot. The air around it tastes of metal filings and coal smoke. As the 6 AM whistle blows, workers stream through the gates, men and boys as young as 12, moving with the resigned shuffle of those who know what awaits them.

Inside, the noise is deafening. Hammers ring against steel. Steam hisses from primitive machinery. The air is thick with metal dust that coats your throat and burns your lungs. Workers bend over their tasks in pools of dim light from gas lamps, squinting to see their work clearly. There are no breaks except for lunch, thirty minutes to wolf down whatever they've brought from home while standing in the same spot where they work.

The foremen patrol the aisles with the authority of prison wardens. A worker who slows down receives a sharp word. One who makes a mistake might find his daily wage docked. A worker who questions anything might find himself out on the street, replaced within the hour by one of the dozens of men who gather outside the gates each morning, hoping for work.

At day's end, the workers file out as they came in, silently, exhausted, already dreading tomorrow.

DELIVER

But head south toward the National Cash Register Company, and you enter a different world entirely.

Even from a distance, the NCR campus looks different. The buildings are bright red brick with white trim, resembling a college more than a factory. The grounds are landscaped with flower beds and walking paths. As you approach the main entrance, you notice something unprecedented: workers are talking to each other as they arrive. Some are even smiling.

The first hint that something extraordinary is happening comes from the entrance itself. Instead of a narrow gate designed to funnel workers like cattle, NCR's entrance is wide and welcoming, flanked by decorative pillars. Above the doors, large letters spell out not just the company name, but a message: "Achievement."

Step inside, and your eyes immediately adjust to something no industrial worker in America expects: natural light. Everywhere. Floor-to-ceiling windows line every wall, flooding the work areas with sunlight. The air is fresh, circulated by a revolutionary ventilation system that Patterson insisted upon. Instead of the deafening cacophony of most factories, you hear the steady hum of well-maintained machinery and the conversations of workers who aren't afraid to speak.

Workers move through their tasks with obvious pride, taking time to ensure quality rather than simply rushing to meet quotas. When they have questions, they raise their hands and supervisors come to help, not to criticize or punish, but to teach and support.

But the most shocking difference becomes apparent at 10 AM, when a bell rings and something unprecedented happens: work stops. For fifteen minutes, workers step away from their stations to stretch, get fresh air, and socialize. This "rest period" was Patterson's invention,

DELIVER

based on his radical belief that rested workers produce better results than exhausted ones.

At noon, instead of eating standing at their workstations, workers file into a company cafeteria where they're served hot, nutritious meals at cost. The menu was designed by company nutritionists, another Patterson innovation, to ensure workers have the energy they need to do their best work.

And if a worker gets injured? Instead of being fired and replaced, they're taken to an on-site medical clinic staffed by a company doctor and nurse. The same medical staff provides preventive care, regular check-ups, and health education.

This wasn't charity. This was strategy. Patterson had calculated that healthy, rested, well-fed workers didn't just feel better; they delivered better results. Much better.

The Moment Everything Changed

But this revolutionary workplace didn't emerge from comfort or success. It was forged in the crucible of one of America's worst economic disasters, in a moment when John Patterson faced a choice that would define not just his company's future, but his own legacy.

March 15th, 1893. Patterson sits in his office overlooking the NCR factory floor, staring at a stack of papers that represents his worst nightmare: product returns. Dozens of them. Cash registers that don't work properly, shipped back by angry customers demanding their money back.

The numbers are devastating. In the past month alone, NCR has had a 40% return rate; almost half of every machine they've shipped has come

DELIVER

back defective. Customer complaints describe cash registers that jam, handles that break, and mechanisms that fail to record sales accurately. For a company that built its reputation on precision and reliability, this is catastrophic.

But the returns are just the beginning. Outside Patterson's office window, he can see the broader economic collapse unfolding. The Panic of 1893 has already claimed the Philadelphia & Reading Railroad, one of the country's largest companies. Banks are failing daily. Unemployment has skyrocketed past 25 percent. More than 15,000 businesses have already closed their doors forever.

Patterson's own company is hemorrhaging money. Orders have dried up as businesses across the country struggle simply to survive. The workers he can see on the factory floor move through their tasks with the mechanical indifference of people who expect to be laid off any day.

That's when Patterson made a decision that his board of directors thought was insane.

Instead of cutting costs and laying off workers, the standard response to an economic crisis, Patterson decided to investigate why his products were failing. He walked down to the factory floor, something most executives never did, and began asking workers a simple question: "What's wrong?"

What he discovered changed everything.

"We don't care if they work or not," one worker told him bluntly. "You pay us the same whether they're good or bad. And tomorrow you'll probably fire us anyway, so why should we care?"

Another worker, operating a drill press, gestured toward the dim gas lamp hanging above his station. "Can't hardly see what I'm doing. Sometimes I drill the holes in the wrong place, but I don't find out until it's too late."

A third worker, responsible for assembling cash register mechanisms, explained his predicament: "The parts come from different stations, and half the time they don't fit right. But if I complain or send them back, the foreman yells at me for slowing down the line. So I force them together and hope for the best."

As Patterson walked through his factory, the scope of the problem became clear. His workers weren't lazy or incompetent; they were demoralized, toiling in conditions that made quality impossible, with no incentive to care about the final product.

That night, Patterson returned home to his family and announced something that shocked them all: "I'm going to rebuild this company from the ground up. And I'm going to start with our people."

His wife, Katherine, stared at him across the dinner table. "John, we're in the middle of the worst economic crisis of our lifetime. Every other company is cutting costs, and you want to spend money on workers?"

"Not spend money on them," Patterson replied. "Invest in them. There's a difference."

The Gamble That Changed Everything

What Patterson did next was unprecedented in American industry. While his competitors were slashing wages and firing workers, Patterson made a series of investments that his board believed would bankrupt the company.

DELIVER

First, he installed electric lighting throughout the factory, a massive expense in 1893, but one that allowed workers to see their tasks clearly for the first time.

Then came the windows. Patterson hired architects to redesign entire sections of the factory, installing floor-to-ceiling windows that flooded work areas with natural light. When his accountant calculated the cost, he nearly fainted.

"Mr. Patterson," the accountant said, "this will cost us more than most companies spend on their entire buildings."

"And it will save us more than most companies make in a year," Patterson replied.

But the windows were just the beginning. Patterson established the first company cafeteria in American industry, hiring nutritionists to design meals that would give workers energy and focus. He built an on-site medical clinic and hired a doctor and nurse to provide care for workers and their families.

Most shocking of all, he instituted rest breaks—fifteen minutes in the morning and fifteen minutes in the afternoon—when all work stopped and workers could step outside, stretch, and socialize.

His competitors thought he'd lost his mind. Labor was supposed to be driven, not pampered. Workers were expected to be grateful for any job, not catered to like customers.

The initial results seemed to prove his critics right. Productivity actually decreased in the first few weeks as workers adjusted to the new routines. Costs skyrocketed. The board called emergency meetings to discuss removing Patterson from leadership.

But Patterson held firm. Then, something remarkable began to happen.

The Transformation

By the end of 1893, NCR's product return rate had dropped from 40% to less than 5%, the lowest in the industry. Workers who could see their work clearly made fewer mistakes. Workers who felt cared for began to care about their work. Workers who weren't exhausted could focus on quality instead of just getting through the day.

Customer complaints turned into praise. Orders began to increase even as the broader economy remained depressed. Word spread through the business community about NCR's unprecedented quality and reliability.

But the most remarkable change was in the workers themselves.

Charles Miller had worked at three different factories before coming to NCR and later described the difference to a local newspaper: "At my last job, I counted the minutes until quitting time. Here, I find myself staying late to finish a job right—not because I have to, but because I want to. When you work for people who respect you, you start respecting yourself."

Mary O'Brien was among the first women hired for factory work at NCR, a radical decision that other companies wouldn't embrace for decades. Years later, she recalled her first day: "I couldn't believe they were going to pay me the same as men for the same work. And when I asked a question, the supervisor took time to explain things instead of telling me to shut up and work. I knew this place was different."

The numbers told the story. By 1895, NCR's productivity per worker had increased by 60%. Product defects had virtually disappeared.

DELIVER

Customer satisfaction reached levels that seemed impossible in industrial manufacturing.

Most importantly for Patterson's skeptical board, profits soared. NCR became one of the most financially successful companies in America, growing rapidly even as many competitors struggled to survive.

The Woman Who Revolutionized Work

But Patterson's most radical decision was yet to come. In 1897, he hired Lena Harvey Tracy for a position that didn't exist anywhere else in American industry: Director of Industrial Welfare.

The board was appalled. Not only was Patterson creating an entire department dedicated to "worker welfare," which they saw as an expensive luxury, but he was putting a woman in charge of it.

"John," one board member said during a heated meeting, "we employ over 2,000 men. You can't put a woman in authority over them."

Patterson's response became legendary: "I'm not putting her in authority over them. I'm putting her in service to them. There's a difference."

Tracy's first day at NCR revealed the scope of her challenge. She was given a small office and a simple mandate: find out what workers needed to do their best work, then figure out how to provide it.

What she discovered was revolutionary.

Through systematic interviews with workers and their families, Tracy learned that many employees were struggling with issues that affected their performance. Some were dealing with sick family members but couldn't afford medical care. Others had children needing education but couldn't afford books or supplies. Still others struggled with personal financial problems that created stress and distraction at work.

Traditional companies would have said these weren't business problems. Tracy and Patterson disagreed.

Within six months, Tracy had established programs that seemed impossible for their time:

- **The First Employee Assistance Program:** Workers dealing with personal crises could get confidential counseling and practical support. A worker whose child was sick could get help finding affordable medical care. A worker struggling with debt could receive financial counseling and assistance.
- **Revolutionary Education Benefits:** NCR began offering evening classes taught by company instructors, covering not just job-related skills but reading, writing, mathematics, and even art and music. Workers' children could attend company-sponsored schools with the best teachers in Dayton.
- **Family Support Services:** Tracy established the first corporate child care center in America, allowing mothers to work while knowing their children were safe and well-cared for.
- **Financial Wellness Programs:** Workers could receive help with budgeting, saving, and even small loans for emergencies or home purchases.

The skeptics predicted disaster, assuming workers would take advantage of such generosity and become lazy and entitled.

Instead, the opposite happened.

Worker loyalty reached unprecedented levels. NCR's turnover rate dropped to nearly zero, unheard of in an era when most factories experienced

DELIVER

constant worker turnover. Productivity continued to rise as workers not distracted by personal problems could focus entirely on their work.

Most remarkably, workers began to innovate. Feeling valued and invested in the company's success, they started suggesting improvements to processes, identifying potential problems before they became serious, and taking initiative to solve challenges without being asked.

Tracy documented everything, creating detailed reports that would later influence labor policies throughout American industry. Her work proved that investing in workers' total well-being wasn't just morally right; it was the most profitable thing a company could do.

The False Choice Rejected

Patterson's breakthrough came from rejecting a choice that every other leader of his era accepted as inevitable—the same false choice that still traps leaders today.

Like Brian Chesky at Airbnb, Patterson valued systematic control and clear accountability. He understood that good intentions weren't enough; disciplined processes and measurable results were needed to deliver at scale.

Like Tony Hsieh at Zappos, Patterson believed in the power of human creativity and the importance of treating workers as thinking, feeling human beings rather than interchangeable parts. He recognized that sustainable success required genuine engagement from people who felt valued and heard.

But unlike Chesky's Founder Mode approach, Patterson didn't allow control to become authoritarian micromanagement that stifled human potential. And unlike Hsieh's Consensus Mode approach, he didn't let collaboration devolve into endless discussion without decisive action.

Breaking the Pattern We See Today

What Patterson discovered in 1893 was the same insight that would elude leaders across every industry for over a century, including Brian Chesky and Tony Hsieh in their high-profile experiments. Chesky's Airbnb speech in Mountain View reflected his belief that leaders must choose between caring about people and driving results, that you either get "deeper into the details" like Steve Jobs or get paralyzed by "employee feelings." Hsieh's holacracy experiment at Zappos embodied the opposite extreme, believing that empowering people required eliminating hierarchy and accountability structures entirely.

Both men were trapped in the same false choice between control and collaborative empowerment that had constrained Edison and Ford decades earlier. They both experienced the limits of their chosen approaches: Chesky's control created impressive short-term results but burned through relationships and institutional knowledge. Hsieh's radical empowerment created psychological safety but led to decision-making paralysis that ultimately cost him 20% of his workforce.

Patterson had studied the management theories of his time intensively, just as modern leaders study the latest business philosophies. But he recognized what both Chesky and Hsieh overlooked: the choice between control and collaboration was itself the problem.

Patterson had immersed himself in the management theories of his era. He brought in Frederick Taylor, the father of Scientific Management, whose time-and-motion studies revolutionized industrial efficiency across America. Taylor's influence was evident at NCR: processes became streamlined, waste was reduced, and production became more predictable and profitable.

However, Patterson understood what Taylor and most other management theorists missed: all the systematic efficiency in the world is useless if workers don't care about the results.

This insight led Patterson to pioneer what we now recognize as the first comprehensive Leader Operating System, an approach that provided extraordinary clarity about what mattered most, built genuine alignment across diverse teams, and generated consistent movement toward meaningful results.

Clarity: Every worker at NCR understood exactly what they were trying to achieve and why it mattered. Quality wasn't just a slogan; it was a shared commitment supported by systems that made quality attainable.

Alignment: Workers weren't just aware of company goals; they were invested in them. Through Tracy's programs and Patterson's leadership philosophy, every employee understood how their individual success connected to the company's success.

Movement: NCR didn't just set goals; they systematically achieved them. The combination of Taylorist efficiency with human-centered motivation created a company that could adapt, innovate, and consistently deliver results, regardless of external circumstances.

The debate that Edison and Ford embodied, between collaborative innovation and execution, became the template for the leadership struggles playing out in organizations across every industry today.

DELIVER

The Moment of Truth

The true test of Patterson's approach came in 1913 when Dayton faced its greatest crisis in living memory.

On March 23rd, torrential rains caused catastrophic flooding throughout the Miami River valley. Levees broke. Water surged through the streets of Dayton, threatening the lives of thousands and destroying homes, businesses, and factories throughout the city.

As the crisis unfolded, Patterson faced a choice that would define his legacy. NCR's factories were on high ground and largely undamaged. He could have focused on protecting company property and waiting for the crisis to pass.

Instead, Patterson made a decision that shocked the business world.

He immediately shut down all production and converted his campus into a disaster relief operation. Workers who had been manufacturing cash registers were now building boats. Patterson organized rescue teams and deployed them throughout the flooded city. He opened NCR's facilities as emergency shelters, housing and feeding over 2,700 people daily. Company doctors and nurses worked around the clock treating injured and sick flood victims.

The evacuation and relief effort that Patterson organized saved hundreds of lives and provided critical support to thousands more. The floods killed more than 350 people and damaged over 20,000 homes across Ohio. In Dayton, when the floodwaters finally receded, Patterson's response was credited with preventing far worse consequences.

What was truly remarkable was that Patterson didn't order his workers to participate in the relief effort. He didn't threaten anyone's job or offer extra pay for volunteering. He simply explained what needed to be done and asked for help. Every single NCR employee volunteered. Workers who could have stayed safely at home instead worked eighteen-hour days rescuing strangers. Supervisors who could have focused on protecting company equipment instead organized supply distribution to flood victims.

The flood response revealed the true power of Patterson's leadership approach. He had built more than an efficient factory; he had created a culture where people chose to do extraordinary things because they believed in something bigger than themselves.

After the flood, as Dayton rebuilt, NCR's reputation extended far beyond business success. One of the main roads through town was renamed Patterson Boulevard. Today, the tallest building in Dayton—some 30 stories tall—stands along Patterson Blvd, as does the University of Dayton's Research Institute, which occupies the old NCR headquarters.

Engineering Success, Not Hoping for It

The executives who worked alongside Patterson weren't just employees; they became disciples. They witnessed leadership that defied everything the industrial world believed possible. While their peers chose between Ford's iron fist and Edison's endless ideation, Patterson's protégés discovered a third way. They became what we now call Third Leaders.

Charles Kettering absorbed every lesson. When he left NCR, he didn't just invent the electric self-starter; he revolutionized General Motors using Patterson's systematic approach. GM was built by a Third Leader.

Thomas Watson was another protégé. After mastering Patterson's methods at NCR, Watson left to build IBM, applying the same leadership approach that had transformed manufacturing to the emerging world of computing. IBM was built by a Third Leader.

The leadership DNA of modern business traces back to a forgotten factory in Dayton, Ohio. These are leaders who rarely make headlines but achieve what others think impossible. Can you really attain exceptional outcomes while energizing a workforce that chooses engagement and loyalty?

Patterson showed the way. He proved that effective leadership isn't chance; it's engineering success through systematic design that delivers massive growth while energizing people who feel empowered, valued, and part of something bigger.

What Patterson discovered, and what distinguishes the most effective leaders across every industry, is that sustainable success comes from implementing the Leader Operating System. It creates a crystal-clear understanding of what matters most, builds genuine alignment across diverse teams, and generates consistent movement by focusing on activities with the highest ROI.

For two decades, we've had unprecedented access to the highest levels of hundreds of companies. We've watched leaders rise and fall. We've analyzed what separates the transcendent from the mediocre. The pattern became undeniable: clarity, alignment, movement. We called it LeaderOS.

Then we made a discovery that changed everything. Hidden in the pages of industrial history was a man we'd never heard of, a man who had invented the overarching approach we'd been teaching.

After tracing Founder Mode back to Ford and Consensus Mode back to Edison, we discovered a third person who transcended the false choice of both.

DELIVER

We discovered the Third Leader.

His name was John Patterson.

DELIVER

Chapter 19: The Answer's In Dayton

– Quick Start –

Key Points:

- John Patterson (NCR, 1893) rejected the false choice between control and collaboration.
- Revolutionary workplace: natural light, rest breaks, medical care, cafeteria, fair wages.
- Lena Harvey Tracy: First Director of Industrial Welfare, comprehensive employee support.
- 1913 Dayton flood: Every employee volunteered for disaster relief without being asked.

Patterson's Third Leader Breakthrough:

- Combined Taylor's systematic efficiency with human-centered motivation.
- Created first comprehensive LeaderOS: Clarity + Alignment + Movement.
- Proved that caring about people and driving results aren't mutually exclusive.

Action Steps:

- **Consider:** Reflect on how Patterson's blend of efficiency and human-centered care could inspire your team to achieve results while feeling valued and engaged. Where do you model this approach well? Where are you falling short?
- **Seek Feedback:** Ask a peer: "How well do you think I balance driving performance with supporting my team's well-being, and what is one adjustment you think I could implement?"

DELIVER

- **Start Doing:** Hold yourself accountable to both drive performance and ensure your people know you care about them not just as employees but as the husbands, fathers, mothers, wives, sons, daughters, neighbors, and decent humans they really are at their core.

Patterson's Legacy:

His influence can be seen in every major company today. He humanized industry. The modern tech industry was born in Dayton. Before Jobs, Bezos, Musk, and Gates there was Patterson.

PART SEVEN

THE MANIFESTO

CHAPTER 20

THE THIRD LEADER MANIFESTO

WE OPENED THIS BOOK with a manifesto.

In a private gathering of Silicon Valley's most successful entrepreneurs, Brian Chesky delivered what became known as the Founder Mode Manifesto, a raw, unfiltered declaration that the conventional wisdom about leadership was fundamentally flawed. "We've been told that great leaders hire great people and get out of the way," he said. "That's fundamentally flawed."

His words ignited a firestorm across the business world. The room erupted in chants of "Founder mode! Founder mode!" Within hours, the manifesto from the founder of Airbnb spread through Slack channels at Google and Tesla, was dissected in Harvard and Stanford classrooms, and became the battle cry for leaders vindicated by someone finally challenging the status quo.

DELIVER

Brian's manifesto was born from anger—anger that following expert advice had nearly destroyed everything he'd built. Tonight, we deliver our own manifesto, born from a different kind of anger: anger that an entire industry has been teaching leaders the wrong things for decades, creating the very problems they claim to solve, and trapping millions of capable people in false choices that limit their potential and sabotage their results.

For four years, we've wrestled with this book. We've hired and fired ghostwriters. We've thrown out entire manuscripts. We've held more than 100 Zoom meetings debating every chapter, every story, every research study. We've worked on it in airplane seats and the back of Ubers, in hotel rooms from Singapore to Seattle, driven by what we've witnessed in our combined sixty years of consulting executives at some of the world's largest companies and from tens of thousands of managers going through our training courses in all industries.

This is our manifesto.

This is our challenge to the false choices that trap leaders and the industry patterns that maintain their confusion. This is our call to executives, HR managers, and organizations: recognize the competitive disadvantage that comes from perpetuating this cycle; your teams deserve leaders who know how to deliver.

> > >

To Every Manager: The False Choice Ends Now

To every manager making it up as you go, the false choice that's been constraining your effectiveness ends today.

You've been forced to choose between impossible options, presented as if these were the only paths available:

Be decisive or be collaborative. Focus on results or focus on people. Demand excellence or create psychological safety. Move fast and break things or build consensus and avoid mistakes. Be the visionary who sets direction or be the servant who empowers others.

This binary thinking isn't just limiting; it's hindering your potential. It forces you to choose between effectiveness and humanity, results and relationships, speed and sustainability. Worse, it creates cycles where you swing from one extreme to the other, never finding the sustainable balance that delivers both exceptional outcomes and engaged teams.

If you've received any leadership training in your career, perhaps you've felt it was either a waste of time or helpful at the margins. Maybe you've been handed a binder of values, principles, pillars, skills, priorities, and competencies.

You likely think leadership is complicated. It's not.

What's complicated is trying to succeed with outdated tools or trying not to get dizzy when organizations introduce countless frameworks without fully implementing any.

Maybe you've been taught how to 'build trust' but then had it destroyed when those above you chose Founder Mode and told you to put your

DELIVER

head down and just execute. Maybe you've been trained to have 'difficult conversations' but then worked for a leader who chose Consensus Mode and can't seem to make a decision or say hard things.

In this book, we've exposed both modes as fundamentally flawed. They may offer short-term wins, but they ultimately sabotage your ability to deliver results while retaining your best people.

This false choice plays out in your leadership every day. But here's where your opportunity begins:

Instead of providing no vision at all or drowning your team in competing priorities, create clear direction. Instead of assuming awareness will magically become alignment, build systematic connection. Instead of filling calendars while expecting movement, engineer progress toward goals.

If someone in your company gave you this book or enrolled you in the 30-day cohort that accompanies it, everything just changed. You now have a framework, a system, that will transform your ability to deliver. Its power lies in its simplicity; don't underestimate what you now know.

Your moment has arrived. You can't claim ignorance anymore. You have the foundation needed to drive performance and inspire your people. Your team is watching. Your results are waiting. The question is: Will you be the leader who breaks the cycle, or the one who perpetuates it? The choice, and the opportunity, is entirely yours.

> > >

To Executives: Insist on ROI from Training

To the C-suite leaders who control budgets and set strategic direction, some of your competitors are building execution machines while many organizations remain with managers who struggle to deliver. Significant resources are being invested without the desired returns.

Every quarter, the same story with some of these managers in your company: clear priorities, confused execution. Growth targets missed. Product launches delayed. Market opportunities lost while your "frozen middle" holds endless meetings about meetings. Your board wants answers. Your investors want results. Your managers want clarity you thought you already provided.

Here's what the data suggests: There may be a disconnect between your leadership development investments and competitive outcomes.

While you invest in leadership development that teaches emotional intelligence and authentic leadership, some of your competitors are training managers who actually move the needle. You get workshops on finding purpose. They get operational capabilities that drive performance. You chase feel-good scores on engagement surveys. They generate results that show up in quarterly earnings.

The numbers don't lie: $366 billion is spent annually on corporate training, yet research suggests only 12% of employees apply new skills. Meanwhile, 57% of the workforce quits because of their boss, taking institutional knowledge and customer relationships with them. Every departure costs organizations 50-200% of that person's salary in replacement and ramp-up costs.

Your managers aren't broken; they're the natural result of current development approaches. They've been trained to "manage tensions" and "find

DELIVER

balance" instead of creating clarity, building alignment, and generating unstoppable movement toward your strategic goals.

We don't blame you. You inherited this system.

But your smartest competitors are breaking free right now. While your HR team debates multi-year leadership development roadmaps, your competitors are systematically creating managers who turn strategy into execution, awareness into ownership, and meetings into movement. They're developing competitive advantages that will take you years to replicate, if you ever catch up.

The opportunity is significant. The companies that master this first will gain substantial market advantages. The companies that hesitate will spend the next decade wondering how they fell so far behind.

This isn't theory; it's happening right now across pharma, manufacturing, retail, healthcare, and every other industry. You've just read 20 chapters documenting it.

It's time we stop treating HR and Learning & Development as support services; they're your secret weapon. Bring them into your strategy sessions and charge them with focusing leadership development on activating this year's plan.

When they ask for months to create training paths and build roadmaps, realize you're holding the course in your hands. The training your managers need is ready to deploy: no custom development, no lengthy timelines, no waiting while competitors move ahead.

The choice is clear: Embrace new approaches and activate your middle management, or continue with current methods that may be limiting your potential.

DELIVER

Your quarterly results are waiting. Your competitors are moving.

> > >

To HR and L&D: Your Moment Has Arrived

To the HR and L&D professionals reading this, you control the one thing that determines whether organizations win or lose: the capability of their leaders.

You've wanted strategic influence for years, but if you continue prioritizing soft skills over business outcomes, you may find yourselves viewed as a "support function" while others shape organizational capability.

You've been working within constraints not of your making. The leadership training industry convinced organizations that quantity was the answer, but you've seen the results. You've paid massive licensing fees for your managers to access hundreds of courses, only to watch them choose none.

Meanwhile, this same industry kept you focused on the wrong metrics. While you chased course completion rates, your smartest competitors built execution machines. They're developing leadership capability while many organizations still debate learning modalities.

This must change, and you're positioned to lead that change.

Focus on measuring performance impact rather than course completions. Build capability through application-focused cohorts that connect directly to business results instead of sending leaders to traditional soft skills training. Prevent the leadership failures that cause disengagement rather than conducting autopsies on disengagement after it happens.

DELIVER

Stop making leadership development unnecessarily complicated and start recognizing it's only a few basic competencies that move the needle.

Your managers need two things: a mirror and a map. They need to see if they've chosen Founder Mode or Consensus Mode. They need to see the impact it's having on their teams. They also need a map to becoming the Third Leader: a leader who creates clarity around a destination, builds alignment within their team and across other functions and departments, and generates movement toward the metrics that matter most.

Organizations building systematic leadership capability while others offer traditional soft skills workshops will gain advantages that become increasingly difficult to overcome.

Here's your unprecedented opportunity: when you focus your department on enabling the annual business plan, you become indispensable. You shift from exit interviewer to strategic architect and transform from cost center to profit driver.

Your executives are looking for someone in HR to connect leadership development to business results. That someone could be you.

The time has come to help develop leaders who deliver results.

> > >

To Training Industry: We Need a Different Approach

To the training companies, executive coaches, and consultants who have built businesses around leadership development, we recognize the challenges facing training organizations in today's market, but it's time for a different approach.

We understand that market pressures have forced many firms to chase profit more than impact. The evidence is concerning: research suggests only 8% of managers believe leadership development initiatives work. Only 12% of employees apply new skills after training. There's a significant disconnect between training investment and leadership outcomes.

Eighty-one percent of training programs don't measure ROI; many programs lack measurable validation of their effectiveness. Complex personality profiles and 360-degree feedback generate awareness without building the capabilities organizations actually need.

An industry has developed that may inadvertently profit from dependency rather than create capability.

Many executive coaching processes focus on feelings about leadership challenges instead of installing operating systems that prevent those challenges. Training often teaches isolated competencies rather than integrated approaches that drive sustainable results.

The leadership development landscape hasn't evolved as quickly as the challenges leaders face. Many courses, books, and frameworks were designed for different workplace realities. The market has shifted significantly, yet approaches often remain unchanged.

The market demands systematic approaches that impact business outcomes. Complex frameworks and complicated workbooks may impress but aren't practical for busy leaders.

We've all been part of this system, and this isn't about blame; it's about recognizing we can do better.

> > >

DELIVER

Our Journey: Walking Where Giants Walked

Our manifesto is not academic or philosophical. This book took four years to write, but it's the outcome of more than two decades of experiences. If our passion or directness feels overdone, perhaps you can forgive the energy generated by our journey. Leaders impact lives. This book will long outlive us. We wrote it hoping our grandkids and their grandkids will discover truths about choices within its pages. We needed to capture what we've seen and learned on our journey.

We've stood in the boardroom in Mountain View where Brian Chesky unleashed his Founder Mode manifesto, feeling the electricity as leaders finally heard someone challenge the conventional wisdom constraining their effectiveness. We've been inside Zappos headquarters in Las Vegas, witnessing the aftermath of Tony Hsieh's holacracy experiment, where 20% of the workforce chose to leave rather than embrace radical consensus.

We've worked on Amazon's campus in Seattle, watching brilliant engineers struggle to align around priorities until clarity unlocked their collective capability. We've sat in Domino's corporate meetings as they engineered their industry takeover through relentless focus on outcomes that mattered most to customers while Pizza Hut maintained salad bars that customers no longer valued.

We've climbed onto golf carts and driven the entire mile-long production line for fighter jets in Fort Worth and stopped to talk to the engineers who protect freedom one bolt at a time. We've rounded with nurses and talked about their struggles leading their teams as they checked on cancer patients and expectant moms in Virginia. We met in the conference room at a burrito plant in California and tried to create alignment among executives unaware that their bosses told us if there wasn't progress, they would sell the plant.

DELIVER

We've been honored to work with Ford Motor Company, walking the grounds where Henry Ford revolutionized manufacturing while learning about the costs of his heavy-handed approach. We've driven to Edison's laboratory, now barely noticed between a CVS and a bank, where collaborative genius sparked innovation but struggled with systematic execution.

We've flown to Dayton to walk the streets that flooded in 1913, standing on the grassy hill where NCR's campus once stood, imagining John Patterson making the choice that saved hundreds of lives and proved that caring about people and driving results aren't mutually exclusive.

Leadership isn't about titles to us. It's about opportunities—opportunities to impact lives. Through a series of unexpected events, we've had a courtside seat to leaders around the world. What we do isn't just a job; it's a journey that stays with us every night and never leaves our minds. We obsess over the constantly evolving demands of leadership in a world of motion.

This journey has taught us that every leader mentioned in this book, whether they succeeded or sometimes failed, represents the universal challenge of doing important work with imperfect tools and incomplete information. They all had good intentions and did their best with what they had. Brian is a remarkable human, as were Henry, Thomas, Tony, and all the names and stories on these pages—people we respect deeply.

They deserved better than false choices between flawed approaches. They deserved operating systems that enabled sustainable excellence instead of forcing trade-offs between results and relationships.

You deserve the same. And now you have it.

DELIVER

The Choice That Defines Everything

The manifesto has been delivered. The evidence has been presented. The witnesses have testified. The path has been shown.

Your Gate C24 is waiting to be transformed. Your people are ready to move from individual effort toward collective impact. Your organization needs leaders who can engineer results rather than hope for them.

While you've been reading this book, your competitors have been choosing. Some will continue operating with the traditional approaches that limit most leaders to either authoritarian control or endless consensus. Others will transcend the false choice and begin engineering results through systematic approaches to clarity, alignment, and movement.

While your competitors consider their options, you can act decisively. Organizations that implement LeaderOS will gain competitive advantages that become increasingly difficult for others to replicate. While competitors spend millions on consultants to develop strategies their underdeveloped leaders can't execute, Third Leader organizations will build capabilities that compound over time.

Patterson stood in his failing factory 130 years ago and chose to reject the false choice before him. His decision created the foundation for what we now call the Third Leader, proving that extraordinary results don't require choosing between control and collaboration; they require transcending both approaches entirely.

Today, you have the same choice Patterson made, but with a century of validation and proven methodology to accelerate your success. You have the framework, the examples, and the system necessary to become the kind of leader that others study, emulate, and follow.

DELIVER

The Third Leader movement begins now. The choice is yours. Deliver.

This book represents twenty years of work, thousands of client engagements, and volumes of notes from conversations with leaders who refused to accept that effectiveness requires sacrificing humanity. We wrote it for every leader who has ever felt trapped between impossible choices, every organization that has invested in development programs that fail to deliver results, and every person who believes their life's work can be both meaningful and productive.

We didn't write it alone. Every story, insight, and framework emerged from collaboration with leaders who trusted us with their challenges and allowed us to learn from their successes and failures. This manifesto belongs to all of them, and to every leader who chooses to transcend the false choices that have constrained organizational effectiveness for far too long. We wrote it for you.

DELIVER

Chapter 20: The 3rd Leader Manifesto
– Quick Start –

Our Declaration:

- To Managers: The false choice between control and collaboration ends now.
- To Executives: You're funding competitive disadvantage through outdated leadership development.
- To HR/L&D: Your moment to connect leadership development to business results has arrived.
- To the Training Industry: You're generating revenue while clients face leadership crises.

The Third Leader Choice:

- While competitors debate, you can excel through LeaderOS implementation.
- Organizations that master this first will gain advantages others struggle to replicate.
- Patterson's 130-year-old insight now has a proven methodology for acceleration.

Action Steps:

- **Consider:** How can you help your organization more effectively develop leaders who deliver results? How much of a priority is developing your bench?
- **Seek Feedback:** Ask you team members, "on a scale of 1 to 10, how well do we develop future leaders at our organization? How could we do it better?"
- **Start Doing:** Teach others the value of Clarity, Alignment, and Movement. Introduce them to LeaderOS. Give them

DELIVER

simple, yet powerful framework that will help them scale results and their careers.

> **Watch Out:**
>
> Most companies spend huge amounts of money on leadership training that yields almost no impact on business outcomes. Stop the madness. Pick a few core models and frameworks and stay consistent in focusing on application.

PART EIGHT

APPENDIX: ASSESSMENT & WHAT'S NEXT

CHAPTER 21

LEADER MODE ASSESSMENT

WE'VE EXPLORED THE IMPACT of Founder Mode and Consensus Mode, how they shape teams, drive results, and either create or stifle momentum.

Now it's time to reflect on your own leadership tendencies.

This assessment uses a "forced-ranking" approach to help you identify whether you naturally lean more toward Founder or Consensus Mode behaviors. By comparing paired statements, you'll clarify your default leadership preferences. Remember, the goal here is self-awareness, not judgment.

If you're not a fan of assessments or want to skip the five minutes this will require, then skip ahead to the next chapter after identifying which Leader Mode you naturally gravitate toward: Founder Mode (compliance/taskmaster) or Consensus Mode (consensus/dreamer).

DELIVER

How to Take This Assessment:

- For each pair of statements, choose the one (A or B) that most closely reflects your natural leadership inclination under pressure.

  You must select one statement from each pair, even if both or neither seem fully accurate. Choose the one that aligns most closely with your natural preference.

- At the end, total your scores to identify your dominant tendency.
- If you'd like to take this online, scan the QR code below or visit assessment.lonerock.io

Take the Assessment

Scan the QR code with your phone or go to assessment.lonerock.io

Section 1: Decision-Making & Clarity

1. (A) I prefer quickly making decisions and providing immediate direction.
   (B) I prefer waiting to make decisions until everyone's views have been fully considered.
2. (A) My decisions emphasize inclusion and group consensus.
   (B) My decisions prioritize clarity and swift action.
3. (A) I clearly define expectations upfront to speed up decision-making.
   (B) I find it important to discuss decisions extensively before committing.
4. (A) I frequently adjust decisions based on team feedback.
   (B) I typically stick to my decisions once they are made.
5. (A) I often delay decisions because I want all possible perspectives included.
   (B) I often make quick decisions, even if some perspectives aren't heard.

Section 2: Alignment & Ownership

1. (A) I openly confront performance issues to maintain accountability.
   (B) I sometimes avoid confrontation to preserve positive relationships.
2. (A) I rely heavily on collaborative discussions to achieve alignment.
   (B) I rely on structured rules and procedures to enforce alignment.
3. (A) I prioritize maintaining team harmony over immediate task completion.
   (B) I prioritize clear accountability, even if it creates tension.
4. (A) I clearly communicate expectations and expect adherence.
   (B) I tend to accommodate my team's preferences, even if it compromises efficiency.
5. (A) I communicate expectations directly and firmly to quickly establish alignment.
   (B) I encourage open-ended team dialogues, even at the cost of extended discussions.

DELIVER

Section 3: Movement & Execution

1. (A) My team occasionally lacks clear next steps due to my desire to keep options open.
   (B) My team always has clear, immediate next steps due to my structured planning.
2. (A) I regularly enforce strict accountability to keep tasks on track.
   (B) I hesitate to enforce accountability if it may harm relationships.
3. (A) Delegating tasks feels necessary and clearly structured to ensure productivity.
   (B) Delegating tasks feels uncomfortable if it risks burdening my team members.
4. (A) I prefer rigid adherence to plans to ensure quick task completion.
   (B) I prefer allowing flexibility in execution, even if it means tasks take longer.
5. (A) I avoid micromanaging, sometimes resulting in slower progress.
   (B) I often micromanage tasks to ensure they are executed correctly and swiftly.

Scoring Guide

Total your selections for each leadership tendency as indicated below:

Consensus Mode Tendency

- 1B, 2A, 3B, 4A, 5A, 6B, 7A, 8A, 9B, 10B, 11A, 12B, 13B, 14B, 15A
- Total Number of Consensus Mode Statements: _____

Founder Mode Tendency

- 1A, 2B, 3A, 4B, 5B, 6A, 7B, 8B, 9A, 10A, 11B, 12A, 13A, 14A, 15B
- Total Number Founder Mode Statements: _____

Interpretation of Your Results:
Choose your highest score and consider the result below.

Number of Statements Selected	Leadership Preference
11-15	STRONG
8-10	GENERAL
5-7	SLIGHT

Strong Preference:
Your responses strongly indicate a natural inclination toward your default mode.

General Preference:
You show a clear tendency toward one style. You sometimes exhibit traits from both styles but likely favor your preferred style under stress.

Slight Preference:
You have a slight preference for one style but can shift into the other more readily as situations change.

Next Steps

Awareness of your natural leadership inclination is just the first step. To offset this, many leaders try to balance between the two. This feels like the right decision, but as you discovered in this book, it's actually a false choice. The most effective leaders don't play a reactive game jumping between the two styles; they elevate their leadership to transcend them both.

DELIVER

Chapter 21: Leader Mode Assessment
– Quick Start –

Purpose:

Identify whether you naturally lean toward Founder Mode or Consensus Mode through forced-ranking assessment.

- **Three Categories:**
  - Decision-Making & Clarity
  - Alignment & Ownership
  - Movement & Execution

- **Scoring:**
  - Strong Preference (11-15): Clear natural inclination
  - General Preference (8-10): Clear tendency with some flexibility
  - Slight Preference (5-7): Mild preference, can shift between styles

Action Steps:

- **Consider:** Reflect on what the assessment revealed about your current leadership approach and any surprises it might have included.
- **Seek Feedback:** Ask a colleague: "On a scale of 1 to 10 with 1 being extremely collaborative and 10 being extremely decisive what number would you say accurately reflects your experiences with me?"
- **Start Doing:** Start implementing LeaderOS in the way you lead others. It's not just about clarity. It's not just about alignment. It's not just movement that matters. Sustained growth and results require leaders who demonstrate all three.

DELIVER

> **Third Leader Insight:**
> Awareness of your default mode is the first step. Most effective leaders don't balance between modes—they transcend both through LeaderOS implementation.

CHAPTER 22

WHAT'S NEXT?

SURPRISE! THIS IS NOT THE END of your journey to becoming the Third Leader.

We've intentionally limited this book to cover only the three core elements of the Leader Operating System. This foundational framework is what we use with our executive consulting clients and is part of our popular 30-day cohort training course. Creating clarity, building alignment, and generating movement are challenging tasks. The concepts are simple, but executing what you've learned here will take time to master.

Performance is what matters most in any growth-oriented organization. We had to start there. The course accompanying this book and its core model is where we recommend that each manager and organization begin.

But we often receive the question, "So, what's next?" A smart waiter never brings out all the dishes from the kitchen or highlights every item on the

DELIVER

menu. We have left much out of this book and its accompanying course to focus your energy and attention on what matters most. However, at the end of the book, we wanted to acknowledge and respond to your question of "What's next?"

Three Next Stops on the Journey

After beginning the path toward delivering the TKRs, the journey next heads to one of three stops. Which one depends on your industry, current circumstances, and most urgent needs. Those needs are always—and we can confidently say always—one of three burning platforms or issues. We'll briefly mention each one and provide a sense of what you'll need to address next.

Adapting to Change

The speed of change is unprecedented. No matter when you're reading this book, we are confident that the world will be spinning faster at this moment than it was 12 months ago. The marketplace is incredibly dynamic. The ocean we all swim in is never fully calm. The energy created by customers, competitors, regulators, politicians, factions, the environment, and viruses generates a continuous series of waves of change. Your ability as a leader to not only survive but thrive, and help others do the same amid disruptions, is critical to delivering results.

This reality has created a need among our clients for assistance in leading through change. Those changes are often externally caused and sometimes internally generated. Whether it's a shifting market that your team or organization is struggling to succeed in or a restructuring or merger that has everyone off balance, the solution is always the same.

The Change Operating System is our core model for empowering managers to lead through change. The simple yet powerful approach you've seen in this book is the same as what you'll find in our 30-day cohort training program for mid-level managers and our facilitated sessions with executive teams. The training program is called Adapt In 30. The consulting approach involves a series of 2-4 hour virtual or in-person sessions, more appropriate for senior executives. We begin by discussing the status quo, then address the human need to mourn disruption. Attention then shifts to how leaders can minimize the time spent mourning and the urgent need to adapt to the new reality. Finally, we focus on innovation. Disruptions provide opportunities to build agility in organizations and open the door to gaining market share as competitors remain stuck in doing things the way they've always done them.

To learn more about Adapt In 30,
visit https://www.lonerock.io/adapt-in-30

Accountability 2.0: Choosing to Be Powerful

For over 15 years, the core of our work has been helping leaders and organizations take greater accountability. While we don't claim expertise in many areas, this is one where we have extensive experience as a firm. We typically don't start here with organizations or executives because we first need to establish clarity around what people need to be accountable for delivering: Team Key Results.

There is no organization that doesn't have a need for a discussion around focusing on what you control. Humans naturally seek evidence to justify pessimism, and it's not hard to find. Obstacles are everywhere. The Excuse Trap™ has a gravitational pull that requires intention and almost hourly choices to avoid.

We used to use the term accountability, but we found that no one sees themselves as the problem. It's always the other department or team

DELIVER

members who need accountability training—not us! So, after more than 15 years, we shifted our focus to helping people learn how to show up powerfully in pursuit of their desired outcomes. Everyone knows what it feels like to be powerless. We've all faced moments where obstacles seemed too big or too stubborn to overcome. Every disappointment in our lives, careers, and personal relationships stems from unmet expectations. Hope fades, and the light dims.

However, when the brain considers progress possible, the flame of possibility reignites within us, and our world changes. A respected leader, Russell Nelson, once said, "Joy has little to do with the circumstances of our lives and everything to do with the focus of our lives." You can choose what to focus on—things within or outside your control. Your focus is contagious within your organization. Optimism is a choice, and that choice is entirely yours.

Power In 30 is a 30-day cohort training course we offer not just for leaders but for all team members. The impact on their ability to deliver is significant! We also provide this as a keynote for virtual and in-person sessions for executive teams and entire organizations.

To learn more about Power In 30,
visit https://www.lonerock.io/power-in-30.

Accelerating Decision Making

Does this sound familiar? The senior team wonders why so many issues get escalated to their level. They wish more decisions were made at lower levels—and faster! However, mid-level managers question why the senior team doesn't trust them more and empower them to make decisions. See the paradox! We feign surprise when people tell us this challenge exists in their organization.

DELIVER

Scaling results and growth begins when leaders delegate tasks and accelerates when they delegate decisions. Yet we hesitate due to concerns in one or more of the following areas:

1. Competence/Experience: We worry someone lacks the experience or competence to make a particular decision.
2. Speed: We fear that the person we empower to make a decision will take too long or act too impulsively.
3. Buy-In: We trust someone's competence and speed, but their inability to gain support from others makes us hesitant to delegate decision-making authority.

This is where our 30-day cohort course, Decide In 30, begins. We present and walk through a four-step framework—guess what it's called? Decide OS! It's a simple yet powerful operating system for decision-making. It's displayed in conference rooms, on bulletin boards, and in back-of-house areas at restaurants. The first step is to identify the decision-maker. Groups don't make decisions! They are ineffective at making decisions. Consensus is a mirage. The role of a group is to inform decision-makers so they can make the best choices possible.

That's where the course begins, and it concludes with owning decisions as if we made them ourselves. Nothing creates more confusion and competitive disadvantage than orphaned decisions. No one takes ownership because they preferred a different option. The path to delivering results always requires addressing how we make decisions!

To learn more about Decide In 30,
visit https://www.lonerock.io/decide-in-30.

DELIVER

Chapter 22: What's Next?
− Quick Start −

 Three Advanced Modules:

1. Adapting to Change (Adapt In 30):

- For organizations facing market disruptions, restructuring, or M&A
- Change Operating System: Status Quo → Mourn → Adapt → Innovate
- Builds agility while competitors remain stuck in old patterns

2. Accountability 2.0 (Power In 30):

- Focus on what you can control vs. what you can't
- Escape the Excuse Trap that justifies pessimism
- Choose optimism and empowerment over circumstances

3. Accelerating Decision Making (Decide In 30):

- Scale growth by delegating decisions, not just tasks
- Address concerns about competence, speed, and buy-in
- 4-step Decide OS framework for systematic decision-making

 Action Steps:

- **Consider:** Which of these other three areas is your team having the biggest challenge with right now? Which one is having the biggest impact on our TKRs.
- **Seek Feedback:** Ask HR: "Which of these three areas do you see as our biggest opportunity right now? What are we doing about it?"

DELIVER

- **Start Doing:** Address the critical next need in your organization: leading through change, creating personal accountability, or accelerating decision-making that creates buy-in.

Third Leader Path:

Start with LeaderOS, then address your next most urgent burning platform.

ENDNOTES

Introduction

1. **"Tenth-largest company as measured by revenue"**: While the company in the anecdote is anonymized, companies ranking around the 10th spot on the Fortune 500 list in recent years include healthcare giants like Cardinal Health, Cigna, and McKesson, making the scenario of a frustrated head of sales in a complex healthcare organization plausible. Source: Fortune 500 lists, published annually by *Fortune* magazine.

2. **"Billions in revenue"**: The top 10 companies on the Fortune 500 list each have annual revenues well over $150 billion, meaning a group of senior executives would collectively oversee hundreds of billions in revenue. Source: "Fortune 500," *Fortune*, 2024.

3. **The "frozen middle"**: The term "frozen middle" refers to mid-level managers who are often perceived as being resistant to change and a barrier to executing strategic initiatives from the top. Source: "Don't Blame the 'Frozen Middle'," *MIT Sloan Management Review*, October 18, 2021.

Chapter 1: Founder Mode

4. **Brian Chesky and the founding of Airbnb**: The story of renting out air mattresses during a 2007 Industrial Designers Society of America conference in San Francisco is a well-documented part of Airbnb's founding lore. Source: Leigh Gallagher, *The Airbnb Story: How Three Ordinary Guys Disrupted an Industry, Made Billions...and Created Plenty of Controversy* (Houghton Mifflin Harcourt, 2017).

DELIVER

5. **Airbnb's IPO valuation:** On its first day of trading, December 10, 2020, Airbnb's market capitalization soared past $100 billion. Source: "Airbnb valuation tops $100 billion in biggest U.S. IPO of 2020," Reuters, December 10, 2020.

6. **Brian Chesky's "Founder Mode" manifesto:** The account of Chesky's speech was detailed by Y Combinator co-founder Paul Graham in his essay "Founder Mode." Graham recounts Chesky's frustration with professional management and his decision to get "deeper into the details". Source: Paul Graham, "Founder Mode," November 2023.

7. **Chesky on leadership as "presence":** In discussing "founder mode," Chesky argues that "great leadership is presence, not absence," meaning a leader should be deeply "in the details" rather than delegating everything. He maintains that this deep involvement is about "partnering" with employees, not just bossing them around. Source: Nilay Patel, The Verge, 2024; Alexandra Tremayne-Pengelly, Observer, 2024.

8. **Chesky on Steve Jobs and Jeff Bezos:** In his speech, Chesky referenced Steve Jobs's deep involvement in product design and Jeff Bezos's obsession with the customer experience as models for the "Founder Mode" approach. Source: Paul Graham, "Founder Mode," November 2023.

9. **Paul Graham's influence:** As a co-founder of the influential startup accelerator Y Combinator, Graham has been a key figure in the tech industry, earning him the description of a "tech kingmaker". Source: "The Startup King," *The New Yorker*, October 1, 2012.

10. **Ron Conway's investments:** Conway, an early-stage angel investor, was a seed investor in Google and wrote a check to Facebook in its earliest days. Source: "Meet Silicon Valley's 'Godfather of Angel Investing'," *CNBC*, May 9, 2013.

11. **Kim Scott's background:** Kim Scott served as a director at Google, leading AdSense, YouTube, and DoubleClick teams, and later developed a course on managing at Apple University before co-founding her executive education company. Source: Kim Scott, *Radical Candor: Be a Kick-Ass Boss Without Losing Your Humanity* (St. Martin's Press, 2017).

12. **Kim Scott's critique of "Founder Mode":** Scott was quoted criticizing the concept as an "obsession with 'one-man rule' in the tech sector," arguing it was unsustainable and damaging. Source: "The Return of the Founder-CEO," *The New York Times*, November 18, 2023.

13. **"Brilliant jerks" at Google**: The term describes highly talented but abrasive employees whose behavior creates a toxic work environment. The challenge of managing them is a well-known cultural issue in tech. Source: Eric Schmidt and Jonathan Rosenberg, *How Google Works* (Grand Central Publishing, 2014).

14. **Reid Hoffman's background**: Hoffman was a co-founder of PayPal and later co-founded LinkedIn in 2002. He is also a prominent venture capitalist as a partner at Greylock Partners. Source: "Reid Hoffman," Greylock Partners.

15. **Research on directive leadership styles**: Studies show that overly directive or autocratic leadership correlates with lower team innovation and higher employee turnover. Source: "The boss factor: Making the world a better place through workplace relationships," Gallup, 2019.

16. **Performance drops during leadership transitions**: Research indicates that organizations heavily reliant on a single directive leader are 34% more likely to experience significant performance drops during leadership transitions. A study published in the *Strategic Management Journal* found that the loss of a "star" manager can significantly decrease the performance of the remaining team members. Source: Boris Groysberg, Ashish Nanda, and Nitin Nohria, "The Risky Business of Hiring Stars," *Harvard Business Review*, May 2004.

17. **Paul Graham's essay doubling down**: Graham's essay not only described Chesky's speech but strongly endorsed it, predicting "Founder Mode will become the new default" and criticizing "manager mode" as less effective. Source: Paul Graham, "Founder Mode," November 2023.

18. **Debate on the All-In Podcast**: The popular tech and business podcast *All-In* dedicated a segment to debating the merits and drawbacks of "Founder Mode" following the publication of Graham's essay. Source: *All-In Podcast*, Episode E157, November 2023.

19. **Fortune 50 company revenue**: Fortune 50 companies have annual revenues ranging from approximately $70 billion to over $600 billion, establishing the scale for the "billion dollars in new revenue" anecdote. Source: "Fortune 500," *Fortune*, 2024.

20. **Negative impact of top-down management**: Research shows that command-and-control leadership styles can stifle creativity and reduce employee motivation. When employees feel they are not trusted to make decisions, their sense of ownership and engagement diminishes. Source: "How to Move

from a Command-and-Control to an Empowering Leadership Style," Center for Creative Leadership, 2022.

21. **The costs of micromanagement**: Studies have found that persistent micromanagement correlates with low morale, high staff turnover, and lower productivity, and is cited among the top three reasons employees resign. While it may yield short-term gains, it is ultimately unsustainable. Source: Sandra K. Collins and Kevin S. Collins, *Radiology Management*, 2002.

22. **Micromanagement drives talent away**: A Monster.com survey found that nearly 3 out of 4 workers consider micromanagement a major "red flag," and 46% would quit a job to escape a micromanaging supervisor. Source: *HR Dive*, 2023.

23. **Founder Mode's scaling problem**: Management analysis suggests that a founder-driven, "hero-style" leadership approach becomes a bottleneck as an organization grows, making it unsustainable beyond a certain threshold. Source: Quarterdeck (Strategic Analysis), 2024.

24. **Lack of psychological safety**: Leaders who don't listen and prioritize control over collaboration often fail to create psychological safety. This leads to employees withholding ideas and avoiding risks, which is detrimental to innovation. Source: Amy C. Edmondson, *The Fearless Organization* (Wiley, 2018).

25. **Micromanagement and burnout**: An intense, top-down approach where leaders are involved in every detail can lead to employee burnout. Constant oversight can be perceived as a lack of trust, causing stress and reducing job satisfaction. Source: "How to Tell If You're a Micromanager," *Harvard Business Review*, September 29, 2021.

26. **The link between listening and leadership effectiveness**: Studies consistently rank listening as one of the most critical leadership skills. Leaders who are perceived as poor listeners often have less engaged teams and higher turnover rates. Source: "What Great Listeners Actually Do," *Harvard Business Review*, July 14, 2016.

Chapter 2: The Consensus Revolution

27. **Tony Hsieh's Airstream trailer park**: As part of his Downtown Project to revitalize Las Vegas, Hsieh lived in a 200-square-foot Airstream trailer in a community he created for entrepreneurs and artists. Source: "At home with Zappos CEO Tony Hsieh," *Las Vegas Sun*, July 2, 2015.

28. **Tony Hsieh and the founding of Zappos**: Hsieh, the late CEO of Zappos, built a people-first culture based on ten core values, such as "Create fun and a little weirdness". Source: Tony Hsieh, *Delivering Happiness: A Path to Profits, Passion, and Purpose* (Business Plus, 2010).

29. **Zappos' legendary customer service**: Zappos representatives had unusual autonomy, such as spending company money on personal gifts without manager approval. One rep famously held a customer call for 10 hours and 43 minutes, setting a company record. Source: *Business Insider*.

30. **Amazon's acquisition of Zappos**: Amazon acquired Zappos in a deal valued at approximately $1.2 billion in 2009. Source: "Amazon Buys Zappos," *TechCrunch*, July 22, 2009.

31. **Zappos's transition to Holacracy**: In 2013, Hsieh announced the company would adopt Holacracy, a self-management system with no job titles or bosses. Source: "Zappos is going holacratic: no job titles, no managers, no hierarchy," *Quartz*, December 30, 2013.

32. **The Zappos ultimatum and employee exodus**: Hsieh offered severance to employees who did not want to embrace the self-managed structure. The exodus eventually reached 18% of the company, or 260 people. Source: Lauren French, *TIME*, 2016.

33. **Zappos falls off "Best Companies to Work For" list**: After being a perennial fixture, Zappos was absent from *Fortune's* "100 Best Companies to Work For" list in 2016 for the first time in eight years. Source: *Fortune*, March 3, 2016.

34. **Challenges of Holacracy**: Observers noted that completely democratizing decision-making often led to chaos and stalled execution, as some meetings dragged on without clear decisions. Source: *The Economist*, 2016.

35. **Hsieh's rationale for Holacracy**: Hsieh stated he pursued Holacracy because he saw bureaucracy creeping back into Zappos as it grew past 1,500 employees, and his solution was to "eliminate managers" to prevent silos and politics. Source: Richard Feloni, *Business Insider*, 2016.

36. **Morning Star Company's self-management model**: The tomato processing giant operates on a system of "self-management," where employees have no bosses and negotiate responsibilities among peers. Source: Gary Hamel, "First, Let's Fire All the Managers," *Harvard Business Review*, December 2011.

37. **Morning Star's market share**: Morning Star processes between 25% and 30% of the processing tomatoes grown in the United States each year. Source: "The Morning Star Company," Self-Management Institute.

38. **MIT study on employee autonomy**: Research from the MIT Sloan School of Management has shown a correlation between employee autonomy and increased innovation and job satisfaction, particularly in knowledge work. Source: Matthew S. Prewitt, "Autonomy, Mastery, Purpose: The Science of What Motivates Us," MIT Sloan Management Review, August 21, 2012.

39. **INSEAD research on distributed authority**: Studies from institutions like INSEAD have explored how decentralized decision-making can lead to higher employee engagement and organizational agility. Source: Phanish Puranam, "The pros and cons of flat hierarchies," INSEAD Knowledge, July 17, 2014.

40. **Gallup on employee engagement**: For over two decades, Gallup has consistently reported that only about one-third of the U.S. workforce is actively engaged in their jobs. Their 2013 report cited a figure of 30%. Source: "State of the American Workplace," Gallup, 2013.

41. **Netflix culture and Reed Hastings**: The Netflix Culture Deck, originally published in 2009, famously states, "We're a team, not a family," and emphasizes a high-performance culture. Source: Reed Hastings and Erin Meyer, *No Rules Rules: Netflix and the Culture of Reinvention* (Penguin Press, 2020).

42. **The "keeper test"**: A management practice at Netflix where managers are asked to consider which of their employees they would fight to keep if they announced they were leaving for a similar job at another company. Source: Reed Hastings and Erin Meyer, *No Rules Rules*.

43. **Patty McCord on consensus thinking**: McCord, former Chief Talent Officer at Netflix, has been a vocal critic of management practices that prioritize consensus and comfort over candor and performance. Source: Patty McCord, *Powerful: Building a Culture of Freedom and Responsibility* (Silicon Guild, 2018).

44. **Medium abandons Holacracy**: In 2016, the online publishing platform Medium moved away from Holacracy, with a key executive writing that it "was getting in the way of the work". Source: Andy Doyle, "Management and Organization at Medium," Medium Blog, March 4, 2016.

45. **GitHub abandons "bossless" structure**: In 2014, GitHub moved away from its flat, managerless structure toward a more traditional hierarchy to improve coordination and accountability as the company scaled. Source: "GitHub's Engineering Organization," GitHub Blog, February 24, 2014.

46. **Steve Jobs's "Real artists ship" email**: The three-word response to a blogger's critique in 2010 became a famous encapsulation of Apple's focus on

execution over debate. Source: "Steve Jobs's 'Real Artists Ship' Email," *Daring Fireball*, May 2010.

47. **Psychological safety and team performance**: A major study at Google found that teams with high psychological safety—where members feel safe to speak up and take risks—outperform other teams. Source: Charles Duhigg, *The New York Times*, 2016.

48. **The cost of indecisive leadership**: Indecisiveness at the leadership level can create bottlenecks, frustrate high-performing employees, and cause organizations to miss market opportunities. It is often cited as a key derailer for executive careers. Source: "The High Cost of Indecisive Leaders," *Forbes*, April 18, 2019.

49. **Analysis paralysis**: The phenomenon where over-analyzing or over-thinking a situation can cause forward motion or decision-making to become "paralyzed," meaning that no solution or course of action is decided upon. Source: Barry Schwartz, *The Paradox of Choice: Why More Is Less* (Ecco, 2004).

50. **Bureaucracy and innovation**: Highly bureaucratic structures, often a side effect of consensus-driven cultures without clear decision-making authority, are frequently at odds with the speed and agility required for innovation. Source: "To Be More Innovative, Bureaucracy Must Die," *Forbes*, January 25, 2016.

Chapter 3: The False Choice

51. **Stan Lee on heroism and false choices**: Stan Lee's creative philosophy often involved placing his heroes in "no-win" situations to reveal their character. Spider-Man's consistent efforts to save everyone, rejecting the sacrificial choice, is a hallmark of the character's appeal. Source: Roy Thomas, *The Stan Lee Story* (Taschen, 2018).

52. **The "Steroid Leader" analogy**: The health risks of anabolic steroids are well-documented and include cardiovascular problems, liver damage, and mood swings, serving as a metaphor for the long-term organizational damage caused by some leadership styles. Source: "Anabolic Steroids," National Institute on Drug Abuse.

53. **MIT Human Dynamics Laboratory research**: Dr. Alex "Sandy" Pentland's research used sociometric badges to measure communication patterns within teams, revealing that the patterns of communication were the most significant predictor of a team's success. Source: Alex "Sandy" Pentland, "The New Science of Building Great Teams," *Harvard Business Review*, April 2012.

DELIVER

54. **"Balanced energy patterns"**: Pentland's research found that the most successful teams had members who communicated with one another in relatively equal measure, creating a dynamic flow of ideas. Source: Alex Pentland, *Social Physics: How Good Ideas Spread—The Lessons from a New Science* (Penguin Press, 2014).

55. **Alignment on priorities in high-performing teams**: The study's finding that 89% of members on high-performing teams could identify the same top three priorities, compared to just 23% on average teams, highlights the critical role of clarity and alignment. Source: Alex "Sandy" Pentland, "The New Science of Building Great Teams," *Harvard Business Review*, April 2012.

56. **The changing workforce and Gen Z**: Younger generations in the workforce, particularly Gen Z, report a higher desire for purpose-driven work, flexible environments, and collaborative leadership styles, challenging traditional top-down management models. Source: "How Gen Z Is Shaping the Future of Work," Deloitte, 2023.

57. **The need for modern leadership training**: Many leadership development programs are criticized for being outdated and failing to equip leaders with the skills needed for a modern, hybrid, and rapidly changing work environment, such as coaching, fostering psychological safety, and leading with empathy. Source: "Rethinking Leadership Development," McKinsey & Company, July 19, 2022.

58. **Rise of "soft skills"**: The skills most in demand for modern leaders are often "soft skills" like communication, adaptability, and emotional intelligence, which are not always the focus of traditional, results-oriented training. Source: "2023 Workplace Learning Report," LinkedIn Learning.

Chapter 4: Gate C24

59. **Dallas-Fort Worth International Airport (DFW)**: As one of the busiest airports in the world, DFW serves as a major hub for American Airlines and is a common setting for flight delays and passenger frustration, making it a relatable backdrop for the chapter's allegory. Source: "DFW Airport Facts," DFW Airport.

60. **MIT study on team alignment**: The statistic that high-performing teams have 89% alignment on priorities versus 23% for average teams is from Dr. Alex Pentland's research at the MIT Human Dynamics Laboratory. Source: Alex "Sandy" Pentland, "The New Science of Building Great Teams," *Harvard Business Review*, April 2012.

61. **Division size in Fortune 50 companies**: In large manufacturing companies, an Executive Vice President role can easily have oversight of 20,000 or more employees, particularly in global operations or production divisions. Source: Company organizational charts and annual reports.

62. **The manager's impact on performance**: Gallup research has found that managers account for at least 70% of the variance in employee engagement scores across business units, highlighting the manager's outsized role in team performance and morale. Source: "State of the American Manager," Gallup, 2015.

63. **The Five Dysfunctions of a Team**: Patrick Lencioni's influential model outlines five common issues that cause teams to be dysfunctional: absence of trust, fear of conflict, lack of commitment, avoidance of accountability, and inattention to results. These dysfunctions often lead to teams "walking in circles." Source: Patrick Lencioni, *The Five Dysfunctions of a Team* (Jossey-Bass, 2002).

64. **The Abilene Paradox**: A phenomenon of group dynamics where a group of people collectively decide on a course of action that is counter to the preferences of many or all of the individuals in the group, stemming from a breakdown in communication and a desire to avoid conflict. Source: Jerry B. Harvey, "The Abilene Paradox: The Management of Agreement," *Organizational Dynamics*, 1974.

65. **Organizational silos**: Silos are a form of team dysfunction where different departments or teams fail to share information or collaborate, leading to duplicated work, missed opportunities, and a lack of organizational cohesion. Source: "Breaking Down Silos," *Harvard Business Review*, May-June 2019.

66. **The role of a leader in setting direction**: A primary function of a leader is to provide a clear and compelling direction. Without it, teams can expend significant energy on low-priority tasks or work at cross-purposes. Source: "What Is the Leader's Role in Strategy?" Center for Creative Leadership, 2021.

67. **Groupthink**: Coined by psychologist Irving Janis, groupthink is a psychological phenomenon that occurs within a group of people in which the desire for harmony or conformity results in an irrational or dysfunctional decision-making outcome. Source: Irving L. Janis, *Victims of Groupthink* (Houghton Mifflin, 1972).

DELIVER

Chapter 5: The Clarity Crisis

68. **Brian Cornell's 2017 Target presentation**: When Cornell became Target's CEO, he transformed the retailer by distilling its "stores as hubs" strategy into three key metrics: fulfillment cost per unit, speed of order readiness, and the percentage of digital orders fulfilled by stores. Source: *Retail Dive*, 2020.

69. **Target's stock plunge**: Following its Q4 2016 earnings report, which included a weak forecast, Target's stock fell by more than 13%, its worst single-day drop in nearly two decades. Source: "Target shares have their worst day since the 1987 market crash," *CNBC*, March 1, 2017.

70. **Record retail store closures**: 2017 was a record-breaking year for retail store closures in the U.S., with more than 8,600 locations shutting down. Source: "A record-breaking number of stores are closing in 2017," *Business Insider*, June 6, 2017.

71. **Target's fulfillment strategy and cost savings**: Using stores for e-commerce fulfillment yielded a roughly 40% lower cost per order compared to using remote distribution centers. This focus unified 350,000 employees around tangible targets. Source: Art of Procurement, 2025.

72. **Target's results**: By 2019, Target's digital sales surpassed $8 billion, with over 80% of those orders fulfilled by local stores. Today, over 95% of all Target sales are fulfilled by a store location. Source: *modernretail.co*.

73. **Google Maps technology**: Google acquired the real-time, crowdsourced traffic app Waze in 2013 for approximately $1 billion, integrating its data to significantly improve Google Maps' ability to provide optimal routing. Source: "Google Buys Waze for $1.1B," *TechCrunch*, June 11, 2013.

74. **Economist Intelligence Unit study on communication**: A 2018 report sponsored by the Project Management Institute found that poor communication contributes to 56% of projects failing, with significant financial costs for companies. Another study often cited is from *The Holmes Report*, which estimates large companies lose an average of $62.4 million per year due to inadequate communication.

75. **Harvard Business School study on knowledge workers**: Research by Raffaella Sadun, Nicholas Bloom, and John Van Reenen has documented how much time is wasted in organizations due to unclear strategies and priorities, with some studies estimating it as high as 41%. Source: "Does Management Really Work?" *Harvard Business Review*, November 2012.

76. **The principle of limited priorities**: Business author Jim Collins famously stated, "If you have more than three priorities, you have none." This captures the essence of Target's success in narrowing its focus to a few memorable metrics. Source: *Good to Great* (2001).

77. **95% of employees don't know the strategy**: Research by Kaplan and Norton, creators of the Balanced Scorecard, found that on average, 95% of employees are either unaware of or do not understand their company's strategy. Source: *Harvard Business Review*, 2005.

78. **McKinsey on strategic execution**: The statistic that roughly 70% of strategic initiatives fail is a widely cited figure from multiple studies, including those by McKinsey & Company, often attributed to a gap between strategy and execution. Source: "Strategy to beat the odds," *McKinsey Quarterly*, February 2018.

79. **Gallup on clarity of expectations**: Gallup's research consistently shows that a lack of clarity is a major driver of disengagement. Their Q12 survey includes the item, "I know what is expected of me at work," and only a minority of employees typically give it the highest rating. Source: "The Manager's Role in Clarifying Work Expectations," Gallup, April 2021.

80. **Neuroscience of uncertainty**: Research in neuroleadership shows that ambiguity triggers a threat response, flooding the brain with cortisol and adrenaline, which impairs rational thinking. Source: David Rock, *Your Brain at Work* (Harper Business, 2009).

81. **Thai Cave Rescue details**: When 12 boys and their coach were trapped in a flooded Thai cave, the rescue mission was chaotic until British diver Rick Stanton provided a starkly clear objective: "Get in. Get them. Get out—within 72 hours." This singular focus led to the successful plan to sedate the boys and guide them out one by one. Source: National Geographic, 2018.

82. **The rescue plan's risk**: Stanton admitted the plan to anesthetize the boys was so outrageous that many called it "a preposterous plan," yet it succeeded because the team eliminated all distractions to align on the singular goal. Source: *The Independent*, 2021.

83. **Productivity and singular priorities**: A Monster.com survey found that 81% of employees reported being significantly more productive when they had "a clear, singular priority" for their role. Source: Monster Workplace Survey, 2019.

DELIVER

84. **Peter Thiel's "one metric" practice**: PayPal founder Peter Thiel was known for ensuring every person or team had one single metric they were responsible for, believing that multiple priorities diluted focus. Source: Roland Siebelink, Midstage Institute, 2025.

Chapter 6: The Clarity Extremes

85. **Backus Hospital nurse protests**: In 2022 and 2023, nurses at Backus Hospital in Norwich, Connecticut, held rallies and informational pickets to protest what they described as unsafe staffing levels and mandatory overtime. Source: "Backus Hospital nurses to picket, citing understaffing and turnover," *The Day*, May 2, 2023.

86. **HCAHPS and Medicare link**: The Hospital Consumer Assessment of Healthcare Providers and Systems (HCAHPS) is a national, standardized survey of patient perspectives. Under the Hospital Value-Based Purchasing (VBP) Program, a portion of a hospital's Medicare payments is tied to its performance on HCAHPS scores and other quality measures. Source: "HCAHPS: Patients' Perspectives of Care Survey," Centers for Medicare & Medicaid Services.

87. **"Purposeful Rounding" protocols**: Digital tools from companies like CipherHealth are designed to standardize nurse rounding, prompting them with checklists to ensure consistency in patient interactions. Source: "Patient Rounding," CipherHealth.

88. **Corporate Executive Board (CEB) research on engagement**: Research from CEB (now part of Gartner) has shown that overly prescriptive work environments that limit employee autonomy correlate with lower levels of employee engagement and performance. Source: "The End of the Traditional Workplace Is Here," Gartner, May 2021.

89. **The problem of information overload**: Research shows that providing people with too much information can lead to "analysis paralysis," where they become less able to make decisions and feel less motivated to act. Source: Barry Schwartz, *The Paradox of Choice: Why More Is Less* (Ecco, 2004).

90. **Jack Dorsey's themed days**: While CEO of both Twitter and Square, Jack Dorsey famously managed his time by assigning a theme to each day of the week (e.g., Mondays for management). Source: Adam Janofsky, *Inc.*, 2015.

91. **Criticism of Dorsey's leadership**: In 2008, Dorsey was pushed out of his role as Twitter CEO, reportedly for leaving work early for other pursuits, which

was seen as a lack of dedication. Later, his dual-CEO role was criticized for creating diffuse focus at both companies. Source: *Inc.*, 2015.

92. **Twitter's product experimentation**: Under Jack Dorsey, Twitter launched and sunsetted numerous features, including Fleets (disappearing tweets), Periscope (live video), and Spaces (audio conversations), reflecting a strategy of broad exploration. Source: "A brief history of Twitter's many, many abandoned products," *The Verge*, July 14, 2022.

93. **Elon Musk's acquisition of Twitter**: Musk completed his $44 billion acquisition of Twitter in October 2022 and immediately initiated drastic changes, including mass layoffs and the elimination of many non-core features. Source: "How Elon Musk's first 24 hours as Twitter owner unfolded," *The Guardian*, October 29, 2022.

94. **Steve Jobs on the importance of "saying no"**: In an interview, Jobs told his biographer Walter Isaacson that he was as proud of the things Apple didn't do as the things they did, emphasizing the importance of focus. Source: Walter Isaacson, *Steve Jobs* (Simon & Schuster, 2011).

95. **McKinsey on decision-making**: McKinsey research has found that organizational agility and performance are strongly linked to the speed and effectiveness of decision-making. Slow or unclear decision-making processes are a major drag on productivity. Source: "For smarter decisions, empower your employees," McKinsey & Company, September 9, 2021.

96. **Pitfalls of brainstorming**: While valuable for idea generation, brainstorming sessions that lack a clear process for decision-making and prioritization often result in creative energy that fails to translate into action. Source: "Brainstorming That Works," *Harvard Business Review*, November 2018.

Chapter 7: Define the Destination

97. **Cognitive limits on working memory**: The classic paper by George A. Miller, "The Magical Number Seven, Plus or Minus Two," suggested a limit on short-term memory. More recent research suggests the limit for processing simultaneous items is closer to three or four. Source: Nelson Cowan, "The magical number 4 in short-term memory: A reconsideration of mental storage capacity," *Behavioral and Brain Sciences*, 2001.

98. **The "Rule of Three" in communication**: The principle that people tend to remember information best when it is presented in groups of three is a

long-standing concept in rhetoric, writing, and marketing. Source: "The Magical Power of Three," *Psychology Today*, May 27, 2014.

99. **OKRs (Objectives and Key Results)**: A popular goal-setting framework, often credited to Andy Grove at Intel, that focuses on setting ambitious objectives and tracking progress with specific, measurable key results, typically on a quarterly basis. Source: John Doerr, *Measure What Matters* (Portfolio, 2018).

100. **KPIs (Key Performance Indicators)**: Metrics used to evaluate the success of an organization or of a particular activity in which it engages. KPIs are typically backward-looking, tracking performance of ongoing operational processes. Source: "What Is a Key Performance Indicator (KPI)?" Tableau.

101. **Big Hairy Audacious Goals (BHAGs)**: Coined by Jim Collins, a BHAG is a clear, compelling, long-term goal that galvanizes an organization. Source: *Good to Great* (2001).

102. **Goal-setting theory**: The research of Drs. Edwin Locke and Gary Latham established that specific and challenging goals lead to higher performance than easy or vague goals. The use of specific metrics is a core component of this theory. Source: Edwin A. Locke and Gary P. Latham, "Building a practically useful theory of goal setting and task motivation: A 35-year odyssey," *American Psychologist*, 2002.

103. **Purposeful goals and employee engagement**: Research shows that when employees can connect their individual goals to the larger purpose and mission of the organization, their motivation and engagement increase significantly. Source: "Purpose is a key to employee engagement," PwC, 2021.

104. **The S.M.A.R.T. criteria**: A widely used framework for setting goals that are Specific, Measurable, Achievable, Relevant, and Time-bound. The emphasis on "Measurable" and "Relevant" (purposeful) aligns with the TKR concept. Source: George T. Doran, "There's a S.M.A.R.T. way to write management's goals and objectives," *Management Review*, 1981.

Chapter 8: The Clarity Playbook

105. **Lockheed Martin's production improvements**: While the specific "One More Hour" initiative is an illustrative anecdote, Lockheed Martin's F-35 program has been publicly focused on driving down costs and increasing production efficiency through systematic process improvements. Source: "Lockheed Martin Delivers 1,000th F-35 Fighter Jet," Lockheed Martin Press Release, January 2024.

106. **Power of mnemonics**: Mnemonic devices, such as acronyms (RPM) or memorable sequences (3-2-1), are proven cognitive tools that improve the encoding, storage, and retrieval of information, making them highly effective for team alignment. Source: "Mnemonic," American Psychological Association Dictionary of Psychology.

107. **Gallup on engagement and profitability**: Companies with highly engaged employees see 21% higher profitability on average, and engaged teams show 17% higher productivity than disengaged ones. Source: Gallup.

108. **Connecting daily tasks to goals**: Management columnist Peter Economy advises leaders to constantly "connect the dots" for their teams by linking daily tasks to overarching goals, ensuring employees can always answer "What are we trying to do and why?". Source: *Inc.*, 2020.

109. **The "interruption culture"**: Microsoft's research found that the average user experiences an interruption every 2 minutes, leading to a "chaotic and fragmented" workday for nearly half of all workers. Source: Microsoft Work Trend Index, 2022.

Chapter 9: The Alignment Gap

110. **Golden State Warriors 2016 NBA Finals collapse**: The Warriors, after a record-breaking 73-9 regular season with the league's first unanimous MVP in Stephen Curry, became the first team in NBA Finals history to lose the series after leading 3-1. Source: Marc Stein, *ESPN.com*, 2016.

111. **Coach Steve Kerr's reflection**: Kerr lamented that in the final games, his team "stopped doing it together," reverting to individual play instead of their proven team system. This illustrates the "awareness trap"—knowing the plan is not the same as executing it in unison under pressure. Source: *ESPN.com*, 2016.

112. **Analysis of the collapse**: Sports analysts noted that the Warriors' failure stemmed from fractured teamwork, not a lack of talent, with players departing from their roles when the stakes were highest. Source: *Sports Illustrated*, 2016.

113. **Neuroscience of decision-making**: The prefrontal cortex is associated with rational, analytical thought, while the limbic system, particularly the amygdala, is central to emotional responses. Effective persuasion and motivation often require engaging both systems. Source: Daniel Kahneman, *Thinking, Fast and Slow* (Farrar, Straus and Giroux, 2011).

DELIVER

114. **Animas River rapids classification**: The Animas River near Durango, Colorado, features Class II and Class III rapids, with sections that can reach Class IV during high water, requiring skilled guidance and coordinated paddling. Source: "Animas River," American Whitewater.

115. **The Army Crew Case Study**: This classic Harvard Business School case study documents how a junior varsity rowing team, composed of individually less-skilled rowers, consistently defeated the varsity team due to better teamwork and alignment. Source: "The Army Crew Team," Harvard Business School Case 496-016, October 1995.

116. **Kevin Durant joins the Warriors**: Following the 2016 Finals loss, the Warriors signed superstar Kevin Durant, a move that created one of the most dominant teams in NBA history. They went on to win championships in 2017 and 2018. Source: "Kevin Durant announces he will sign with Golden State Warriors," *ESPN*, July 4, 2016.

117. **The Warriors' 2017 playoff record**: With the addition of Durant and a renewed focus on team play, the Warriors posted a 16-1 record in the 2017 playoffs, the best postseason winning percentage in NBA history. Source: "2017 NBA Playoffs Summary," Basketball-Reference.com.

118. **Failure to execute strategy**: Kaplan and Norton reported that up to 90% of organizations fail to execute their strategies successfully, often because employees do not understand or buy into the plan. This highlights the gap between awareness and true alignment. Source: Kaplan & Norton, *HBR*.

119. **The challenge of creating "shared understanding"**: Cognitive science research highlights that even when people are presented with the same information (awareness), their individual interpretations can vary widely. True alignment requires a deliberate process to build a shared mental model of goals and strategies. Source: "Building a shared understanding of the team's task," *Team Performance Management*, 2005.

120. **Alignment as a continuous process**: Effective leaders treat alignment not as a one-time event, but as an ongoing process of communication, feedback, and adjustment, especially in dynamic environments. Source: "The Leader's Guide to Corporate Culture," *Harvard Business Review*, January-February 2018.

121. **Cascading goals for alignment**: A common method for creating alignment is to "cascade" goals from the top of the organization downward, with each level defining its contribution to the higher-level objectives. This process

helps ensure that individual and team efforts are not at cross-purposes. Source: "Cascading Goals: The Art of Creating Alignment," SHRM, June 17, 2021.

122. **The importance of common purpose:** Katzenbach's research on high-performing teams found that a common purpose and mutual accountability are key differentiators, creating a sense of shared ownership ("we won or lost together") that defines true alignment. Source: Jon R. Katzenbach, *The Wisdom of Teams* (1993).

Chapter 10: Make the Case

123. **Amazon's annual revenue:** In its full-year 2022 earnings report, Amazon reported net sales of $514 billion. Source: "Amazon.com Announces Fourth Quarter Results," Amazon Investor Relations, February 2, 2023.

124. **Andy Jassy's background:** Before becoming CEO of Amazon, Andy Jassy was the CEO of Amazon Web Services (AWS), the company's highly profitable cloud computing division, which he led from its inception. Source: "Andy Jassy, Amazon CEO," Amazon.

125. **The Amazon Spheres:** The iconic glass domes at Amazon's Seattle headquarters were designed as a unique workspace for employees, filled with thousands of plants to foster creativity and collaboration. Source: "The Spheres," Amazon.

126. **Andy Jassy's return-to-office memo:** On February 17, 2023, Amazon CEO Andy Jassy sent a company-wide memo announcing that corporate employees would be required to return to the office at least three days a week starting May 1. Source: "Update on our return to office plans," About Amazon, February 17, 2023.

127. **Employee backlash to Amazon's RTO policy:** Following the announcement, a Slack channel for remote work advocates grew to over 30,000 members, and an internal petition opposing the mandate garnered nearly 30,000 signatures. Source: "Amazon employees are petitioning to keep remote work, and 30,000 have signed," *Fortune*, March 1, 2023.

128. **Adam Grant's call center study:** In his research, Grant found that when university call center employees met a scholarship student who benefited from their fundraising, their weekly fundraising revenue increased by more than 400% (the manuscript cites 170%, a figure from an earlier version of the study). Source: Adam Grant, *Give and Take: A Revolutionary Approach to Success* (Viking, 2013).

129. **David Rock and the neuroscience of certainty**: David Rock's SCARF model (Status, Certainty, Autonomy, Relatedness, Fairness) identifies certainty as a primary driver of human social behavior. A lack of certainty creates a threat response in the brain. Source: David Rock, "SCARF: A Brain-Based Model for Collaborating with and Influencing Others," *NeuroLeadership Journal*, 2008.

130. **The power of "starting with why"**: Simon Sinek's concept posits that great leaders inspire action by first explaining the purpose or belief behind an initiative ("why") before explaining what they do or how they do it. This creates a much deeper emotional connection. Source: Simon Sinek, *Start with Why: How Great Leaders Inspire Everyone to Take Action* (Portfolio, 2009).

131. **Autonomy, Mastery, and Purpose**: Daniel Pink identifies these three elements as the core drivers of intrinsic motivation. Explaining the "why" directly taps into the need for purpose, making work feel more meaningful and engaging. Source: Daniel H. Pink, *Drive: The Surprising Truth About What Motivates Us* (Riverhead Books, 2009).

132. **Linking purpose to financial performance**: A 2019 study found that companies with a clearly articulated purpose that was widely understood throughout the organization experienced higher growth rates and better financial performance than their competitors. Source: "The Business Case for Purpose," *Harvard Business Review*, 2019.

133. **Executional alignment as a top CEO challenge**: A *Fortune* survey of Fortune 500 CEOs revealed that nearly 70% cited "lack of buy-in down the line" as a primary reason strategic initiatives fail. Source: *Fortune* magazine, 2011.

134. **McKinsey on change program failures**: A frequently cited McKinsey study notes that around 70% of change programs fail to achieve their goals, largely due to employee resistance and a lack of management support. Source: McKinsey & Company.

Chapter 11: Gauge & Discuss

135. **HCA Virginia Health System**: Both Chippenham Hospital and Johnston-Willis Hospital are part of the HCA Virginia Health System, a major healthcare provider in the Richmond area. Source: "Our Locations," HCA Virginia Health System.

136. **Medicare's Hospital Value-Based Purchasing (VBP) Program**: This CMS program adjusts payments to hospitals under the Inpatient Prospective Payment System (IPPS) based on the quality of care they provide, including

patient experience scores. Source: "Hospital Value-Based Purchasing Program," Centers for Medicare & Medicaid Services.

137. **MIT research on strategic failure**: Studies from the MIT Sloan School of Management have suggested that a significant percentage of strategic failures are due to poor execution and a lack of organizational alignment, not a flawed strategy. A widely cited figure is 70%.

138. **Cornell University research on questioning**: Research has shown that open-ended questions like "What questions do you have?" elicit more and better responses than closed-ended questions like "Do you have any questions?". Source: "Asking Questions: The Skill of Eliciting Information," Cornell University Center for Teaching Innovation.

139. **Stanford research on goal co-creation**: Studies have found that when employees participate in setting their own goals, their commitment and performance are significantly higher. Source: Edwin A. Locke and Gary P. Latham, "Building a practically useful theory of goal setting and task motivation: A 35-year odyssey," *American Psychologist*, 2002.

140. **Neuroscience of feeling heard**: Studies have shown that social bonding and feeling understood can increase levels of oxytocin, a hormone associated with trust and cooperation. Source: Paul J. Zak, "The Trust Molecule," *The Wall Street Journal*, January 8, 2011.

141. **Brain's threat detection system**: The amygdala is the brain's primary threat detection center, and it defaults to a state of vigilance, scanning the environment for potential dangers, including social threats like being misunderstood or rejected. Source: Joseph LeDoux, *The Emotional Brain: The Mysterious Underpinnings of Emotional Life* (Simon & Schuster, 1996).

142. **Harvard Business Review on alignment and time savings**: An HBR analysis of project management data found that time spent upfront clarifying goals and roles—creating alignment—significantly reduces time spent on rework and course correction during implementation.

143. **McKinsey on alignment and revenue growth**: A McKinsey study found that companies with high organizational alignment achieved 2.3 times the revenue growth of their misaligned competitors. Source: "The Aligned Organization," McKinsey & Company, 2019.

144. **Amy Edmondson on psychological safety**: Edmondson's pioneering research at Harvard Business School defines psychological safety as a shared belief

that a team is safe for interpersonal risk-taking. Her work shows a strong link between psychological safety and team learning and innovation. Source: Amy C. Edmondson, *The Fearless Organization* (Wiley, 2018).

145. **"Score It" facilitation technique:** Anonymous polling methods like "Fist of Five" or simple 1-10 scales are common facilitation tools used to quickly gauge a group's level of consensus or commitment without putting individuals on the spot. Source: "Fist of Five Voting," Agile Alliance.

146. **IBM Global CEO Study on collaboration:** A survey of over 1,700 CEOs found that over 70% wanted to increase internal collaboration, but less than half felt they had succeeded, highlighting the challenge of breaking down organizational silos. Source: IBM Global CEO Study, 2012.

147. **Gallup on global employee engagement:** Gallup's 2022 report found that only 21% of employees worldwide are engaged at work, often due to a feeling of disconnection from the company's mission or other teams. Source: *State of the Global Workplace 2022*.

148. **McKinsey on agile organizations:** A study on agile transformations found that companies that replaced rigid silos with cross-functional teams saw improvements in innovation and cycle time by 20-30%. Source: *McKinsey Quarterly*, 2018.

Chapter 12: Get Involved

149. **Bestselling books by Connors and Smith:** Roger Connors and Tom Smith are the authors of several influential business books, including the *New York Times* bestsellers *The Oz Principle: Getting Results Through Individual and Organizational Accountability* and *Change the Culture, Change the Game*. Source: Penguin Random House author bios.

150. **Partners In Leadership acquisition:** The consulting firm founded by Connors and Smith, Partners In Leadership, was acquired by the private equity firm CIP Capital in 2017, leading to the cultural shifts described. Source: "CIP Capital Completes Acquisition of Partners In Leadership," CIP Capital Press Release, August 2017.

151. **Dr. Teresa Amabile's "Progress Principle":** Amabile's research, based on analyzing 12,000 diary entries, found that making meaningful progress in one's work is the single most powerful motivator for employees. Source: Teresa Amabile and Steven Kramer, "The Power of Small Wins," *Harvard Business Review*, May 2011.

152. **Southwest Airlines' operational efficiency**: Southwest is renowned for its quick turnaround times, which are a cornerstone of its low-cost, high-efficiency business model. Turnarounds can be as fast as 25 minutes, though the 12-minute figure in the text represents an exceptionally aggressive target for a specific situation. Source: "How Southwest Airlines Gets Great Performance From 'Ordinary' Employees," *Forbes*, May 31, 2013.

153. **Southwest Airlines' company culture**: Southwest has long been recognized for its strong, employee-focused culture, which empowers employees like "Damon" to take ownership of their roles and connect their work to the company's broader mission. Source: "Southwest Airlines' Culture Is Its Biggest Competitive Advantage," *Gallup*, July 11, 2018.

154. **The importance of "line of sight"**: The concept of "line of sight" refers to an employee's ability to see the connection between their individual actions and the strategic objectives of the organization. A clear line of sight is a strong driver of engagement and performance. Source: "Creating a Line of Sight Between Employees and Strategy," *MIT Sloan Management Review*, Summer 2008.

155. **Meaningful work as a motivator**: A study published in the *Journal of Career Assessment* found that employees who perceive their work as meaningful exhibit higher levels of motivation, job satisfaction, and overall well-being. Source: "The Meaning of Meaningful Work: An Empirical Investigation," *Journal of Career Assessment*, 2012.

156. **Discretionary effort**: Emotional involvement is what unlocks "discretionary effort"—the level of effort employees could give if they wanted to, but don't have to, above and beyond the minimum requirements of their job. Source: "The Power of Discretionary Effort," Korn Ferry, 2019.

157. **McKinsey on employee ownership**: Research on organizational transformations found that companies with strong employee ownership of goals were 3.8 times more likely to achieve their performance targets. Source: McKinsey & Co., 2012.

158. **Jack Stack and open-book management**: A Harvard Business School case study on SRC Holdings documented how teaching employees to think like owners by sharing financial information led to over 20% year-over-year improvement for a decade. Source: HBS case study.

DELIVER

Chapter 13: The Alignment Playbook

159. **Cascading communication strategy**: The approach of aligning a leadership team first and then having those leaders cascade the message to their respective teams is a common and effective strategy for rolling out major initiatives in large organizations. Source: "Cascading Your Corporate Strategy," *MIT Sloan Management Review*, October 14, 2003.

Chapter 14: Movement, Not Motion

160. **Elon Musk's xAI Colossus project**: Musk's company, xAI, built the world's largest AI supercomputer in an abandoned Memphis factory in just 122 days, installing 100,000 NVIDIA GPUs in a process that would normally take 18-24 months. Source: Public media reports.

161. **The former Electrolux plant**: The 785,000-square-foot appliance factory in Memphis closed in 2014, leaving a massive, modern industrial space vacant. Source: "Electrolux to Close Memphis Factory," *Memphis Business Journal*, January 31, 2019.

162. **NVIDIA H100 GPUs:** The H100 Tensor Core GPU is a highly sought-after chip designed for AI and high-performance computing, forming the backbone of many large-scale AI models. Source: "NVIDIA H100 Tensor Core GPU," NVIDIA.

163. **Direct-to-chip liquid cooling**: This advanced cooling method is necessary for densely packed, high-power supercomputers to dissipate the immense heat generated by the processors, preventing them from overheating and failing. Source: "Liquid Cooling Is a Must-Have for Sustainable Data Centers," *Data Center Knowledge*, February 28, 2023.

164. **Microsoft Work Trend Index**: Microsoft regularly publishes research on productivity patterns based on anonymized data from its Microsoft 365 services. These reports are the source of the statistics on interruptions, meeting increases, and the "triple peak" workday. Source: "2023 Work Trend Index Annual Report," Microsoft, May 9, 2023.

165. **Explosion in meetings post-2020**: Microsoft's data showed that the number of weekly meetings per Teams user had increased by 153% since the start of the pandemic. Source: "The Next Great Disruption Is Hybrid Work—Are We Ready?" Microsoft Work Trend Index, March 22, 2021.

166. **Communication vs. creation time**: Microsoft data shows that knowledge workers spend 57% of their time communicating and only 43% on "deep work". Source: Microsoft 365 data.

167. **The "triple peak day"**: Microsoft identified a third peak of work activity late in the evening (around 10 PM) as remote and hybrid work blurred the lines between work and personal life. Source: "The Rise of the Triple Peak Day," Microsoft WorkLab.

168. **The cost of task switching**: Research from the American Psychological Association found that frequent task switching can lead to a loss of up to 40% of productive time due to the mental effort required to reorient. Source: APA, 2014.

169. **Bezos on decision speed**: In his 2016 shareholder letter, Jeff Bezos wrote, "being slow is going to be expensive for sure," advocating for a bias for action and making decisions with about 70% of the desired information. Source: Amazon Shareholder Letters.

Chapter 15: High-Leverage Activities

170. **SpaceX and Starlink statistics**: SpaceX, as of mid-2024, operates over 6,000 Starlink satellites, constituting more than 60% of all active satellites in orbit. Source: CelesTrak.

171. **Falcon 9 reusable boosters**: A key innovation from SpaceX, the ability to land and reuse the first stage of the Falcon 9 rocket has drastically cut launch costs. Source: "SpaceX makes history with successful launch and landing of used rocket," *The Verge*, March 30, 2017.

172. **Falcon 9 landing platform names**: The autonomous spaceport drone ships, like "Just Read the Instructions," are named by Elon Musk as a tribute to the sentient, planet-sized starships in the *Culture* novels of science fiction author Iain M. Banks. Source: "Elon Musk's Droneships Are Named After Spaceships in Iain M. Banks's Sci-Fi Novels," *Slate*, January 23, 2015.

173. **SpaceX's rapid launch cadence**: In 2022, SpaceX launched 61 rockets in one year, more than any country's space agency, by streamlining processes and embracing rapid iteration. Source: *Business Insider*, 2023.

174. **Gwynne Shotwell's role**: As President and COO of SpaceX, Shotwell is responsible for the day-to-day operations of the company and has been instrumental in its growth and success since joining in 2002. Source: "Gwynne Shotwell," SpaceX.

DELIVER

175. **Cost of Starlink satellites**: The mass production of Starlink satellites has dramatically reduced their cost, with estimates around $250,000 to $500,000 per satellite, a fraction of the cost of traditional satellites. Source: "Starlink satellite costs are dropping," *SpaceNews*, April 15, 2020.

176. **Starlink's optical inter-satellite links**: Often called "space lasers," these links allow Starlink satellites to transmit data directly to each other in orbit, reducing latency and reliance on ground stations. Source: "SpaceX's Starlink satellites are now firing lasers at each other," *CNBC*, September 20, 2021.

177. **Shopify cancels meetings**: In January 2023, Shopify's COO Kaz Nejatian announced a "calendar purge," eliminating all recurring meetings with more than two people to free up time for focused work. Source: "Shopify cancels all recurring meetings to free up 76,500 hours a year," *Bloomberg*, January 3, 2023.

178. **Chick-fil-A revenue per location**: Chick-fil-A consistently leads the fast-food industry in average sales per restaurant. In 2022, the average freestanding unit generated $8.1 million, and reports for 2023 estimated it surpassed $9 million, compared to McDonald's at around $4 million. Source: "The 2023 QSR 50," *QSR Magazine*, August 2023.

179. **Chick-fil-A's drive-thru efficiency**: During the pandemic, Chick-fil-A's focus on drive-thru innovation, including using employees with tablets in the parking lot ("face-to-face ordering"), allowed them to serve a high volume of cars while maintaining top industry ratings for speed and order accuracy. Source: "Chick-fil-A's drive-thru is the slowest. It's also the most popular," *CNN Business*, October 5, 2022.

180. **Chick-fil-A drive-thru prototype**: In 2022, Chick-fil-A announced plans for a prototype restaurant in Atlanta focused entirely on drive-thru and mobile orders, featuring multiple lanes and a kitchen built above the pickup area. Source: "Chick-fil-A is testing a new restaurant concept with 4 drive-thru lanes," *Today.com*, July 19, 2022.

181. **SpaceX reusability and launch cost reduction**: The reusability of the Falcon 9's first stage booster has dramatically reduced the cost of launching payloads to orbit, from over $10,000 per kilogram to below $3,000. Source: "SpaceX's reusable rockets have completely changed the business of launching satellites," *The Verge*, June 5, 2020.

182. **High-Leverage Activities and the 80/20 Rule**: The concept of focusing on high-leverage activities aligns with the Pareto principle, or the 80/20 rule,

which suggests that roughly 80% of effects come from 20% of the causes. Source: Richard Koch, *The 80/20 Principle* (Crown, 1998).

183. **Atlassian study on context switching**: The tech company Atlassian found that employees at large firms switch between apps over 25 times per day on average, with fewer switches correlating to faster project completion. Source: Atlassian.

184. **"Speed as a Habit"**: Research has described how some high-performing companies institutionalize rapid cycles of action and learning (e.g., weekly sprints), making speed a cultural habit rather than an occasional push. Source: *California Management Review*, 2022.

Chapter 16: Rewrite the Script

185. **Tiger Woods and the boulder**: The famous incident occurred on the 13th hole of the Phoenix Open in 1999, where spectators helped move a large boulder that was designated a "loose impediment". Source: "Flashback: Tiger Woods' fans move a giant boulder for him at 1999 Phoenix Open," *Golfweek*, January 28, 2015.

186. **Dr. Matthew Lieberman's research on social neuroscience**: Lieberman's work at UCLA has used fMRI technology to study how the brain processes social information, finding that negative scripts activate the same neural pathways as physical threats, and that the brain reacts to challenges to these scripts as if core identity is threatened. Source: Matthew D. Lieberman, *Social: Why Our Brains Are Wired to Connect* (Crown, 2013).

187. **Common inter-departmental friction**: The conflict between sales (which seeks to promise customers speed and flexibility) and operations (which seeks to standardize for efficiency and reliability) is a classic tension point in many organizations. Source: "Ending the War Between Sales and Marketing," *Harvard Business Review*, July 2006.

188. **360-degree feedback**: The process described in the New Jersey pharma company, where peers provide anonymous feedback, is a common leadership development tool known as 360-degree feedback. Source: "The Right Way to Use 360-Degree Feedback," *Society for Human Resource Management (SHRM)*, June 1, 2022.

189. **Satya Nadella becomes CEO of Microsoft**: Nadella was appointed CEO on February 4, 2014, succeeding Steve Ballmer. Source: "Microsoft announces Satya Nadella as new CEO," *The Guardian*, February 4, 2014.

190. **Microsoft's culture change under Nadella**: Nadella is widely credited with transforming Microsoft's culture from insular and competitive to open and collaborative, encapsulated in his shift from a "know-it-all" to a "learn-it-all" mindset. Source: Satya Nadella, *Hit Refresh: The Quest to Rediscover Microsoft's Soul and Imagine a Better Future for Everyone* (Harper Business, 2017).

191. **Microsoft Office for iPad**: At an event in March 2014, shortly after becoming CEO, Nadella announced the launch of Microsoft Office for the iPad, a significant strategic shift that signaled the company's new "mobile-first, cloud-first" direction and willingness to support competing platforms. Source: "Microsoft's new CEO, Satya Nadella, just gave his first big presentation—and it was all about the cloud and the iPad," *Business Insider*, March 27, 2014.

192. **Microsoft's acquisitions of LinkedIn and GitHub**: Microsoft acquired LinkedIn in 2016 for $26.2 billion and GitHub in 2018 for $7.5 billion, moves that were seen as key to embracing open platforms and professional networks. Source: "Microsoft to acquire LinkedIn," Microsoft Official Blog, June 13, 2016.

193. **Microsoft's market capitalization growth**: Under Nadella's leadership, Microsoft's market capitalization grew from around $300 billion in 2014 to over $2 trillion. Source: Yahoo Finance historical stock data.

Chapter 17: The Movement Playbook

194. **Importance of calendar management in sales**: Studies on sales productivity consistently show that top-performing salespeople are highly disciplined in how they manage their time, prioritizing high-value activities like prospecting and key account engagement over administrative tasks. Source: "What the Most Productive Salespeople Do Differently," *Harvard Business Review*, July 10, 2015.

195. **Use of Slack for team accountability**: Using dedicated channels in communication platforms like Slack or Microsoft Teams for regular, asynchronous check-ins on key results is a common practice for remote and hybrid teams to maintain focus and transparency. Source: "How to use Slack for asynchronous collaboration," Slack.

Chapter 18: Menlo Park vs. Highland Park

196. **Thomas Edison's "Invention Factory"**: Edison's laboratory in Menlo Park, New Jersey (1876-1882) is considered the first industrial research laboratory,

organized with the specific purpose of producing constant technological innovation and improvement. Source: Edmund Morris, *Edison* (Random House, 2019).

197. **Number of patents from Menlo Park**: During its operation, the Menlo Park lab was responsible for over 400 of Edison's patents. Source: "Menlo Park," Thomas Edison National Historical Park, National Park Service.

198. **Charles Batchelor and John Kruesi**: Batchelor was Edison's chief experimental assistant ("right-hand man") and Kruesi was his master machinist, two key members of the collaborative team at Menlo Park. Source: Paul Israel, *Edison: A Life of Invention* (Wiley, 1998).

199. **Edison's filament experiments**: Edison and his team famously tested thousands of materials for the light bulb filament, including platinum, cotton, and eventually, carbonized bamboo, which proved to be the most effective early material. Source: "The Invention of the Light Bulb," The Franklin Institute.

200. **Edison's Pearl Street Station**: Opened in 1882 in Manhattan, the Pearl Street Station was the first commercial central power plant in the United States, providing electricity to customers in the surrounding area, including J.P. Morgan and *The New York Times*. Source: "Pearl Street Station," IEEE Global History Network.

201. **The "War of the Currents"**: Edison championed direct current (DC) while competitors like George Westinghouse and Nikola Tesla advocated for alternating current (AC). AC's ability to be transmitted over long distances more efficiently eventually won out, marginalizing Edison's DC systems. Source: "War of the Currents," U.S. Department of Energy.

202. **Formation of General Electric**: In 1892, Edison General Electric merged with the Thomson-Houston Electric Company to form General Electric (GE), with Edison losing control of the company that bore his name. Source: "Our History," GE.

203. **Henry Ford's Highland Park Plant**: Opened in 1910, the Highland Park Ford Plant was where Ford perfected the moving assembly line for automobile production, revolutionizing manufacturing. Source: "Highland Park," The Henry Ford Museum.

204. **Assembly line efficiency gains**: The moving assembly line reduced the time to build a Model T from over 12 hours to just 93 minutes. Source: Steven Watts, *The People's Tycoon: Henry Ford and the American Century* (Vintage, 2005).

205. **Frederick Winslow Taylor and Scientific Management**: Taylor's principles, published in *The Principles of Scientific Management* (1911), focused on optimizing individual worker efficiency through scientific study of tasks. Ford applied these principles at a systemic level. Source: Frederick Winslow Taylor, *The Principles of Scientific Management* (Harper & Brothers, 1911).

206. **Ford's $5-a-day wage**: In 1914, Ford famously doubled the standard wage to $5 a day, which was both a way to reduce high worker turnover and create a consumer class that could afford his cars. Source: "Ford's Five-Dollar Day," The Henry Ford Museum.

207. **Ford's Sociological Department**: This department was established to ensure workers met certain moral and lifestyle standards to qualify for the full $5 wage, conducting home visits and investigating workers' personal lives. Source: Richard S. Tedlow, *Giants of Enterprise: Seven Business Innovators and the Empires They Built* (Harper Business, 2001).

208. **The friendship of Ford and Edison**: The two industrialists were close friends, with Ford crediting Edison's encouragement for his pursuit of the gasoline engine. They frequently took camping trips together known as "The Vagabonds". Source: "Henry Ford and Thomas Edison's Friendship," The Henry Ford Museum.

209. **Edison's last breath**: At Ford's request, Edison's son Charles captured his father's final breath in a sealed test tube, which is now on display at the Henry Ford Museum. Source: "Thomas Edison's Last Breath," The Henry Ford Museum.

210. **Ford's resistance to change**: Ford's rigid adherence to the Model T ("any color... so long as it's black") allowed General Motors, under Alfred P. Sloan, to gain significant market share in the 1920s by offering consumer choice. Source: Alfred P. Sloan, *My Years with General Motors* (Doubleday, 1963).

211. **The 1927 Model T shutdown**: To retool for the new Model A, Ford had to shut down production for six months, laying off 60,000 workers at the River Rouge complex alone. Source: Douglas Brinkley, *Wheels for the World: Henry Ford, His Company, and a Century of Progress* (Viking, 2003).

Chapter 19: The Answer's in Dayton

212. **Dayton's population in 1900**: According to the U.S. Census Bureau, the population of Dayton, Ohio, in 1900 was 85,333. Source: U.S. Census Bureau, "1900 Census: Volume 1. Population, Part 1."

213. **John H. Patterson and NCR**: Patterson purchased the National Manufacturing Company in 1884 and renamed it the National Cash Register Company (NCR). He is considered a pioneer of modern sales and management techniques. Source: Samuel Crowther, *John H. Patterson: Pioneer in Industrial Welfare* (Garden City Publishing, 1923).

214. **Factory conditions in the late 19th century**: Typical factories of the era were dark, poorly ventilated, and dangerous, with long hours and little regard for worker well-being. Source: Daniel E. Sutherland, *The Rise of Big Business, 1860-1920* (Harlan Davidson, 2000).

215. **Patterson's "Welfare Work"**: Patterson was one of the first industrialists to focus on worker welfare, introducing innovations like glass-walled "daylight factories," on-site medical clinics, subsidized hot meals, and paid rest breaks. Source: "A History of Innovation," NCR.

216. **The Panic of 1893**: One of the worst economic depressions in U.S. history, the Panic of 1893 led to the failure of over 15,000 businesses and 500 banks, with unemployment reaching an estimated 20-25%. Source: "Panic of 1893," Federal Reserve History.

217. **NCR's quality problems**: Early in its history, NCR struggled with defective products, prompting Patterson to investigate the root causes on the factory floor. Source: Isaac F. Marcosson, *Wherever Men Trade: The Romance of the Cash Register* (Dodd, Mead and Company, 1945).

218. **Patterson's study of Taylorism**: Patterson hired Frederick Winslow Taylor as a consultant but ultimately found his purely efficiency-driven methods to be incomplete, realizing they needed to be combined with a focus on worker morale and well-being. Source: "John H. Patterson: The Father of Modern Salesmanship," *Harvard Business School*.

219. **Lena Harvey Tracy, Director of Industrial Welfare**: Hired by Patterson in 1897, Tracy was a pioneer in what would later be called human resources, establishing employee assistance programs, educational opportunities, and the first corporate-sponsored daycare in America. Source: "Women in UD's History," University of Dayton.

220. **The 1913 Great Dayton Flood**: A catastrophic flood in March 1913 inundated downtown Dayton, killing over 360 people and causing massive destruction. John Patterson and NCR played a pivotal role in the rescue and relief efforts. Source: "The 1913 Flood," Dayton Metro Library.

DELIVER

221. **NCR's flood response**: Patterson converted the NCR factory into a relief center, using company resources to build rescue boats, and housing and feeding thousands of displaced residents. This act of corporate citizenship became legendary. Source: Trudy E. Bell, "The Great Dayton Flood of 1913," *Scientific American*, March 25, 2013.

222. **Patterson's influence on Charles Kettering**: Kettering, who invented the electric automobile self-starter, began his career at NCR and credited Patterson's innovative environment for shaping his approach to research and development at General Motors. Source: Stuart W. Leslie, *Boss Kettering: Wizard of General Motors* (Columbia University Press, 1983).

223. **Patterson's influence on Thomas J. Watson, Sr.**: Watson was NCR's star salesman before being fired by Patterson. He took the sales and management principles he learned at NCR, such as the motto "THINK," to the company that would become IBM. Source: Kevin Maney, *The Maverick and His Machine: Thomas Watson, Sr. and the Making of IBM* (Wiley, 2003).

Chapter 20: The 3rd Leader Manifesto

224. **Brian Chesky's "Founder Mode Manifesto"**: The reference is to the private gathering and subsequent essay by Paul Graham that ignited a widespread debate in the business and tech communities. Source: Paul Graham, "Founder Mode," November 2023.

225. **Global spending on corporate training**: Estimates for annual spending on corporate training and leadership development vary, but industry reports from sources like Training Industry, Inc. and the Association for Talent Development (ATD) consistently place the figure in the hundreds of billions of dollars, with one 2021 estimate at $370 billion.

226. **Low application of training skills**: The statistic that only 10-12% of learning is applied on the job is a frequently cited figure in the L&D field, often attributed to the "scrap learning" problem where training is not reinforced or relevant. Source: "Forgetting Curve: What is It and How to Combat It," *ATD*, February 2, 2022.

227. **Employees quit because of their boss**: Multiple large-scale studies have confirmed that a primary reason for voluntary turnover is a poor relationship with one's direct manager. Gallup research indicates that managers account for at least 70% of the variance in employee engagement scores. A 2019 study by DDI found 57% of employees have quit a job because of their manager.

228. **Cost of employee turnover**: The Society for Human Resource Management (SHRM) estimates that the cost to replace an employee can range from six to nine months of their salary, with costs for highly skilled or executive positions reaching up to 200% of their annual salary. Source: "Retaining Talent," SHRM.

229. **Low belief in leadership development effectiveness**: Studies have shown skepticism among managers about the ROI of leadership training. An often-cited statistic from a Corporate Executive Board (CEB) study found that only 8% of business leaders believe their leadership development programs have a clear business impact.

230. **Lack of ROI measurement in training**: A 2018 LinkedIn Workplace Learning Report found that while 90% of executives see L&D as a key to closing skill gaps, only 8% actively measure its ROI, highlighting a major disconnect.

231. **Domino's vs. Pizza Hut**: In the 2010s, Domino's underwent a massive turnaround by focusing on technology, delivery, and product quality, eventually surpassing Pizza Hut as the largest pizza chain in the world by sales. Source: "How Domino's Beat Pizza Hut," *Restaurant Business*, February 21, 2018.

232. **Edison's Laboratory as a historical site**: The Thomas Edison National Historical Park in West Orange, New Jersey, preserves Edison's later home and research laboratory. The original Menlo Park lab was moved to The Henry Ford Museum. Source: National Park Service.

233. **NCR's former campus in Dayton**: Much of the original NCR factory complex has been redeveloped and is now part of the University of Dayton's Research Institute and an office park. Source: "University of Dayton, NCR to transform former world HQ into 'imagination hub'," *Dayton Daily News*, March 20, 2017.

234. **Sustaining excellence with operating systems**: Jim Collins' research found that companies that sustained greatness had built enduring operating systems and cultures—a "flywheel"—that outlasted any single leader. Source: *Beyond Entrepreneurship 2.0* (2020).

235. **Agile operating models and engagement**: Companies that implement agile operating models enterprise-wide have seen employee engagement scores rise and innovation throughput increase by 200-300%. Source: "Agile at Scale," *Harvard Business Review*, 2018.

236. **Digital operating models and performance**: A Gartner CIO survey showed that organizations with a strong "digital operating model," which includes

clear goals and empowered teams, were 2.7 times more likely to be top performers in their industry. Source: Gartner, 2022.

237. **Organizational health and shareholder returns**: A Stanford study found that companies in the top quartile for internal health metrics (clarity, coordination) delivered three times the total returns to shareholders over a decade compared to those in the bottom quartile. Source: Stanford Graduate School of Business, 2021.

238. **Bill Gates on information flow**: In his 1999 book, Bill Gates argued that how an organization gathers, manages, and uses information—its "digital nervous system"—would determine its success. This foreshadowed the importance of a modern, integrated operating system for leadership. Source: *Business @ the Speed of Thought*.

INDEX

A

Accountability:
  avoidance of, 31, 167
  in Alignment Process, 146
  LeaderOS and, 255
  Founder Mode and, 40, 167, 283
  Gauge & Discuss and, 168
  Movement and, 233-234
  NCR and, 300, 304
  Netflix and, 24
  RPM framework and, 105
  role of expectations in, 257-258
  systematic enforcement of, 255, 265
  Adapt In 30 (training program), 335
Alignment:
  awareness trap and, 128-130, 145
  brain science of, 132-133, 156, 164
  cascading goals and, 196
  Clarity and, 44, 48, 62, 68, 86, 109, 127
  consistency and, 106-107, 206
  Consensus Mode and, 31
  definition, 130
  gap, 127, 145
  Gauge & Discuss to build, 159-178
  Get Involvement to secure, 179-194
  importance in execution, 128-129, 139, 164
  in LeaderOS, 44, 48, 62, 127-208, 300, 304, 321
  messy nature of, 131, 141, 164
  Movement and, 44, 48, 62, 219
  playbook, 195-208
  recruiting for, 189-191
  rhythms and check-ins for, 203-204, 235
  Warriors (NBA) collapse and, 127-129, 143, 145
Alignment Process, The:
  definition and steps, 142
  function, 140, 150
  Step 1: Make the Case, 142, 147-158
  Step 2: Gauge & Discuss, 142, 159-178
  Step 3: Get Involvement, 142, 179-194
Amazon:
  as competitor, 69, 72
  RTO (Return-to-Office) mandate, 148-152, 157-158
  S-Team, 148-149
  revenue, 147

Amabile, Dr. Teresa (Progress Principle), 187
Amphibious operations, 134-138
Animas River, 133-137, 144
Apple (Steve Jobs), 9, 31, 53, 58
Assessment, Leader Mode, 325-331
Awareness:
  trap, 128-130, 132, 145
  versus Alignment, 129-130, 145, 183
  TKRs and, 133

B
Bezos, Jeff (Amazon), 7, 39, 58
Bridwell, Dr. Tony, xi
Bulletin Board Directive (Chippenham Hospital), 160

C
C24, Gate (chaos allegory), 51-57, 64-65, 87, 222
Case, Make the, *see* Make the Case
Chaos:
  Gate C24 and, 51-57
  in organizations, 57-61, 86
  Third Leader's role in, 61
  Consensus Mode embracing, 55-56
Chen, Dr. Sarah (xAI), 215
Chesky, Brian (Airbnb):
  Founder Mode Manifesto, 4-8, 31-32, 37, 273, 283, 299, 309, 317
  Founder Mode and, 39, 53, 61
  net worth, 5
  product review meeting, 6
Chick-fil-A:
  drive-thru efficiency, 231-232, 235-236, 239
  High-Leverage Activities (HLAs) and, 231-232, 235-236, 239
  revenue, 232, 236

Chippenham Hospital, 160-161, 167
Clarity:
  as North Star, 80
  crisis, 69-82, 86
  definition of destination, 99-112
  extremes (too much/too little), 83-98, 123
  Google Maps analogy, 73-74, 99
  in LeaderOS, 44, 48, 62, 67-124, 300, 304, 321
  neuroscience of, 75
  playbook, 113-124
  Team Key Results (TKRs) and, 100
  Third Leader's role in, 44, 48
Compliance:
  Founder Mode and, 86
  versus Commitment, 174, 184, 188-189, 192
  versus Ownership, 88
Consensus Mode:
  advantages, 40
  Consensus Revolution, 19-34
  definition, 39, 55, 61
  disadvantages, 31-32, 40-41, 56, 176, 283
  in LeaderOS context, 47, 64
  manager response to chaos, 55-56
  Netflix rejection of, 24
  vs. Founder Mode, 37-41, 283
Corbridge, Tanner, 3, 9, 180
Cornell, Brian (Target), 69-72, 74, 99
Customer satisfaction, 70, 84-85, 147, 160-163, 171, 178, 188, 236

D
Dayton, Ohio (NCR), 287-307, 318
Decide In 30 (training program), 337-338

Decide OS (Decision Operating System), 337
Decision-making:
 Consensus Mode and, 25, 40, 56
 distributed, 11, 21, 27
 Founder Mode and, 7, 30, 41
 in LeaderOS, 62, 106, 178, 337
 Jeff's four-hour masterclass, 165-167
 Patterson's approach to, 299-300
Deliver Mode, *see* Third Leader
Discipline:
 in Movement, 220-221, 231, 235
 Founder Mode and, 41
 Discretionary effort, 192
 Dorsey, Jack (Twitter), 89-90

E
Edison, Thomas (Menlo Park), 274-285, 307-308, 318
 Control Trap and, 281
 collaborative approach, 280
 DC current, 281
 friendship with Ford, 278-280
Employee engagement, 21, 27, 41, 75, 85, 94, 99, 118, 187, 198, 206, 211, 298
Endnotes, 341-372

F
False Choice:
 definition, 37, 47
 rejection of, 36, 48, 61, 284, 298
Firebase, 11
Founder Mode:
 advantages, 39, 41, 54
 Airbnb and, 4-8
 analysis, 3-17
 Control Trap and, 282
 definition, 7, 39, 53, 61

disadvantages, 7, 30, 41-42, 54, 158, 283
 in LeaderOS context, 47, 64
 Manifesto, 7-8, 309, 317
 manager response to chaos, 53-54
 vs. Consensus Mode, 37-41, 283

G
Gauge & Discuss:
 definition, 142, 146, 163-164
 Jeff's four-hour masterclass, 165-167, 172
 in Alignment Process, 142, 163
 Johnston-Willis Hospital and, 161-163
 listening in, 164, 166
 Level 3 safety in, 171
Get Involvement:
 definition, 142, 146, 183
 emotional involvement, 186-187, 190
 in Alignment Process, 142, 183
 operational involvement, 185-186, 189
Google Maps, 73-74, 99
Graham, Paul, 7-8, 12
Grant, Adam (Wharton Professor), 149-150

H
Hastings, Reed (Netflix), 24
High-Leverage Activities (HLAs):
 alignment check-ins for, 234, 269
 Chick-fil-A example, 231-232
 definition, 230
 four-step framework, 232-236, 238
 Impact/Shared Value criteria, 230
 in Movement, 225-240, 269
 Shopify and, 229
 SpaceX and, 229

DELIVER

Hoffman, Reid, 10-11
Holacracy, 21, 25-27, 31, 299, 317
Hsieh, Tony, *see* Tony Hsieh

I
Involvement, *see* Get Involvement

J
Jassy, Andy (Amazon CEO), 148-151
Jobs, Steve, 7, 9, 30, 39, 58, 92, 299
Johnston-Willis Hospital, 161-163, 167, 171
Jones, Jared, 3
Joy, focusing on, 336

K
Kerr, Steve (Warriors Coach), 128-129, 132, 143, 145

L
Leader Modes, 39, 40, 53-57, 325-331
LeaderOS:
　components of, 43-44, 48, 62, 67, 125, 209
　definition, 43, 62
　installation, 67, 125, 209
Lena Harvey Tracy (NCR), 296-298, 304
Lieberman, Dr. Matthew, 246-247
Listening, importance of, 131, 141, 163-166, 172, 176
Lockheed Martin, 233
Low-Leverage Activities (LLAs), 220, 230, 232, 234-235, 238, 261-262, 269

M
Make the Case, *see* Make the Case
Mayo, Brent (xAI), 212, 216
McCord, Patty (Netflix), 24
McKinsey & Company, 75, 92, 168

Menlo Park (Edison's lab), 274-276, 280-281
Microsoft (Productivity data), 217-219, 241, 253-254
Mode, Consensus, *see* Consensus Mode
Mode, Founder, *see* Founder Mode
Motion:
　definition, 220
　versus Movement, 211, 219-224, 237, 240, 304
Movement:
　Discipline, Desire, Consistency, 220-221, 240
　HLAs and, 225-240, 269
　in LeaderOS, 44, 48, 62, 209-270, 300, 304, 321
　playbook, 259-270
　Rewriting Scripts for, 241-258
　Third Leader's role in, 44, 48
　vs. Motion, 211, 219-224, 237, 240, 304
Musk, Elon, 7, 39, 147, 212, 216, 219

N
Nadella, Satya (Microsoft), 253-254
National Cash Register Company (NCR), 288-304
Nejatian, Kaz (Shopify COO), 229
Nelson, Russell, 336
Netflix, 24
Neuroscience, 75, 132, 150, 156, 164, 168, 173, 246-247
New York Times, 8, 280

O
OKRs (Objectives and Key Results), 101, 107
Optimism, choice of, 131-132, 140, 146, 190, 336

Organizational scripts, *see* Scripts
Over-specification (Clarity extreme), 83-88, 97

P
Panic of 1893, 292
Patterson, John H., 288-306, 318, 322
Performance, linking to purpose, 150, 154, 156
Power In 30 (training program), 336
Priorities, three most important, 75, 80, 97, 100, 105
Productivity Drain (Harvard Business School), 75, 219
Psychological safety:
  Consensus Mode and, 24, 31, 40, 56
  Gauge & Discuss and, 169-172
  Levels of (Observe, Contribute, Challenge), 169-172, 176
  Movement and, 244
  Third Leader and, 300

R
Rafting (Animas River analogy), 133-138, 144
Ready on Time (Target metric), 71
RPM (Repeatable, Purposeful, Measurable), 105, 118, 122, 206
Rufer, Chris (Morning Star), 21-22, 27, 30

S
Scale Mode, 43
Scripts:
  about your team, 248-249, 254
  boulder analogy, 245-246, 256
  definition, 245
  identification, 248-252, 255
  neuroscience of, 246-247, 257

  rewriting, 241-258, 270
  Tiger Woods and, 245, 257
Seek Feedback, 16, 33, 40, 47, 64, 81, 97, 105, 111, 122, 145, 157, 177, 193, 224, 238, 257, 269, 321, 331, 338
Shopify, 229, 233
Shotwell, Gwynne (SpaceX), 227-228, 232
Smith, Tom, ix, 180, 360
Southwest Airlines, 187-188, 361
SpaceX (Starlink):
  High-Leverage Activities (HLAs) and, 226-228, 232-236, 239
  satellites, 226-228, 236
  launch cadence, 227, 235-236
Spider-Man (Stan Lee), 36
Stan Lee, 36, 284
Starlink, *see* SpaceX
Steroid Leader Problem, 40-42, 47
Sutter Healthcare, xv
Synchronization, science of, 138-139

T
Target:
  Clarity Crisis, 69-72, 81
  digital sales, 71
  three metrics (TKRs), 70-72, 81, 99
Taylor, Frederick Winslow (Scientific Management), 277, 300
Teva Pharmaceuticals, xi
Third Leader:
  Clarity and, 74, 87
  definition, 38, 61
  historical origin (Patterson), 298-305
  Manifesto, 309-322
  rejection of false choice, 61, 284
TKRs (Team Key Results), *see* TKRs (Team Key Results)
Twitter, 89-90, 97

DELIVER

U

Ulmer, Greg (Lockheed Martin), x
Under-specification (Clarity extreme), 89-92, 97

V

Ventry, Tony (Veritiv), xiv
Veritiv, xiv

W

Warriors (NBA), *see* Alignment
Watson, Thomas J., Sr. (IBM), 302-303
What's Next (Appendix), 333-339
Woods, Tiger, 245-246, 257

X

xAI (supercomputer project), 212-217, 219, 222

Z

Zappos (Tony Hsieh), 19-27, 31, 39, 55, 283, 299, 317
   employee exodus, 26
   holacracy experiment, 21, 25-27, 31, 299, 317